LIBRARY
LEWIS-CLARK STATE COLLEGE
LEWISTON, IDAHO

D1108499

LIBRARY

# Peculiar Portrayals

Mormons on the Page, Stage, and Screen

# PECULIAR PORTRAYALS
Mormons on the Page, Stage, and Screen

Edited by
Mark T. Decker and Michael Austin

Utah State University Press
Logan, Utah

Copyright © 2010 Utah State University Press
All rights reserved

Utah State University Press
Logan, UT
USUPress.org

ISBN 978-0-87421-773-5 (paper)
ISBN 978-0-87421-774-2 (e-book)

Manufactured in the United States of America
Printed on acid-free, recycled paper

Library of Congress Cataloging-in-Publication Data

Peculiar portrayals : Mormons on the page, stage, and screen / edited by Mark T.
Decker and Michael Austin.
     p. cm.
 Includes bibliographical references and index.
 ISBN 978-0-87421-773-5 (pbk. : alk. paper) -- ISBN 978-0-87421-774-2 (e-book)
 1. Mormons in mass media. I. Decker, Mark T. II. Austin, Michael, 1966-
 P94.5.M67P43 2010
 700'.4382893--dc22
                          2010000780

# Contents

*Introduction*      *1*

1.  Center and Periphery: Mormons and American Culture in
    Tony Kushner's *Angels in America*

    *Cristine Hutchison-Jones*      5

2.  Four Consenting Adults in the Privacy of Their Own Suburb:
    *Big Love* and the Cultural Significance of Mormon Polygamy

    *Michael Austin*      37

3.  Teaching *Under the Banner of Heaven*: Testing the Limits of
    Tolerance in America

    *Kevin Kolkmeyer*      62

4.  Avenging Angels: The Nephi Archetype and Blood Atonement
    in Neil LaBute, Brian Evenson, and Levi Peterson, and the
    Making of the Mormon American Writer

    *J. Aaron Sanders*      87

5.  Elders on the Big Screen: Film and the Globalized Circulation
    of Mormon Missionary Images

    *John-Charles Duffy*      113

6.  "I Constructed in My Mind a Vast, Panoramic Picture": *The
    Miracle Life of Edgar Mint* and Postmodern, Postdenominational
    Mormonism

    *Mark T. Decker*      144

7.  Jane Austen in Mollywood: Mainstreaming Mormonism in
    Andrew Black's *Pride & Prejudice*

    *Juliette Wells*      163

8.  Reality Corrupts; Reality Television Corrupts Absolutely

    *Karen D. Austin*      183

*About the Contributors*      *197*

*Index*      *199*

# Introduction

Although always an object of both popular and scholarly curiosity, Mormons and Mormonism have seen increasing scrutiny during the previous decade. For example, the Church of Jesus Christ of Latter-day Saints (LDS Church) understandably used the 2002 Salt Lake Winter Olympics as a pretext to mount an extensive public-relations campaign that capitalized on the extensive media attention that Olympic host cities typically receive. In spite of a bribery scandal, this effort was largely successful, resulting in generally positive stories on television and in newspapers and magazines.

Unfortunately for the church, however, the media have also reported stories that do not present Mormons in the best light, like the 2008 raid on the polygamist compound at the Yearning for Zion ranch in Texas. And while the ranch was the property of fundamentalist Mormons who have no ties to the LDS Church, the full implications of that distinction were probably lost on many viewers and readers. Indeed, it is possible that the frequent repetition of the lack of connection between Warren Jeffs's church and the one headquartered in Salt Lake City by a dutiful and risk-averse media actually intensified the popular connection between polygamy and mainstream Mormonism. One could not, say, watch the pioneer-dress-wearing YFZ mothers who appeared on *Larry King Live* to plead for the return of their children without being reminded of the history that all Mormons share.

Participation in politics by individual Mormons, as well as the institutional LDS Church, has also generated media coverage and increased scrutiny. That coverage has generally aligned Mormons and Mormonism with the Right in America, Harry Reid notwithstanding. The tearfully partisan Glenn Beck is not the only prominent Mormon on the right. The media has not always presented the church or its members as polarizing figures. Mitt Romney's failed, but highly visible, bid for the Republican presidential nomination—as well as his quieter, but equally unsuccessful, bid to be John McCain's running mate—generated a great deal of press coverage. While some of that attention added to the "will America vote for a Mormon?" meme, much of it stressed the attractiveness of the putatively moderate former Republican governor of heavily Democratic

1

Massachusetts. After all, what's not to like about a generically attractive, Ivy League–educated entrepreneur with a seemingly stable family life and bipartisan credentials? The LDS Church's 2008 decision to support California's Proposition 8, which denied gays and lesbians the right to marry, however, not only placed the institution well to the right on the American political spectrum but also allowed opponents of the measure to wonder publicly why a church that had once openly advocated polygamy was now encouraging its members to donate more than 50 percent of the funding of an effort to define marriage as the union of one man and one woman.

Mormons have often referred to themselves as a "peculiar people," implying that their devotion to their faith and the unique truth of their gospel sets them apart from the rest of the world. But for many people who are unfamiliar with the faith, Mormons are just peculiar. Most people simply don't have the time to think deeply about a group of people who try to present themselves as neat and orderly members of the American mainstream while they are simultaneously haunted by the specter of their nineteenth-century eccentricities. Instead, most people, when they think about Mormons at all, take at face value a conflicted public image with a long history. Well before the 2002 Winter Olympics, the 2008 presidential campaign, the raid on the YFZ ranch, or the controversy surrounding Proposition 8 captured the attention of the news media, Americans had easy access to pejorative literary and filmic depictions of Mormons and Mormonism. Many unsavory Mormons populated the pulp novels of the nineteenth century, and more respectable authors like Mark Twain crafted critical depictions of Mormon customs and theology. Silent film audiences were sometimes treated to the spectacle of beautiful women entrapped by scheming Mormon polygamists.

Contemporary portrayals of Latter-day Saints have been no less problematic. For example, Tony Kushner's *Angels in America* focuses on a politically dangerous Mormon character whose religion has turned him into a hypocrite. Lighter entertainment sometimes features Mormon characters best described as absurd, such as the missionary-turned-porn-star in *Orgazmo*. And while *Big Love's* portrayal of polygamist and businessman Bill Henrickson is sympathetic, the show's appeal rests heavily upon its creation of a fundamentalist Mormon suburban surrealism. Even authors who had a Mormon upbringing often create peculiar Mormon characters, such as the sometime-Mormon main character of returned Mormon missionary Brady Udall's *The Miracle Life of Edgar Mint*, who finds his life permanently altered when the postman runs over his head.

Although peculiar Mormon characters have haunted America's literary and filmic imagination for decades, few studies have investigated this cultural phenomenon. There has been much comment on the uniqueness of Mormonism as a religion and historical phenomenon, yet it is also true that Mormons are unique literary characters that may represent a peculiarly American trope. Naturally Mormon intellectuals have sometimes attempted to explain their faith's place in American culture to Mormon audiences. And prominent non-Mormon intellectuals have written about the faith's uniquely American characteristics. But there has not been a concerted effort to explore the ways that Mormons and Mormonism have been characterized in literature and film. This collection of articles provides a broad perspective on the way Mormons and Mormonism are depicted in contemporary fiction, theater, and film that begins to map out the peculiar terrain these characters inhabit.

As with most rudimentary exercises in physical or intellectual cartography, however, *Peculiar Portrayals* creates a map that is more suggestive than definitive. Individual articles clarify the texts and issues they address, but tantalizing gaps remain. For example, astute readers will notice that most—but not all—of the essays in this volume focus on texts whose authors or creators are male. Unfortunately, in the diverse group of texts that explicitly discuss Mormons and Mormonism for a national, secular audience, male authorship or auteurship is typical. And because it is difficult to trace thematic continuity among works like *Under the Banner of Heaven* and *Orgazmo*, essays are not grouped into categories but are instead offered on their own merits.

As readers will see, each article finds Mormons and Mormonism interacting with notions of Americans and America in ways that are both peculiar and familiar. Cristine Hutchison-Jones's "Center and Periphery: Mormons and American Culture in Tony Kushner's *Angels in America*" concludes that the playwright's texts are not so much anti-Mormon as anti–Mormon orthodoxy. Consequently, Mormonism signifies the tendency for radical American movements to degenerate into hidebound, reactionary orthodoxy, a trend that Kushner finds deeply troubling. Michael Austin's "Four Consenting Adults in the Privacy of Their Own Suburb: *Big Love* and the Cultural Significance of Mormon Polygamy" sees the HBO series as a meditation on the way Americans describe "normal" families that is designed implicitly to inform contemporary debates about gay marriage. Kevin Kolkmeyer's "Teaching *Under the Banner of Heaven*: Testing the Limits of Tolerance in America" uses empirical evidence gathered in a composition classroom—refreshing for a literary study—to argue that an ethnically and religiously diverse group of working-class New York City freshman can relate to the cognitive dissonance of the Mormon experience because both groups find themselves simultaneously inside and outside of American culture. J. Aaron Sanders's "Avenging Angels: The Nephi Archetype and Blood Atonement in Neil LaBute, Brian Evenson, and Levi Peterson, and the Making of the Mormon American Writer" concludes that Mormon authors writing for a national audience about the violent aspects of Mormon culture are actually participating in a broader American investment in violence as a means of self-definition. John-Charles Duffy's "Elders on the Big Screen: Film and the Globalized Circulation of Mormon Missionary Images" argues that globalized popular culture readily turns the carefully crafted and easily recognized image of Mormon missionaries to its own ends. Mark T. Decker's "I Constructed in My Mind a Vast, Panoramic Picture": *The Miracle Life of Edgar Mint* and Postmodern, Postdenominational Mormonism" suggests that it is possible to create nuanced portrayals of Mormons and Mormonism that escape the hagiography-or-condemnation binary by creating postmodern, post-Mormon characters. Juliette Wells's "Jane Austen in Mollywood: Mainstreaming Mormonism in Andrew Black's *Pride & Prejudice*" proposes that oblique presentation of Mormon cultural mores by means of a cognate cultural context can produce a narrative that explains a peculiar lifestyle without antagonizing a broad audience with little professed interest in the minutia of Mormon life. And Karen D. Austin's "Reality Corrupts; Reality Television Corrupts Absolutely" offers a broad, but insightful, overview of Mormon participation in reality-television programs, arguing that Mormon participants either act as naïve foils for more urbane cast members or, if they happen to be gay, embody cultural contradictions inherent in American life.

Of course, the lack of a total picture that characterizes this volume does not preclude greater understanding of the peculiar place fictive Mormons have in the American cultural imagination. An incomplete map, after all, is better than no map at all. And hopefully, an incomplete map can motivate others to fill in the gaps.

# Center and Periphery

*Mormons and American Culture in Tony Kushner's*
Angels in America

CRISTINE HUTCHISON-JONES

Literature and film have long provided ample evidence of mainstream America's conflicting and conflicted perceptions of and feelings about Mormons and their beliefs, and Tony Kushner's *Angels in America: A Gay Fantasia on National Themes* is a case in point. Immediately accorded canonical status when it premiered in New York in 1992, critics labeled *Angels* "the most thrilling American play in years,"[1] and scholars have since declared that "*Angels* restored to American theatre an ambition it has not enjoyed since the days of Eugene O'Neill or Arthur Miller."[2] Winner of the 1993 Pulitzer Prize for drama (for *Part I: Millennium Approaches)* and two Tony Awards for best play (1993 for *Millennium Approaches* and 1994 for *Part II: Perestroika)*, *Angels* has also enjoyed international success with audiences. Since 2003, the HBO Films adaptation has garnered further critical accolades (two Screen Actors Guild Awards, five Golden Globes, and eleven Emmys, including outstanding writing for a miniseries, movie, or dramatic special for Kushner's screenplay), and the DVD release has created a much wider audience for Kushner's work than the stage could offer.[3] Within this acclaimed exploration of AIDS, queer identity, and the conservative politics of the Reagan era, Kushner portrays three Mormon characters whose struggles with their sexual identity, love, politics, and religion are central to his larger vision.

In the afterword to *Perestroika*, Kushner points out, "We organize the world for ourselves, or at least we organize our understanding of it; we reflect it, refract it, criticize it, grieve over its savagery and help each other to discern, amidst the gathering dark, paths of resistance, pockets of peace and places from whence hope may be plausibly expected."[4] Just so, Kushner *uses* his play and the status it has granted him as a public intellectual to reflect, refract, criticize, and even grieve over Mormons and their place in the epic of American history as he sees it. In so doing, his play offers startling insights into the dark and difficult place of Mormonism in the American imagination.

## Literature Review

Mormons, with the reputation they gained during the twentieth century as all-American conservatives,[5] are not an obvious choice for a playwright seeking to explore issues of queer identity and the AIDS crisis in 1980s New York. But in fact, Mormons were among the first things Kushner knew he wanted to write about in *Angels in America*: "All I knew," he says, "was that I wanted to write about gay men, Mormons and Roy Cohn."[6]

In spite of this fact—and the remarkable presence of important Mormon characters in the play—Mormonism has often gone unnoticed by commentators: "only 68 of 370 reviews mentioned Mormons at all" according to a 1999 survey of critical responses to the plays.[7] When it is noted, little is actually said. Whereas reviewers and scholars have minutely dissected Kushner's representations of Jews, homosexuals, and blacks, the importance of religious identity for the play's Mormons is often relegated to the status of window dressing, as when one scholar remarked on "Mormon Family Values" in the play without any explanation of what he meant by the phrase.[8] Others simply refer, as did one reviewer, to the presence of "some extraordinary Mormons" in the play.[9]

Not surprisingly, Mormon reviewers and scholars have paid far greater attention to the importance of Mormons and Mormonism in *Angels in America*. This scholarship has reached a limited audience, however, even by the standards of scholarly work, being published in such journals as *Dialogue: A Journal of Mormon Thought* and the *Journal of Mormon History*. Nor do such treatments situate Kushner's representation of Mormons within the history of American images of Mormonism. Instead, they focus on the potential impact of *Angels* on the faith of Mormon viewers, the relative positive or negative value of interpretations of those characters, or even the parallels that can be drawn between Mormon theology and Kushner's own theological perspective in the play.[10]

## So Why Mormons?

While Kushner's play is, first and foremost, an exploration of the place of the homosexual community in American culture and the devastation wrought in it by the combination of AIDS and political inaction in the 1980s, on a deeper level, it is also an exploration of minority experience in the United States. Kushner assembles a group of people whose only commonality is their marginal status at the fringes of national culture: Jews, Mormons, women, African Americans, homosexuals. Though these groups are generally not connected to one another, their outsider status unites them.

Although he clearly seeks to explore the experience of otherness, visible or not, Kushner anchors the story in Prior Walter, the only WASP (white Anglo-Saxon Protestant) in the play.[11] This identity initially seems to privilege Prior, but in fact it also leaves him a blank slate. Because Prior does not carry a significant residue of any religious culture, unlike virtually every other major character in the play, he proves a receptive vessel for the Jewish and Mormon cultural ideas that his experiences teach him. Though he does not accept every religious idea presented to him, most notably the conservative proscriptions of the Angel, he does not have to overcome strong, inherited religious ideas to assimilate new ones. Further, Prior's WASP background makes him ripe for the influence of both Jewish and Mormon traditions because it looks to Judaism as a direct ancestor and serves as the cultural as well as religious ground in which Mormonism appeared in the nineteenth century.

Kushner places Prior at the end of an ancient line of Walters, a line that can be traced back through New England to the Mayflower and, further, to England. In fact, early in the play, his lover Louis declares that "there's a Prior Walter stitched into the Bayeux tapestry," thus carrying his family back into the eleventh century—shortly after the beginning of the current millennium.[12] But with Prior, a gay man who will have no children (a circumstance noted by the ghosts of two prior Priors who serve as heralds to the Angel), the line will die out. Thus, while his pure WASP status may reinforce "the largest of the cultural themes of *Angels in America:* the resistance that biological descent and inherited tradition, embodied here in the body of the WASP, pose to political change," the natural result for Kushner is that the line is fizzling out because it has not adapted to changing historical and cultural realities.[13] Prior himself acknowledges that such a fate awaits—or has already overtaken—America's WASP heritage: in the play's final scene, he notes that the trees in Central Park are "New England transplants. They're barren now."[14]

Prior's WASP status also connects him to the American prophet whose experiences he will shortly recapitulate. Joseph Smith Jr., the Mormon prophet, was also a Yankee WASP descended from English immigrants to the New World. In fact, both sides of his family were eminently respectable middle-class New Englanders in his grandparents' generation.[15] Thus, the truly American religion—as Mormonism has been designated by observers—is as rooted in Yankee Puritan stock as the WASP mainstream that Kushner dismisses as sterile.

Here Kushner highlights the artificiality of distinctions of race, class, and sexuality that he himself is exploring. Although Mormons were represented (from outside) as a separate ethnic group as early as the middle of the nineteenth century, this distinction was largely artificial.[16] By labeling Mormons as an ethnic other, scholar Terryl Givens asserts, "threatening proximity has been transformed into manageable distance."[17] This strategy was necessary, he argues, because Mormonism was "very hard to see. Mormons were, after all, usually ethnically identical with one's neighbors and even one's family."[18] Just as Allen J. Krantzen has speculated that Kushner knew what he was doing in assigning Prior Anglo-Saxon ethnic status and then undercutting that identity by tying Prior's family to the Bayeux tapestry—woven by the eleventh-century *French* conquerors of England—the connection between Prior's WASPishness and that of the prophet Joseph Smith undercuts assumptions about the tangible ethnic difference between Mormons and other Americans.[19]

Mormonism's Yankee roots do not, however, change the fact that the group was accorded outsider status shortly after it appeared in upstate New York in 1830.[20] It shares this status as *other* with the other religious community depicted in *Angels in America*—Judaism—which Kushner represents as the immigrant other in counterpoint to Mormonism's native origin.

But Mormonism shares more with Judaism than simple outsider status. Kushner himself has noted the similarities of practice and belief between the two communities, including their shared focus on a text, emphasis on actions over beliefs, experience of diaspora, and emphasis on gathering.[21] These similarities are by no means accidental because Joseph Smith and his early followers saw the Church of Jesus Christ of Latter-day Saints as, among other things, a restoration of the religion of ancient Israel. This Hebraic emphasis fostered early Mormonism's focus on the tribes of Israel, temple worship, and patriarchal blessings as well as bloodlines and also had a profound impact on the Mormons' understanding of their trek west as a recapitulation of the biblical exodus.[22]

Further, along with homosexuals, the two religious communities share a history of oppression at the hands of the majority in the United States. Both have negotiated, with some success, the tricky process of accommodating to American culture while maintaining a sense of their religious and cultural distinctness. So while some scholars argue that "the archetype for the transformation of identity, which is the mark of queer experience and survival in the play, is the wandering, rootless, shape-shifting Jew who never finds a home,"[23] in fact, the Mormons and their protracted migration west in the nineteenth century provide another example of the "rootless, shape-shifting" other.[24]

The forms that intolerance toward Mormons, Jews, and homosexuals have taken in the United States share a number of commonalities. Certainly relevant to Kushner is the fact that "bigotry toward scapegoats often takes similar forms, painting the pariah group as inhuman sexual predators, especially dangerous to children."[25] Just as late-nineteenth-century anti-Semitic propaganda employed images of lascivious, sexually perverse Jews, anti-Mormon materials from the nineteenth and early-twentieth century abound with images, both frightening and humorously demeaning, of wicked old Mormon polygamists with captive harems of innocent young women.[26]

Some other prominent themes shared by anti-Semitic and anti-homosexual propaganda that Kushner explores in *Angels in America* include the power of the suspect community to manipulate government and economy, control the media, and acquire (through unethical and sometimes illegitimate means) ubiquitous wealth.[27] These themes, too, are readily apparent in material on the Mormons, much of which is not avowedly anti-Mormon. For example, John Heinerman and Anson Shupe's book *The Mormon Corporate Empire: The Eye-Opening Report on the Church and Its Political and Financial Agenda*, originally published in 1986 and reissued in 1988, grounds its exploration of Mormonism in the story of the church and community's economic prowess and its political implications. Even Richard and Joan Ostling's more balanced and respectful 1999 book *Mormon America: The Power and the Promise* (reissued in 2007 as "revised and updated for the 2008 election") includes chapters with titles like "Mormons, Inc." and "The Power Pyramid."[28] Thus, Mormons are a natural part of Kushner's community of suspect outsiders.

For each of Kushner's characters, "the marginality of each of these religious traditions is shown to contribute to the individual's sense of his or her place (or lack of place) in the structures of power."[29] In spite of the clout he has achieved in his life and career as a Republican power broker, Roy Cohn is also keenly aware that the Judaism he barely acknowledges even to himself makes him an easy target because he will always be seen in some quarters as "some sort of filthy little Jewish troll."[30] Roy's other mark of outsider status—the homosexuality that he viciously denies, along with the AIDS infection that is killing him—is also an issue not of identity but power. Thus, Roy tells his doctor that a homosexual is not a man who has sex with other men but one without power: "Roy Cohn is a heterosexual man . . . who fucks around with guys."[31] In the same way, Mormonism disempowers the Pitts in the eyes of the play's other characters: Roy uses Joe's Mormonism to trivialize him, and Joe's religion invites the suspicion that eventually leads Louis to abandon him. And Joe's wife, Harper, talking to her mother-in-law, Hannah, speaks for all three Mormon characters, struggling to leave behind the apparent cultural isolation that Mormonism has imposed on them yet unable to embrace the more liberal culture that beckons all of Kushner's characters: "You have less of a place in this world than I do if that's possible."[32]

But Kushner is not just using the experience of other, longer-standing minority groups to illuminate the contemporary marginalization of the homosexual community. He also sees the country's behavior toward such minorities as a barometer of tensions in the mainstream: "It always seems to me that in the concerns of any group called a minority and called oppressed can be found the biggest problems and the central identity issues that the country is facing."[33] Scholars of the experience of religious minorities in the United States would agree; put another way, the experiences of "subordinate peoples or groups have typically been represented in ways that justify the inequality of power relations and serve to rationalize or reinforce the identity, interests, or agenda of those in positions of dominance."[34] Thus, the story of marginalized people becomes a window into the minds of those at the helm of the central or dominant culture.

For Kushner, America's marginalization of Jews and Mormons results in part from a sense of the otherworldliness of both traditions as embodied in their millennial traditions. Just as Jews end the yearly celebration of the Passover meal with the hope for a new future—"Next year in Jerusalem"—Mormonism was founded on the hope and expectation of Christ's imminent second coming and the construction of a new Zion.[35] These beliefs open up Kushner's exploration of history and its end, as well as providing a platform for the supernatural visitations and visions that permeate the play.[36] Such hope for the future, tinged with millennial expectation, is also an important part of America's national identity.[37]

But while American millennialism focuses on the nation itself as the new Promised Land, Jews and Mormons look outside the nation both culturally and physically—Jerusalem for Jews; and Deseret, the nine-teenth-century Mormon name for Utah, which was not a United States territory when the Latter-day Saints settled there.[38] But unlike postmil-lennial visions of the advent of God's kingdom as generally peaceful, Kushner's vision of the future carries with it both the weight of the past and a sense of impending (and perhaps already-occurring) apocalypse: "The most dangerous thing is to become set upon some notion of the future that isn't rooted in the bleakest, most terrifying idea of what's piled up behind you."[39]

Thus, for Kushner, Mormonism becomes part of a conscious strat-egy to guide his viewers toward a progressive perspective on history and human relations where community is no longer based on tribe. Not family, nor ethnicity, nor religion determines human interactions in the glimpse of the ideal that Kushner gives in the play's epilogue. Now acceptance, not just tolerance, is the only legitimate principle guiding human behavior.

Within Kushner's proposed framework for human interaction, Judaism represents both the failure and the promise of the American progressive liberal tradition that Jews embraced in the early twentieth century. But while Louis is repeatedly ridiculed throughout the play for the meaninglessness of his progressive political platitudes—none of which are backed up by his actions—the epilogue nonetheless finds him comfortably situated in Kushner's ideal community. His words are little changed, but his very presence—his return to Prior in spite of both Prior's sickness and his refusal to take Louis back as a lover—clearly demon-strates that Louis has learned to stand by the principles he espouses.[40]

Mormonism is a similar cautionary tale. Mormons represent the fail-ure of a homegrown, radical political, social, and economic critique that at one time separated itself from the nation (albeit not wholly volun-tarily) and lived one of the most successful communitarian experiments in American history. Kushner views the abandonment of this project as a great failure, which is compounded by the extent to which Mormons have become part of the conservative American mainstream: "Now, they're right wing and horrible."[41]

## "The Delicate Ecology of Your Delusions"

For Kushner perhaps the most important of all of Mormonism's char-acteristics that it shares with Judaism is prophecy. But just as his use of various other aspects of Mormon belief and history is slyly ambivalent, so, too, is his relationship to the "prophets" in his play. Not only is the prophecy that Prior Walter receives from the Angel of America one that Prior—along with the playwright—rejects, but in fact it is never clear whether Prior's visions are meant to be revelation or madness.

Prophetic tradition is clearly a part of both of the religions that Kushner is mining for his characters' experiences, and Prior's visionary experiences clearly derive from both Judaism and Mormonism. The Angel of America's Mormon roots are evident to anyone who knows the story of the prophet Joseph Smith: like the Angel Moroni, she comes to Prior at night in his bed, announces a great work that he is to carry out, and tells him of a book to which she will lead him. The book is buried much as the Book of Mormon was, though instead of being first uncovered on a nearby hillside, it is under the floorboards in the kitchen of Prior's apartment (Joseph Smith used a similar hiding place, placing the golden plates under the family hearthstone after he had retrieved them from the Hill Cumorah). What Prior "unearths" is "a large book with bright steel pages," reminiscent of the metal plates on which Joseph Smith claimed the Book of Mormon was written. Accompanying the book is "a pair of bronze spectacles with rocks instead of lenses"—which the Angel identifies as "Peep-stones"—that allow Prior to read the book.[42] Kushner clearly counts on the fact that Joseph Smith's story is familiar to *Angel's* viewers from sources as varied as the Book of Mormon itself, ubiquitous Mormon missionaries (who, in part, inspired Kushner's interest in writing about the tradition), and general American lore.

Unlike Joseph Smith, Prior Walter does not welcome this angelic visitation, greeting the Angel with a tone that belongs more to reluctant prophets of the Hebrew Bible: "Go away."[43] Also unlike Joseph Smith, Prior's task is not to translate the book.[44] Instead, like the biblical Ezekiel, Prior *consumes* the prophecy he is destined to relate, internalizing the text when the Angel presses it to his body and declares, "Vessel of the BOOK now: . . . On you in you in your blood we write have written [*sic*]."[45]

In a sign that brings the two traditions together, Kushner endows (or saddles) Prior with a limp even before he sees the Angel.[46] The most obvious parallel, which Kushner indirectly draws in the play, is to the biblical patriarch Jacob, later called Israel, who wrestled an angel and won but was injured in the contest and left with a limp.[47] Joseph Smith, too, had a limp, the result of a childhood bone infection that nearly killed him.[48] Thus, Prior's leg pain—a symptom of his infection with HIV—is also an outward physical sign of his role as prophet.

Just as Prior is not reducible to a Hebrew Bible prophet or Joseph Smith, the Angel, too, is fully Kushner's own. While he acknowledges that the angelic presence in Mormonism is part of why he chose that tradition to shape the plays ("the prototypical American angel is the Angel Moroni"[49]), he also maintains a sharp distinction between Joseph Smith's angel and Prior's: "The thing that appeared to Joseph Smith, to tell him where the book was hidden, was not ever actually described as an angel in his writing. He calls it a personage in robes of surpassing whiteness. It's not described as having wings. This is Prior's angel, not Joseph Smith's. Prior's angel would definitely have wings."[50]

Kushner repeatedly suggests in the play that Judaism and Mormonism are important not only to his construction of the Angel but to Prior's as well. The nature of visions—delusion or prophecy?—is addressed repeatedly throughout the play: by visionaries (Prior and Harper), by a level-headed realist (Belize), and by some who are in between (Hannah, whose perspective mirrors that of Belize—until she encounters the Angel).

Belize feels that Prior's visions are clearly an attempt to deal with what is happening to him because of his illness: the pain, the physical breakdown, and, perhaps most importantly, Louis's abandonment. Prior also thinks that the visions may all be in his head but for a very different reason: dementia brought on by AIDS. Yet Belize, a nurse, does not think so: "This is not dementia. And this is not real. This is just you, Prior, afraid of what's coming, afraid of time."[51]

Belize is often the voice of reason and humanity in the play, and his perspective on Prior's so-called prophecy hints at Kushner's own. The argument for the cultural origins of Joseph Smith's prophecy is certainly at the heart of Fawn McKay Brodie's classic biography of Smith, *No Man Knows My History*, which Kushner has acknowledged as an important source for his representation of Mormonism.[52] Brodie asserts that Smith's prophetic labors—from the Book of Mormon to the *The Doctrine and Covenants*—sprang not from God but from Smith's mundane environment. Thus, the Book of Mormon can be seen, she argues, as Smith reckoning with various popular issues of his time, including the purported Hebraic origins of Native Americans and the search for the true Christian church.[53] Just as Brodie sees Smith constructing his visions from events and ideas in his community and his family, Belize interprets Prior's visions as personal responses to his needs and fears.

Brodie also attributes some of Smith's prophetic assertions to psychological factors.[54] Kushner explores this view of prophecy in the character of Harper, Joe's frustrated, anxiety-ridden, Valium-addicted wife, whose hallucinatory visions at times appear to be utter madness and at others—primarily when they bleed into Prior's visions—are "the very threshold of revelation."[55] When Harper is alone (or with her imaginary friend Mr. Lies) in her hallucinations, madness has the upper hand: she wanders the city for days, imagining that she is in Antarctica, finally drawing the attention of the police when she chews down a tree to begin building her Antarctic civilization. But when she shares her visions with Prior, both begin to see things that do not make any sense apart from some shared revelatory experience. As Harper tells Prior during their first such encounter, "I don't understand this. If I didn't ever see you before and I don't think I did then I don't think you should be here, in this hallucination, because in my experience the mind, which is where hallucinations come from, shouldn't be able to make up anything that wasn't there to start with, that didn't enter it from experience, from the real world. Imagination can't create anything new, can it? It only recycles bits and pieces from the world and reassembles them into visions . . . ."[56]

This explanation for visions as hallucinations constructed by the individual imagination is reinforced by the fact that we first see the actress who plays the Angel not in winged glory but in the far more mundane role of Emily, the nurse who cares for Prior during his first major medical crisis—well before he lays eyes on the Angel.[57] But such an explanation cannot account for Prior and Harper, who have never met in the "real" world, coming together in their visions.

Prior and Harper share information with one another in these visions that they seemingly could not have acquired any other way: Prior tells Harper that Joe is homosexual (information that Harper likely already knew but Prior could not have); Prior discovers that Louis has a new lover and that he is, in fact, Harper's Mormon husband. Thus, because it is in the context of one of these shared visions that Prior first hears the Angel, she can be seen as part of the reality of these revelatory experiences.

And yet Kushner, ever sly, pulls back from allowing viewers to consider these visions truly prophetic when he has Prior allude to *Alice in Wonderland* after he first meets Harper: "People come and go so quickly here . . . ."[58] Even more damning for those who see Prior's visions as revelation is the scene when he awakens in the hospital, having just returned from heaven, and delivers Dorothy's lines from *The Wizard of Oz*: "I've had a remarkable dream. And you were there, and you . . . and you. . . . And some of it was terrible, and some of it was wonderful, but all the same I kept saying I want to go home. And they sent me home."[59] Just as he resorts to Lerner and Loewe's musical *My Fair Lady* to cope with the appearance of his dead ancestors, Prior turns to the annals of popular culture to express his doubts about the reality of his revelations.

Prompted, no doubt, by such moments in the play, reviewers and scholars generally describe the visions, particularly Harper's, as hallucinatory, rather than prophetic.[60] Kushner encourages this view when he refers, in his notes on the text, to "the Book hallucination," remarking that "it's OK if the wires show, and maybe it's good that they do."[61] In his essay "*Angels in America:* The Millennium and Postmodern Memory," Stanley B. Garner Jr. argues that Kushner has restored magic to the theatrical stage precisely so that he can knock it down and expose it for the sham that it is.[62] Kushner has said as much himself: "I think there's value to the power of a really, sort of almost overwhelmingly convincing illusion that's sometimes both working and not working at the same time. . . . You believe it and don't believe it simultaneously, which engages a certain part of your brain that has to do with being skeptical about the nature of what you're experiencing in life."[63] The play's angelic visions, then, are meant to inspire belief at the same time that they ask viewers to question what they are seeing, just as Kushner seeks to inspire skepticism in his audience about the accepted norms and values of the world outside the theater.

But does the play itself draw any conclusions about the nature of revelatory experience? According to Kushner, no: "Whether the Angel is real, imagined, or hallucinated is something I want the audience to wrestle with, as the characters do."[64] But the text tells a different story; as David Savran argues, "The play's undecidability is, in fact, always already resolved because the questions that appear to be ambivalent in fact already have been decided consciously or unconsciously by the text itself."[65] In fact, the message of the play is that prophecy is a form of insanity, and insanity a form of prophecy.[66] As Prior tells Belize, when Belize is trying to convince him both that he is not crazy and his visions are not real, "Maybe I am a Prophet. Not just me, all of us who are dying now. Maybe we've caught the virus of prophecy."[67] Thus, Prior's prophecy is both real in itself and a consequence of his illness, but this connection to AIDS does not detract from its power. In fact, in the world of the play, the connection to Prior's struggle with the AIDS virus has the effect both of elevating prophecy and making it more real. As the characters must struggle with life (and with angels) to win anything of value, Prior's battle with prophecy gives him hard-won insight into the nature of the world and the human community in particular.

As Kushner validates prophetic vision as a tool people can use to cope with the realities of everyday life—an assertion that is justified by the activities of the Hebrew prophets after whom Prior's experiences are in part modeled—he once again turns to Joseph Smith as the archetypal

American prophet. While fully embracing Brodie's view that Smith's visions were firmly rooted in his cultural milieu, Kushner tells us such mundane origins do not detract from the power of revelation. As Joe's mother, Hannah, recently arrived from Salt Lake City and on a hiatus from her day job at the Mormon Visitor's Center in New York City, tells Prior, "He had great need of understanding. Our Prophet. His desire made prayer. His prayer made an angel. The angel was real. I believe that."[68] While Hannah believes that Smith's prayer generated the Angel Moroni—the angel was "made," not brought or called—this does not, for her, invalidate Smith's role as prophet or the religious visions he described. Revelation is a serious business, even when its origins are thoroughly human.

Kushner's directions for staging *Perestroika* bear this out. When defining the nature of the play as a comedy, he explains,

> it's not farce; all this happens only through a tremendous amount of struggle, and the stakes are high. The Angel, the scenes in Heaven, Prior's prophet scenes are not meant to occasion lapses into some sort of elbow-in-the-ribs comedy playing style. The Angel is immensely august, serious and dangerously powerful *always*, and Prior is running for his life, sick, scared and alone. A CAUTIONARY NOTE: The play is cheapened irreparably when the actors playing the Angel and *especially* Prior fail to convey the gravity of these situations. A Prior played for laughs is death to this enterprise! Every moment must be played for its reality, the terms always life and death; only then will the comedy emerge.[69]

Life is absurd, both painful and funny at the same time. And because prophecy is portrayed, in the world of the play, as a perfectly reasonable tool for dealing with life, it is intensely awesome and, at the same time, ridiculous. In short, prophecy—whether from Prior Walter or Joseph Smith—is only, and yet sublimely, human.

## The Emblem of Conservative America

While Kushner confronts the origins of Mormonism through Prior's recapitulation of the prophet Joseph Smith's experiences, he engages contemporary Mormonism through his characters Joe and Harper Pitt, a young married couple, and Joe's mother, Hannah. All of the members of the Pitt family are in some sense actively Mormon; though we never see or hear about a Sunday service or local congregation in the play, Joe wears temple garments (as does Harper in the film), his mother volunteers at the Mormon Visitor's Center in New York City, and all three characters pay lip service to what Mormons do and do not do, believe and do not believe. Their Mormonism is a prominent and pervasive presence in the play, from Joe's first scene (which is only the play's second), when he tells his mentor, Roy Cohn, that he is a Mormon, until his last appearance (in the penultimate scene of the play), when he tries to return to his wife to lead the only good life he believes in—that of a straight, married, Mormon man.

Kushner employs the Pitts' Mormonism as a form of shorthand, deploying familiar stereotypes to build individual characters and illuminate their worldviews. Piety and clean living are essential to the Pitts' understanding of who they should be, if not who they actually are. Joe reveals his Mormonism to Roy to justify his request that Roy not take the name of God in vain.[70] Harper, during her first meeting with Prior in what, for her, is a pill-induced hallucination, tells him, "I'm not *addicted*. I don't believe in addiction, and I never . . . well, I *never* drink. And I *never* take drugs. . . . It's terrible. Mormons are not supposed to be addicted to anything. I'm a Mormon."[71] And when a drunk Joe calls her, Hannah ignores the content of his conversation and chastises, "Drinking is a sin! A sin! I raised you better than that."[72]

This pervasive conservative piety relates to more than personal deportment. It also reveals a wealth of biases and political views. Joe is the clerk for a conservative Republican judge, and his services extend to writing his boss's court opinions. His mentor, the only historical figure in the play (although he is, Kushner notes, thoroughly fictionalized), is Roy Cohn, the powerful Republican "fixer" and former aide to Senator Joe McCarthy. And Joe is not just an opportunist, using the conservatism of the Reagan era to build a career—he is a devotee: "America has rediscovered itself. Its sacred place among the nations. And people aren't afraid of that like they used to be. This is a great thing. The truth restored. Law restored. That's what President Reagan's done. . . . He says, 'Truth exists and can be spoken proudly.' And the country responds to him. We become better. More good."[73] Joe believes in President Reagan and his politics as fervently as he does in Joseph Smith and his religious legacy—if not more so.

Finally, in a scene in the Diorama Room at the Mormon Visitor's Center, Kushner emphatically reminds viewers of the Mormons' pioneer past.[74] While the scene functions as space for Prior and Harper's second shared vision, at the same time the looming presence of the automatonic pioneer family in their covered wagon links Mormonism and Mormons to a past in which they were driven west by the dominant culture's violent intolerance, to their present association with conservative (heterosexual, child-rearing) family values, and with the ongoing migratory character of American life reviled by the Angel but celebrated by Kushner.[75]

Although Kushner respects the Mormon past, his interest in writing about the Saints stems from altogether different feelings about contemporary Mormonism: "Mormons always seem much nicer people than what they wind up visiting on themselves and the rest of Utah. That contradiction is very interesting."[76] Individual Mormons may be nice, but their ultraconservative political views are insidious. It is these political implications of Mormonism, and not the religion itself, that offend Kushner.[77] Louis can accept his new lover, Joe, in spite of his religion, but he cannot forgive Joe's political conservatism, exemplified by his ties to Roy Cohn and his authorship of judicial decisions that deny equal rights to homosexuals. In the same way, while Kushner acknowledges that he finds Mormons "decent, hard-working, serious, intelligent," and "good-hearted,"[78] he, too, cannot forgive Joe for the conservatism that is so thoroughly a part of his cultural values: "When I was working on Joe, I wanted to write a conservative man that I actually liked. I didn't finally succeed [laughs]."[79]

At the same time that Kushner openly condemns Joe Pitt for the conservative social and political values that the playwright depicts as characteristic of Joe's Mormon faith, he is also using Angels to expose the hypocrisy he sees as inherent to such conservatism. Harper is trapped in a loveless marriage from which she escapes through an addiction to Valium; Hannah is, at least at first, a hard, unsympathetic character in total opposition to the stereotypical image of the happy, nurturing Mormon wife and mother; like his mentor, Joe is secretly homosexual, even as he uses politics to condemn homosexuality. And all of them are terribly, painfully unhappy. Joe explains his wife's failures thus: "Everyone thinks that Mormons don't come from homes like that, we aren't supposed to behave that way, but we do. It's not lying, or being two-faced. Everyone tries very hard to live up to God's strictures. . . . The failure to measure up hits people very hard. From such a strong desire to do good they feel very far from goodness when they fail."[80] Anything less than orderly, sober, kind, heterosexual perfection is simply un-Mormon. But that kind of perfection, Kushner tells us, is not real. As Harper tells Prior about the Mormon Visitor's Center, "This isn't a place for real feelings."[81] It is impossible to maintain the façade without sacrificing some part of your humanity.

The part of himself that Joe believes he must sacrifice is erotic love because his homosexuality is harshly condemned by his church. This is tantamount to blasphemy for Kushner, for whom the elevation of homosexuality in American culture to a place of not just tolerance but total acceptance is an avowed goal. To illustrate the destructive force of such repression, he taps into a stereotype that expands upon the image of the secret polygamist in the pantheon of twentieth-century myths about Mormons: the repressed sexual deviant. As Latter-day Saints have become an object of ridicule for their embrace of the conservative sexual values that were once used to condemn them, such images declare that sexual deviance—including polygamy, homosexuality, and violence—is the result of "an excessive devotion to conservative notions about sexual morality." Thus, the LDS Church represents the "institutionalization of repressed passion" and "sexual deprivation."[82]

Examples of these stereotypes abound. Secret, abusive polygamy has been a staple among representations of Mormonism since the nineteenth century, when popular novels (some claiming to be memoirs) explored the alleged horrors of the lives of polygamous wives. In the early twentieth century, popular Western writer Zane Grey made Mormon polygamists the villains of some of his most popular novels.[83] Alan Drury's 1959 Pulitzer Prize–winning novel, *Advise and Consent*, features a young Utah senator by the name of Brig Anderson caught in a scandal when one of his colleagues discovers a secret homosexual rendezvous (director Otto Preminger adapted the novel into a film in 1962).[84] Writer Natalie R. Collins's mystery novels declare a direct link between Mormon sexual repression and the subjugation and abuse of women.[85] Most recently, HBO's television series *Big Love* follows the exploits of a modern-day polygamist.[86]

In the vein of these representations of the secret, dangerous sex lives of religiously conservative Mormons, Joe's denial of his homosexuality is slowly destroying him:

> Does it make any difference? That I might be one thing deep
> within, no matter how wrong or ugly that might thing is, so long as
> I have fought, with everything I have, to kill it. . . . For God's sake,
> there's nothing left, I'm a shell. There's nothing left to kill.
>     As long as my behavior is what I know it has to be. Decent.
> Correct. That alone in the eyes of God.[87]

Joe's self-denial is also destroying his wife, who knows that sex is at the heart of her marital—and thus her mental—instability: "You think you're the only one who hates sex; I do; I hate it with you; I do. I dream that you batter away at me till all my joints come apart, like wax, and I fall into pieces. It's like a punishment. It was wrong of me to marry you.

I knew you. . . . It's a sin, and it's killing us both."[88] Joe's violence against Harper is never active; it lies in his complete disregard for her. When he looks at her he sees "*Nothing.*"[89]

It is true that the Mormon characters in *Angels in America* defy the expectations that others place on them relative to their religion and their politics. For example, Louis, when he is comforted by Joe during an emotional breakdown at work in their fateful first meeting, responds with surprise, "What a nice man," as though he cannot believe that a staunch Republican is also a kind person.[90] And when, in their first encounter, Hannah escorts Prior to the hospital because he is in the throes of another medical crisis, he distrusts her kindness to a homosexual man like him because she is a Mormon: "I wish you would be more true to your demographic profile. Life is confusing enough."[91] But when these characters stray from strict obedience to the beliefs and behaviors apparently demanded by their faith, it leads to trouble. Joe, of course, ends up having a sexual relationship with Louis that finally destroys his marriage. Hannah appears, at play's end, to have left her conservatism behind altogether: she is an accepted part of Prior's self-made family—in which the other three members are all openly gay men. Her assimilation into Prior's world is so complete that "she looks like a New Yorker, and she is reading the *New York Times.*"[92]

Both Hannah's and Harper's redemptions are foreshadowed in the play by their ongoing inability to "pass" (in Joe's words) as good Mormons. As Joe tells Roy, "I know I married her because she . . . because I loved it that she was always wrong, always doing something wrong, like one step out of step."[93] Harper herself acknowledges to Prior that she is a "Jack Mormon": "It means I'm flawed. Inferior Mormon product."[94] Hannah's failures are revealed throughout the play: she "takes a furtive drag" of a friend's cigarette when she believes no one is looking; the same friend tells her, "I decided to like you 'cause you're the only unfriendly Mormon I ever met";[95] and, perhaps most damning, she does not like men, leading many commentators to argue that her self-avowed aversion, combined with the sexual experience she shares with the female-bodied Angel, indicate that she is a lesbian.[96] These women escape the conservative culture surrounding their religion—and Kushner's final condemnation—because they were already out of step with the social values of Mormon culture. But Joe, who never questions any aspect of Mormon religion or culture, cannot escape.

## Final Redemption

The play's epilogue is supremely hopeful. In the words of one reviewer, *Angels* "goes out in a blaze of compassion"; "the uplift is real and salutary."[97] Prior is still alive and in relatively good health, and he has found a new "family": Louis, still his friend if no longer his lover; Belize, still challenging and humanizing everyone, especially Louis; and the transformed Hannah. Having left her husband and taken back her life by taking up Kushner's call for movement and migration, Harper is on a plane, and we can be hopeful for her sanity and prospects. Even Roy Cohn has received forgiveness, if only on his deathbed.[98] But what of Joe?

In his final appearance in the play, Joe attempts to reconcile with Harper in an effort to get back on track in his conservative, straight, married life, telling her that he has "done things, I'm ashamed. But I have changed. I don't know how yet, but. . . . Please, please, don't leave me now."[99] The audience (and the playwright) may see this as disingenuous; after all, Joe has just tried to get back together with Louis and failed when Louis refused to forgive him for his "legal fag-bashing."[100] But Joe is not simply looking for someone to take care of him now that his first attempt at a gay relationship has fallen apart: this, his second return to Harper, is another effort to remake himself, to conquer the angel he is wrestling and begin again his struggle to be a good Mormon and, as he sees it, a good man.[101] Harper, however, is already embracing her new path to self-discovery after her final shared vision with Prior, which took place in heaven. Her response to Joe's plaintive request for a return to the lie they have lived together is to slap him—hard—and hand him two of her vision-inducing Valium with the instructions, "Get lost. Joe. Go exploring."[102] Joe is last seen sitting alone in his Brooklyn apartment. While the play's other characters are all adopting Prior's very human prophecy of movement, migration, and change, Joe is silent and static, unmoving and seemingly unmoved.[103]

Why is it that Joe cannot be remade as almost every other character in *Angels* has been? In some sense, it is because he is a Mormon. To be specific, it is because he cannot, finally, repudiate the conservative values—both theological and political—that Mormonism represents in Kushner's play. In the brave new world that Kushner brings into being at the end of *Angels in America*, varieties of race, religion, and, most importantly, sexual orientation are irrelevant in the face of the overwhelming fact that human beings all deserve full inclusion in the community—especially the American one. Change is embraced as both inevitable and valuable. But even in his moments of greatest freedom, Joe cannot imagine such a liberal (and, in Kushner's vision, liberated) world. For Joe even "time is conservative, it moves slow."[104]

Unlike his pioneer ancestors, whose mass exodus beyond the borders of the United States was an act of both self-preservation and intentional radical separation, undertaken in part so that the Mormons could live out their religious and social experiment beyond the reach of the conservative culture that would have squelched their attempts at change and difference, Joe is stuck in the heart of America's conservative culture, unable or unwilling to move to a periphery where he can embrace the difference that Kushner celebrates. Thus, Joe's contemporary conservative Mormonism "is part of the problem: it is an overly institutionalized, guilt-producing, conservative religion that stands in the way of meaningful social change."[105] Moreover, Mormonism is, on some level for Kushner, intellectually indefensible: "It's so dumb. It's naïve and disingenuous. It's like Grandma Moses, the celestial and the terrestrial heavens with all this Masonry incorporated into it. It's American gothic."[106] Joe's failure, for which the playwright ultimately condemns him, is that he clings without question to what Mormonism has become: settled—physically and intellectually—and unable to move with the changing times.[107]

This is not to say that religion has no place in the ideal world that Kushner is building. Religion is part of the culture in which every person grows to adulthood in the United States and cannot—and should not—be wholly abandoned or denied any more than a person's sexuality. Thus, when Joe offers to remove his sacred Mormon temple garment if Louis asks him, Louis responds, "How can you stop wearing it if it's a skin? Your past, your beliefs . . . ."[108] In the same way, although Louis is a decidedly secular Jew, Belize expects that anyone who identifies himself as Jewish will be able to handle something as basic as chanting Kaddish, and Louis proves him right (albeit with a bit of supernatural assistance from Ethel Rosenberg's ghost).[109]

Faith is, in fact, a positive asset, as evidenced by the religious story that dominates the epilogue, a scene that showcases the ideal community that Kushner is promoting. The story of the Angel Bethesda and the healing fountain that she once opened at Jerusalem, which will again flow at the coming of the millennium, is not the property of a single character: Prior prompts the telling of the story; Louis relates its Jewish origins; Belize speaks of the fountain's healing powers; and finally the re-formed Hannah explains the story's millennial implications. In fact, Prior tells us, it is Hannah who first shared the story with him, presumably turning once again to her Mormon heritage to help explain and categorize the angelic experiences that they have shared.[110]

What Kushner is saying, in contemporary American style, is that it is okay to be *spiritual* but not *religious*, with that term implying institutional affiliation. While those characters who find themselves do not abandon religious ideas, they no longer rely on institutions to supply and interpret those ideas for them. In this light, Joe's sin is not his ongoing faith but his uncritical acceptance of the tenets of that faith—and its social and political implications—as laid out for him by a church. He does not approach his belief in the supernatural with the healthy skepticism that Kushner hopes to inspire in viewers, whereas Hannah's belief is acceptable precisely because it is her own, not that of an institutionalized authority, and it is rooted in a reasonable perspective on life tempered both by her experience and her humanity.[111]

## From Stage to Screen:
## Taking the Edge Off?

Director Mike Nichols's 2003 film adaptation of *Angels in America*, for which Kushner wrote the screenplay, significantly softens his critique of Mormonism when compared with the text of the play. The way his treatment shifts from the play to the film is echoed in a review in *The New Yorker:*

> the opening credits of "Angels" offer an astonishing effect, which beautifully sets the stage, as it were, for the movie. The camera moves across the entire United States, high above the clouds and sometimes right through them, and you feel that you're flying with it as it passes over the Golden Gate Bridge, up and over the Arch in St. Louis, past the Sears Tower in Chicago, past the Empire State Building, finally descending into Central Park and stopping at the statue of the angel in Bethesda Fountain, whose face, to your surprise, comes alive, lifting its blank, grave eyes to stare into your own.[112]

In spite of the fact that Kushner's characters do not mention either St. Louis or Chicago in the play or the film, these cities' brief appearances are noted in the review. The only city and landmark in the credits that is not mentioned is the second to appear: after leaving San Francisco, the camera dips below the clouds to reveal the Mormon Temple in all its grandeur at the heart of Salt Lake City. Similarly Mormonism remains a presence in Kushner's film script, but it is far less significant than it was in the play.

While the film maintains Mormonism as the religious representation of a conservative American ideology that has no place in the ideal world Kushner posits, many of the sharpest direct critiques—those delivered by the Mormons themselves—are gone: the pivotal scene in the Diorama Room at the Mormon Visitor's Center—where Harper's open disaffection from Mormonism first becomes obvious in the play—is substantially rewritten, eliminating many of her sharpest comments; the early scene in which Hannah decides to leave Salt Lake City and reveals her distance from Mormonism in her furtive smoking and the disdain with which she speaks of the Latter-day Saints ("It's a hard place, Salt Lake: baked dry. Abundant energy; not much intelligence")[113] is gone altogether.

The most significant change of all is Joe Pitt's status at the end of the story. As early as 1994, Kushner indicated that in spite of his failure to create Joe as a conservative character he could like, he did not believe that Joe was beyond redemption: "He gets somewhere and will ultimately be redeemable, in *Angels*, part three."[114] This view is more evident in the film than in the play: while Joe is still not "saved" at the end, the audience's last sight of him is no longer a forlorn figure alone in his apartment immediately after his wife has left him. Instead, the morning after his wife leaves (and after his mother, Hannah, begins her transformation in earnest through her encounter with the Angel), Hannah is walking down the street in Brooklyn when she bumps into her son. He is on his way to work, and he looks terrible. Hannah, after ascertaining that Harper has left him ("Good for her."), asks if he will be home that night and tells him she will make dinner. It is clear that she intends to take care of her son, and since her redemption is so clear at the end of both the film and the play, we have reason to hope that she will help Joe along his own path to self-discovery and wholeness.

The action in this new scene unfolds over the voices of a choir, anachronistically dressed in clothes reminiscent of those worn by the Mormon family in the Diorama Room at the Visitor's Center, singing in the street. The hymn is "Shall We Gather at the River":

> Shall we gather at the river,
> Where bright angel feet have trod,
> With its crystal tide forever
> Flowing by the throne of God?
> Yes, we'll gather at the river,
> The beautiful, the beautiful river;
> Gather with the saints at the river
> That flows by the throne of God.[115]

The obvious message is one of hope: Hannah—and perhaps Joe—with the other characters is part of a new gathering like that of the Latter-day Saints in the nineteenth century. They are coming together in a new community founded on ideals of reform and the certainty of divine presence in their lives. But the hymn also reflects a warning that Kushner did not deliver at the end of the play: just like past Jewish and Mormon migrants, who sought safety and meaning in new communities that challenged the conservative ideals of America in their own times, Kushner's newly liberated American homosexual spiritual community is also at risk of settling down, becoming complacent in its rootedness. Kushner seems aware, ten years after he won the Pulitzer Prize for his vision of a new American community, that even the utopia he imagines can be corrupted if, as the Angel demands, it stops moving with the flow of history.[116]

## Conclusion

Terryl Givens argues in his book on nineteenth-century American anti-Mormonism that "the imaginatively rendered instances of the 'Mormon Problem' and the creative solutions to that problem that fiction made possible have a great deal to tell us about how identity can be threatened, manipulated, and constituted."[117] *Angels in America* bears many of the marks of an anti-Mormon text, including Kushner's clear skepticism about a prophet modeled on Joseph Smith and his devastating portrayal of Mormon Joe Pitt. But despite Kushner's clear animosity toward orthodox Mormonism, this is not an anti-Mormon text: Mormonism is not his primary target in the play. Rather it is a representative, alongside the politics of the Republican Party that dominated the United States under President Ronald Reagan, of the broader evil of institutionalized reactionary conservatism. It is not, in the end, his Mormonism that Joe must abandon to be part of Kushner's ideal community—his mother, Hannah, carries and indeed celebrates the residue of her religious beliefs in the utopia of the epilogue—but the archconservative mores that drive him to deny the rights of homosexuals and indeed even his own homosexuality. Thus, the entity that Kushner models as dangerous and subversive is not Mormon faith but the complex of conservative institutions and politics to which it is tied in the contemporary United States.

There is a fine line between Kushner's use of anti-Mormon images and rhetoric and actual anti-Mormonism, but it is a line that Kushner carefully maintains in the text. What Kushner is doing in *Angels in America* is critiquing particular (conservative) aspects of Mormon belief and culture that he does not consider essential to Mormon religiosity.

This is evidenced by the fact that Hannah does not give up her faith to enter the utopian community of the epilogue: the belief in Joseph Smith and his visions (particularly the Angel Moroni) that she defends to Prior even before she confirms the existence of angels by her encounter with the Angel of America is clearly reflected in her becoming the source of the story of the Angel Bethesda's return.[118] Elsewhere Kushner has spoken positively of certain aspects of Mormon theology, particularly those that he thinks reflect Judaism: the emphasis on practice over belief and the deemphasis of damnation, the centrality of a text, the importance of diasporic experience in forming identity, and the positive theology of the body.[119] Kushner distinguishes these aspects of Mormonism from the conservative social and political values that he condemns in Joe and Jewish Roy Cohn, which he clearly sees as distinct from religion. Kushner believes that it is possible (and perfectly acceptable, as evidenced by Hannah's presence in the epilogue) to be Mormon—albeit a different kind of Mormon, clearly defined by liberal social values—without espousing the dangerous conservative values that find voice in Roy's and Joe's Republican politics. The politics associated with Joe's conservative Mormon outlook that Kushner finds irredeemable are not, in his view, essential to being a Mormon believer.

For Kushner, Mormons and Mormonism represent both the positive good of American creative energy and the dangerous stagnation of such creativity into conservative institutions that threaten to destroy American society. He calls for skepticism from both his characters and his audience about theological and political ideas, Mormon and otherwise, and he shows that such skepticism is utterly at odds with the kind of conservatism that orthodox Mormonism represents in the play. Finally, he demands that his characters reject the rigid conservatism of the contemporary Church of Jesus Christ of Latter-day Saints and Reagan-era Republican politics to rebuild the nation on liberal progressive values, the only values that Kushner believes can create a sustainable American community that will survive the violence of history. While the Angel Moroni may still be *the* American angel, his journey from the margins to the conservative center demands that now he, like that center, must be rejected: "An angel is just a belief, with wings and arms that can carry you. It's naught to be afraid of. If it lets you down, reject it. Seek something new."[120]

# Notes

I would like to thank Professor Terryl Givens of the University of Richmond and Professor Peter Hawkins of Yale Divinity School for reading multiple drafts of this essay and providing me with incredibly valuable feedback.

1. Rich, Review, "Angels in America; Millennium Approaches; Embracing All Possibilities in Art and Life."
2. Freedman, "Angels, Monsters, and Jews," 91.
3. *Angels in America*, directed by Mike Nichols.
4. Kushner, *Angels in America*, 289. Further quotations from the play will be cited with the title of the part, *Millennium Approaches* or *Perestroika*, and the page number.
5. Shipps, "Surveying the Mormon Image since 1960." See also Shipps, "From Satyr to Saint," in *Sojourner in the Promised Land*, 51–97.
6. Kushner, quoted in Bruce Weber, "Angels' Angels."
7. Stout, Straubhaar, and Newbold, "Through a Glass Darkly," 140.
8. Miller, "Heavenquake," 66.
9. Canby, "Sunday View: Two 'Angels,' Two Journeys, in London and New York."
10. See Pace, "Review: Mormon Angels in America," 191–97; Stout, Straubhaar, and Newbold, "Through a Glass Darkly"; and Austin, "Theology for the Approaching Millennium," 25–44.
11. Prior specifically identifies himself this way in his first scene, only minutes into the play. See *Millennium Approaches*, 26.
12. Ibid., 57.
13. Frantzen, "Prior to the Normans," 138.
14. *Perestroika*, 278.
15. Brodie, *No Man Knows My History*, 1–4. Kushner acknowledges his indebtedness to Brodie's book in "The Theater and the Barricades," an interview with Craig Kinzer, Sandra Richards, Frank Galati, and Lawrence Bommer, in *Tony Kushner in Conversation*, 197. Brodie portrays Smith as a scoundrel and a fraud but also a man of genius. For a more respectful biography, see Richard Bushman, *Joseph Smith and the Beginnings of Mormonism* or *Joseph Smith: Rough Stone Rolling*. Bushman discusses Smith's family background in *Beginnings of Mormonism*, 11–29. *Joseph Smith and the Beginnings of Mormonism* would have been available to Kushner when he was writing *Angels in America*, though I have found no indication that he referred to it.
16. See Givens, *Viper on the Hearth*, 17–18. The separate ethnic identity of the Mormon community achieved scholarly respectability after Thomas O'Dea asserted it in *The Mormons*. I am especially indebted to Professor Givens's work, which is currently the most sustained scholarly exploration of the reception and representation of Mormonism in American culture.
17. Givens, *Viper on the Hearth*, 18.
18. Ibid., 6.
19. The invisibility of Joe Pitt's Mormonism within the play supports this breakdown of ethnic distinctions. Joe's mentor and political father figure, Roy Cohn, does not know that Joe is a Mormon until he tells Roy

(*Millennium Approaches*, 20–21), and later his lover Louis is incredibly distressed to find out that he has unknowingly "spent a month in bed with a Mormon!" (*Perestroika*, 197).

20.  In *Viper on the Hearth*, Givens asserts that this outsider status was imposed on Mormons from the outside. R. Laurence Moore argues, however, that Mormons themselves embraced the designation of "other," and that, in fact, status as what Moore calls a "religious outgroup" helped the Mormons to flourish. See "How to Become a People, 25–47.

21.  See, for example, Savran, "Tony Kushner Considers the Longstanding Problems of Virtue and Happiness," 101–2.

22.  Shipps, "Difference and Otherness," 83–84.

23.  Freedman, "Angels, Monsters, and Jews," 92. In her essay "Wrestling with Angels: A Jewish Fantasia," Ailsa Solomon also posits unique parallels between the experiences of the Jewish and homosexual communities in the United States.

24.  During the first twenty years of the church's existence, Latter-day Saints were forced out—sometimes with extreme violence—of communities in New York, Pennsylvania, Ohio, Missouri, and finally Illinois, where Joseph Smith was murdered in 1844.

25.  Solomon, "Wrestling with Angels," 121. Many of these accusations have been leveled against other minorities as well, including the African American community of which Prior's friend Belize is the play's sole representative.

26.  See Givens, *Viper on the Hearth*. Examples include the popular *Female Life among the Mormons: A Narrative of Many Years' Experience among the Mormons* (London: Routledge, 1855); Sir Arthur Conan Doyle's first Sherlock Holmes mystery, *A Study in Scarlet* (1887); and classic Western writer Zane Grey's novels *The Riders of the Purple Sage* (1912) and *The Rainbow Trail* (1915).

27.  Solomon, "Wrestling with Angels," 121–22.

28.  Heinerman and Shupe, *The Mormon Corporate Empire*; Ostling, *Mormon America*.

29.  Kruger, "Identity and Conversion in *Angels in America*," 152.

30.  *Millennium Approaches*, 73.

31.  Ibid., 51–52.

32.  *Perestroika*, 200 (italics in the original).

33.  Kushner, quoted in Savran, "Tony Kushner Considers," 26.

34.  Givens, *Viper on the Hearth*, 14. See also Franchot, *Roads to Rome*, especially xvii–xxvii.

35.  See Brodie, *No Man Knows My History*, 101–2, 121. David Savran gives an overview of millennial expectations in early Mormonism and ties it to Kushner's idea of millennium in "Ambivalence, Utopia, and a Queer Sort of Materialism," 216–19. For a more in-depth exploration of early Mormon millennialism, see Underwood, *The Millenarian World of Early Mormonism*.

36.  It is no accident that the crowning angelic story of the play, related in the epilogue in *Perestroika*, features the Angel Bethesda. While the story comes from Jewish tradition, the source in *Angels in America* is the Mormon Hannah. See *Perestroika*, 279.

37.  See Tuveson, *Redeemer Nation*.

38.  Since the late nineteenth century, American Jews have focused increasingly on Jerusalem and the Middle East—a change largely due to the growth of the Zionist movement in the last century (see Sarna, *American Judaism: A History,* 200–206). In 1830 Joseph Smith declared Missouri was the Mormon Promised Land, but after the community was forced out of Missouri and, later, Illinois, Brigham Young called the Saints to gather in the Salt Lake Valley in Utah: "For the time has come for the Saints to go up to the mountains of the Lord's house, and help to establish it in the tops of the mountains" (Young, quoted in Arrington, *Brigham Young, American Moses,* 156). In his biography of Young, former LDS Church historian Arrington refers to the settlement in Deseret as "the new Zion" (151). In their book *The Mormon Experience: A History of the Latter-day Saints in America,* Arrington and Davis Bitton write, "To the Mormon pioneers of 1846 the eastern United States assumed the role Europe had traditionally occupied in the greater American consciousness, while the unsettled Great Basin offered the promise of a new world. Rebaptism . . . underscored a desire by the Mormons to put behind them the misunderstanding, dissension, persecution, and temptations of contemporary American society and to build a new and better civilization in the Zion of their mountain stronghold," 110.

39.  Kushner, quoted in Savran, "Tony Kushner Considers," 25. Kushner frequently cites the work of Jewish Marxist philosopher Walter Benjamin (for whom he named the character Prior Walter) as foundational both to his own ideas about history and progress and, more specifically, to his construction of history and time in *Angels in America.* In fact, his Angel is modeled on Benjamin's discussion of Paul Klee's 1920 painting *Angelus Novus* in the essay "Theses on the Philosophy of History." See Savran, "Ambivalence," 210–12.

40.  Ailsa Solomon interprets the play's ongoing criticism of Louis, the play's primary Jewish character, as an assertion "that American Jews, having achieved a level of comfort and even clout in the United States, have abandoned their commitment to erotic and political liberation." "Wrestling with Angels," 131.

41.  Kushner, quoted in Savran, "Tony Kushner Considers," 103.

42.  *Perestroika,* 172–73. Joseph Smith described these "spectacles" in *The History of the Church,* 1:35. Fawn Brodie calls the spectacles "peep-stones" (*No Man Knows My History,* 21) and connects them to Smith's use of magical stones, popular in contemporary folk practices, for treasure digging. See also Bushman, *Joseph Smith and the Beginnings of Mormonism,* 69–78, 82; and D. Michael Quinn, *Early Mormonism and the Magic Worldview.* For Kushner on the peep-stones, see William Harris, "Theatre: The Secret of Angels."

43.  *Perestroika,* 149. Kushner repeatedly refers to the prophet Jonah, who refused his call to prophecy and was subsequently punished: "But the Lord provided a large fish to swallow up Jonah" (Jon. 1:17; all biblical citations are from The New Oxford Annotated Bible, New Revised Standard Version with Apocrypha). For example, the Angel responds to Prior's refusals by telling him, "You can't outrun your occupation, Jonah." *Perestroika,* 179. And when Prior asks Hannah what God does to

prophets who refuse their vision, she tells him, "He...Well, he feeds them to whales." *Perestroika*, 236.

44. In fact, when Prior briefly dons the peep-stones, he quickly tosses them aside with the words, "That was terrible! I don't want to see that!" *Perestroika*, 172. Like the Book of Mormon, the contents of the Angel of America's book are not important; rather, each book is a sign that confirms the prophetic mission of the one who receives it. See Terryl Givens, *By the Hand of Mormon*, 63–64.

45. *Perestroika*, 180. Capitalization in the original. See Ezek. 3:1–3. Similarly the prophet Isaiah receives the gift of prophecy after an angel touches a burning coal to his lips (Isa. 6:6–9). Mormonism's reflection of the prophetic tradition of the Hebrew Bible is not accidental but part of Joseph Smith's "restoration of Israel" in the early Mormon period. See Shipps, "Difference and Otherness," especially 83–84; and Shipps, *Mormonism*, especially 37, 53.

46. Prior first experiences pain in his leg during his earliest medical crisis (*Millennium Approaches*, 54).

47. See Gen. 32:24–31. In a striking reversal of the biblical wrestling match, Prior wrestles the Angel in an intentional recapitulation of Jacob's story and leaves her with a leg injury (*Perestroika*, 251).

48. See Brodie, *No Man Knows My History*, 8; and Bushman, *Joseph Smith and the Beginnings of Mormonism*, 33.

49. Savran, "Tony Kushner Considers," 102.

50. Kushner, quoted in Adam Mars Jones, "Tony Kushner at the Royal National Theatre of Great Britain," 26.

51. *Perestroika*, 181. Belize also notes a parallel between Louis's abandonment of Prior and the Angel's story of God's abandonment of heaven and his angels: "I smell a motif. The man that got away." *Perestroika*, 177.

52. Like Brodie, Kushner views the Book of Mormon as a novel in the tradition of American epic fiction (Jones, "Tony Kushner at the Royal National Theatre," 24); see also Brodie, *No Man Knows My History*, 48, 413.

53. On Brodie as the modern source of the argument for the cultural origins of the Book of Mormon, see Givens, *By the Hand of Mormon*, especially 5, 161, and 202. Givens points out that many of Brodie's claims reflect those put forward in anti-Mormon literature of the nineteenth century. For an overview of nonsupernatural explanations for the origins of the Book of Mormon, see Givens, *By the Hand of Mormon*, 155–84.

54. Brodie, *No Man Knows My History*, 413–17; also discussed in Givens, *By the Hand of Mormon*, 159.

55. *Millennium Approaches*, 39.

56. Ibid., 38.

57. In the film, this connection between the nurse and the Angel is reinforced by Emily's prominent tattoo of angel's wings on her upper arm.

58. *Millennium Approaches*, 40.

59. *Perestroika*, 270.

60. Frank Rich, in his review of *Millennium Approaches* in the *New York Times*, is fairly typical in describing the play as "a space large enough to accommodate everything from precise realism to surrealistic hallucination." Review, "Angels in America; Millennium Approaches."

61. *Millennium Approaches*, 11.

62. Garner, "Angels in America," 173–84.
63. Kushner, "Kushner: Interview."
64. Kushner, quoted in Harris, "The Secret of Angels."
65. Savran, "Ambivalence, Utopia, and a Queer Sort of Materialism," 209.
66. Deborah Geis makes this argument in "The Delicate Ecology of Your Delusions: Insanity, Theatricality, and the Thresholds of Revelation in Kushner's *Angels in America*"; see especially 200.
67. *Perestroika*, 182.
68. Ibid., 235.
69. Ibid., 142 (italics and capitalization in the original).
70. *Millennium Approaches*, 21. Roy responds, with apparent delight, "Mormon. Delectable. Absolutely. Only in America."
71. Ibid., 38 (italics in the original).
72. Ibid., 82. For a discussion of the emergence of the stereotype of the squeaky-clean, all-American Mormon, see Shipps, "From Satyr to Saint," 72–73.
73. *Millennium Approaches*, 32.
74. *Perestroika*, 192–202.
75. In addition to his appreciation of contemporary Mormons' "immense industry, diligence, and faith," Kushner has also stated his admiration for early Mormonism, particularly the experimentation with collective ownership and other economic alternatives to capitalism (Savran, "Tony Kushner Considers," 103; Kinzer, Richards, Galati, and Bommer, 208–9).
76. Kushner, quoted in Jones, "Tony Kushner at the Royal National Theatre," 25.
77. Kushner's conflation of the religious and the political is consistent throughout the play. As Louis informs the audience in the play's epilogue to *Perestroika*, "Only in politics does the miraculous occur," 278. Politics, then, fulfills a role in the contemporary world that in the past was satisfied by religion, and Kushner seems to be telling viewers that politics have in fact superseded religion in human society. Thus, Joe's religious conservatism finds expression in his politics, and Kushner condemns both. This is a consistent theme in twentieth-century American representations of Mormonism; as Terryl Givens notes, whereas Mormons were once regarded as dangerous because of their strange and marginal beliefs (such as polygamy and theocratic governance), "it is now because Mormons occupy what used to be the center that they fall into contempt." *Viper on the Hearth*, 164. See also Shipps, "From Satyr to Saint" and "Surveying the Mormon Image"; and Mario S. DePillis, "The Emergence of Mormon Power since 1945," 1–32. DePillis calls Mormons "a social icon" of American conservatism and "the last innocent Americans," 6. The article includes an extended discussion of *Angels in America*, but I disagree with DePillis's interpretations of the play on almost every point. In particular his failure to discuss the epilogue that closes *Perestroika* (he incorrectly asserts that the play ends with Prior Walter's death of AIDS [6]), in which the Mormon Hannah plays a central and positive role, undermines his argument that Kushner has no respect for Mormonism.
78. Kushner, quoted in Jones, "Tony Kushner at the Royal National Theatre," 25; and Harris, "Secret of Angels."
79. Kushner, quoted in Savran, "Tony Kushner Considers," 103.

80. *Millennium Approaches*, 59.
81. *Perestroika*, 198.
82. Givens, *Viper on the Hearth*, 162.
83. See *The Riders of the Purple Sage*, originally published in 1912, and its sequel *The Rainbow Trail*, published in 1915. Both of these books have been adapted into multiple films, the most recent airing on Turner Network Television (TNT) in 1996, directed by Charles Haid.
84. *Advise and Consent*, directed by Otto Preminger.
85. See *Wives and Sisters* and *Behind Closed Doors*. A Kirkus review of *Wives and Sisters* calls the book an "expert depiction of a young woman's struggle with the oppressive 'family values' of one kind of fundamentalism." Quoted on the book's Amazon sales page, available online at http://www.amazon.com (accessed July 2, 2009).
86. *Big Love*, Anima Sola Productions.
87. *Millennium Approaches*, 46.
88. Ibid., 43.
89. *Perestroika*, 239 (italics in the original). According to David Savran, in *Angels* "it is not homosexuality that is pathological, but its denial." "Ambivalence, Utopia, and a Queer Sort of Materialism," 227.
90. *Millennium Approaches*, 34.
91. *Perestroika*, 236.
92. Ibid., 277.
93. *Millennium Approaches*, 59.
94. *Perestroika*, 193.
95. *Millennium Approaches*, 88.
96. *Perestroika*, 236.
97. Richards, "Sunday View: 'Angels' Finds a Poignant Note of Hope."
98. After Roy's painful death from AIDS, Kushner bestows forgiveness on him in the form of the Kaddish, the Jewish prayer for the dead, which Louis, at Belize's urging and with the help of Roy's old archenemy, Ethel Rosenberg, chants for him (*Perestroika*, 255–57). Roy has a life beyond death in the play, and a scene not usually played (Kushner notes in the introduction to *Perestroika* that the scene is expendable) finds him in an unidentified, but hellish, atmosphere, offering to defend God in a lawsuit Prior has just urged the angels to press against him. Even burning in the afterlife, Roy is finding purpose and fulfillment (*Perestroika*, 274). See also Harold Bloom, introduction to *Tony Kushner*, 4.
99. *Perestroika*, 272.
100. Ibid., 242.
101. See *Millennium Approaches*, 55–56, where Joe tells Harper of his childhood understanding of the story of Jacob wrestling the angel and compares his current struggle with his sexuality to Jacob's "fierce and unfair" battle.
102. *Perestroika*, 273.
103. Ibid., 274–75.
104. Ibid., 204.
105. Austin, "Theology for the Approaching Millennium," 43.
106. Kushner, quoted in Savran, "Tony Kushner Considers," 102.
107. According to Oskar Eustis, the artistic director of the Eureka Theatre Company in San Francisco, which originally commissioned *Angels* in

1987, "The idea [at the heart of the play] had to do with the exodus history of America. . . . You set out from an oppressive old place, go into the wilderness and reinvent yourself, start a new community free of the plagues of the old one. And yet you can never do that, really." Eustis, quoted in Bruce Weber, "Angels' Angels." Thus, the religious story at the core of both Judaism and Mormonism is central to Kushner's agenda. While it is impossible to escape the problems of the home society, the attempt to reject oppression and build something new is clearly a good thing: in the end, it is what Prior and his new "family" do in the midst of the conservative culture they reject.

108. *Perestroika*, 203.
109. Ibid., 254–57.
110. Ibid., 279.
111. Kushner's ideas about the proper attitude toward faith and the supernatural is discussed in the text in the section "The Delicate Ecology of Your Delusions."
112. Franklin, "America, Lost and Found."
113. *Millennium Approaches*, 88.
114. Kushner, quoted in Savran, "Tony Kushner Considers," 103.
115. Verse 1 and refrain; words and music by Robert Lowry, 1864.
116. Kushner's attitude toward the shift of new religious communities from their original dynamic (and often reactionary) origins toward the static respectability of institutions reflects the views of the sociologist Max Weber. See *Max Weber on Charisma and Institution Building*. His perspective also agrees with H. Richard Niebuhr's argument that new religious minorities in the United States—which have not yet institutionalized—are essential to the vitality and relevance of religion in the nation. See *The Kingdom of God in America*.
117. Givens, *Viper on the Hearth*, 4.
118. *Perestroika*, 235, 279.
119. See, for example, Savran, "Tony Kushner Considers," 101–2; and Jones, "Tony Kushner at the Royal National Theatre," 25.
120. *Perestroika*, 237.

# Bibliography

*Advise and Consent*, directed by Otto Preminger. Warner Home Video, 2005.
*Angels in America*, directed by Mike Nichols. HBO Home Video, 2004.
Arrington, Leonard J. *Brigham Young, American Moses*. Urbana: University of Illinois Press, 1986.
Arrington, Leonard J., and Davis Bitton. *The Mormon Experience: A History of the Latter-day Saints in America*. 1st paperback ed. Urbana: University of Illinois Press, 1992.
Austin, Michael. "Theology for the Approaching Millennium: *Angels in America*, Activism, and the American Religion." *Dialogue: A Journal of Mormon Thought* 30, no. 1 (Spring 1997): 25–44.
*Big Love*. Anima Sola Productions, 2006 to present.

Bloom, Harold. Introduction to *Tony Kushner*. Bloom's Modern Critical Views, edited by Harold Bloom. Philadelphia: Chelsea House Publishers, 2005.

Brodie, Fawn McKay. *No Man Knows My History: The Life of Joseph Smith*. 2d ed. New York: Vintage Books, 1995.

Bushman, Richard. *Joseph Smith and the Beginnings of Mormonism*. Urbana: University of Illinois Press, 1984.

———. *Rough Stone Rolling*. New York: Alfred A. Knopf, 2005.

Canby, Vincent. "Sunday View: Two 'Angels,' Two Journeys, in London and New York." *New York Times*, January 30, 1994. http://www.nytimes.com (accessed June 3, 2008).

DePillis, Mario S. "The Emergence of Mormon Power since 1945." *Journal of Mormon History* 22, no. 1 (Spring 1996): 1–32.

Drury, Alan. *Advise and Consent*. Garden City, NY: Doubleday, 1959.

Franchot, Jenny. *Roads to Rome: The Antebellum Protestant Encounter with Catholicism*. The New Historicism: Studies in Cultural Poetics. Berkeley: University of California Press, 1994.

Franklin, Nancy. "America, Lost and Found." *The New Yorker*, December 8, 2003. http://www.newyorker.com (accessed June 6, 2008).

Frantzen, Allen J. "Prior to the Normans: The Anglo-Saxons in *Angels in America*." In *Approaching the Millennium: Essays on* Angels in America, edited by Deborah R. Geis and Steven F. Kruger, 134–50. Ann Arbor: University of Michigan Press, 1997.

Freedman, Jonathan. "Angels, Monsters, and Jews: Intersections of Queer and Jewish Identity in Tony Kushner's *Angels in America*." *PMLA* 113, no. 1 (January 1998): 90–102.

Garner, Stanley B. Jr. "Angels in *America*: The Millennium and Postmodern Memory." In *Approaching the Millennium: Essays on* Angels in America, 173–84.

Geis, Deborah. "The Delicate Ecology of Your Delusions: Insanity, Theatricality, and the Thresholds of Revelation in Kushner's *Angels in America*." In *Approaching the Millennium: Essays on* Angels in America, 199–212.

Geis, Deborah R. and Steven F. Kruger, eds. *Approaching the Millennium: Essays on* Angels in America. Ann Arbor, MI: University of Michigan Press, 1997.

Givens, Terryl. *By the Hand of Mormon: The American Scripture That Launched a New World Religion*. New York: Oxford University Press, 2002.

———. *The Viper on the Hearth: Mormons, Myths, and the Construction of Heresy*. New York: Oxford University Press, 1997.

Grey, Zane. *The Rainbow Trail*. New York: Grossett & Dunlap, 1915.

———. *The Riders of the Purple Sage*. New York: Grossett & Dunlap, 1912.

Harris, William. "Theatre: The Secret of Angels." *New York Times*, March 27, 1994. http://www.nytimes.com (accessed June 6, 2008).

Heinerman, John, and Anson Shupe. *The Mormon Corporate Empire: The Eye-Opening Report on the Church and Its Political and Financial Agenda*. Boston: Beacon Press, 1985.

Jones, Adam Mars. "Tony Kushner at the Royal National Theatre of Great Britain." In *Tony Kushner in Conversation*, edited by Robert Vorlicky, 18–29. Ann Arbor: University of Michigan Press, 1998.

Kinzer, Craig, Sandra Richards, Frank Galati, and Lawrence Bommer. "The Theater and the Barricades." In *Tony Kushner in Conversation*, 188–216.

Kruger, Steven F. "Identity and Conversion in *Angels in America*." In *Approaching the Millennium: Essays on* Angels in America, 151–69.

Kushner, Tony. *Angels in America: A Gay Fantasia on National Themes.* 1st combined paperback ed. New York: Theatre Communications Group, 2003.

———. "Tony Kushner: Interview." *Angels in America*, HBO Films. Available online at http://www.hbo.com/films/angelsinamerica/cast/kushner_interview.html (accessed May 20, 2008).

Miller, James. "Heavenquake: Queer Analogies in Kushner's America." In *Approaching the Millennium: Essays on* Angels in America, 56–77.

Moore, R. Laurence. "How to Become a People: The Mormon Scenario." In *Religious Outsiders and the Making of Americans*, 25–47. New York: Oxford University Press, 1986.

Niebuhr, H. Richard. *The Kingdom of God in America*. Chicago: Willett, Clark & Company, 1937.

O'Dea, Thomas. *The Mormons*. Chicago: University of Chicago Press, 1957.

Ostling, Richard, and Joan Ostling. *Mormon America: The Power and the Promise*. San Francisco: HarperSanFrancisco, 1999.

Pace, David. "Review: Mormon Angels in America." *Dialogue: A Journal of Mormon Thought* 27, no. 4 (Winter 1994): 191–97.

Quinn, D. Michael. *Early Mormonism and the Magic Worldview*. Rev. ed. Salt Lake City: Signature Books, 1998.

Rich, Frank. Review, "Angels in America; Millennium Approaches; Embracing All Possibilities in Art and Life." *New York Times*, May 5, 1993. http://www.nytimes.com (accessed May 29, 2008).

Richards, David. "Sunday View: 'Angels' Finds a Poignant Note of Hope." *New York Times*, Nov. 28, 1993. http://www.nytimes.com (accessed June 3, 2008).

*The Riders of the Purple Sage*, directed by Charles Haid. Arner Productions for Turner Network Television (TNT), 1996.

Sarna, Jonathan. *American Judaism: A History*. New Haven, CT: Yale University Press, 2004.

Savran, David. "Ambivalence, Utopia, and a Queer Sort of Materialism: How *Angels in America* Reconstructs a Nation." *Theatre Journal* 47, no. 2 (May 1995), 207–27.

———. "Tony Kushner Considers the Longstanding Problems of Virtue and Happiness," *American Theatre*, October 1994, 20–27, 100–104.

Shipps, Jan. "Difference and Otherness: Mormonism and the American Religious Mainstream." In *Minority Faiths and the American Protestant Mainstream*, edited by Jonathan Sarna, 81–109. Urbana: University of Illinois Press, 1998.

———. "From Satyr to Saint: American Perceptions of the Mormons, 1860–1960," in *Sojourner in the Promised Land: Forty Years among the Mormons*, 51–97. Urbana: University of Illinois Press, 2000.

———. *Mormonism: The Story of a New Religious Tradition*. Urbana: University of Illinois Press, 1985.

———. "Surveying the Mormon Image since 1960." In *Sojourner in the Promised Land: Forty Years among the Mormons*, 98–123.

Solomon, Ailsa. "Wrestling with Angels: A Jewish Fantasia." In *Approaching the Millennium: Essays on* Angels in America, 118–33.

Stout, Daniel A., Joseph D. Straubhaar, and Gayle Newbold. "Through a Glass Darkly: Mormons as Perceived by Critics' Reviews of Tony Kushner's *Angels in America.*" *Dialogue: A Journal of Mormon Thought* 32, no. 2 (Summer 1999): 133–57.

Tuveson, Ernest. *Redeemer Nation: The Idea of America*'s Millennial Role. Chicago: University of Chicago Press, 1968.

Underwood, Grant. *The Millenarian World of Early Mormonism.* Urbana: University of Illinois Press, 1993.

Weber, Bruce. "Angels' Angels." *New York Times,* April 25, 1993. http://www.nytimes.com (accessed June 6, 2008).

Weber, Max. *Max Weber on Charisma and Institution Building: Selected Papers,* edited and with an introduction by S. N. Eisenstadt. Chicago: University of Chicago Press, 1968.

# 2

# Four Consenting Adults in the Privacy of Their Own Suburb

Big Love *and the Cultural Significance of Mormon Polygamy*

MICHAEL AUSTIN

*The article of the Mormonite doctrine which is the chief provocative to the antipathy which thus breaks through the ordinary restraints of religious tolerance, is its sanction of polygamy; which, though permitted to Mahomedans, and Hindoos, and Chinese, seems to excite unquenchable animosity when practised by persons who speak English, and profess to be a kind of Christians.*

—John Stuart Mill, *On Liberty*

## I.

When HBO premiered its polygamy-themed series *Big Love* in March of 2006, both polygamy and Mormonism had been the focus of considerable attention for the better part of the decade. In February of 2002, the world came to Salt Lake City for the Winter Olympics. Four months later a fourteen-year-old girl named Elizabeth Smart was abducted from her home in Salt Lake City by—the world found out nine months later—a homeless couple claiming God's mandate to make her the husband's plural wife. In 2003 Jon Krakauer's *Under the Banner of Heaven*, the best-selling Mormon-themed book of the new millennium, started its run. And during the same year that *Big Love* premiered, a Mormon senator from Nevada became the leader of the new Democratic majority in the Senate, and the Mormon governor of Massachusetts emerged as a top contender for the Republican nomination for president of the United States.

In many ways, Mitt Romney was an ideal presidential candidate: an attractive, articulate, wealthy governor of a liberal state who had a solid reputation for getting results. But he was a Mormon, and for more than a year, op-ed pages across the country obsessed over the question, "Can a Mormon be president?" More often than not, the answer was no. In an article for the *New York Times Magazine* entitled "What Is It about Mormonism," Harvard law professor Noah Feldman attempted to explain why the majority of Americans felt uncomfortable voting for a Mormon for president. After a largely sympathetic portrayal of the Mormon faith, he concluded with the lament that "the soft bigotry of cultural discomfort may stand in the way of a candidate whose faith exemplifies values of charity, self-discipline and community that we as Americans claim to hold dear. Surely, though, the day will come when we are ready to put prejudice aside and choose a president without regard to what we think of his religion."[1]

The depth of Feldman's analysis is impressive, but his insight does not quite rise to the level of the unnamed Massachusetts politician quoted in a *New York* magazine article several months earlier: "Let's be honest," he said, "Mormons are weird."[2] The more serious Romney's candidacy became, the more pundits tried to get to the roots of Mormon weirdness: they reject the Athanasian Creed, they wear funny underwear, they think that the Garden of Eden was in Missouri. But anybody who has paid attention to American culture for any part of the past 150 years knows that all of this is incidental. What John Stuart Mill understood in 1859 is still true today: it's all about polygamy.

Though it was officially abandoned in 1890, the practice of plural marriage has always symbolized, summed up, and circumscribed the weirdness of the Latter-day Saints. A 2007 Pew survey taken during the height of the Romney campaign bears this out, reporting that "polygamy" or "bigamy" was the most frequent response when participants were asked to describe Mormonism with a single word—followed, in turn, by "family," "cult," and "different."[3] This perception is reflected in news reports. A Lexus-Nexus search of articles written between April 2006 and April 2008 showed that of 120 articles mentioning Romney's religion, 26 (22 percent) also discussed polygamy or plural marriage. The same percentage of articles about Mormonism or Mormons generally also discussed polygamy (219 out of 995).[4] Nearly 120 years after Latter-day Saints abandoned polygamy, then, more than one in every five media references to Mormonism still brings up the practice.

Contrast this attention to polygamy with that given to another controversial nineteenth-century religious belief: the Roman Catholic doctrine of papal infallibility. This doctrine, proclaimed by the First Vatican Council in 1869, was frequently ridiculed, caricatured, and misrepresented by the same popular press that savaged the Mormons, and it was regularly invoked, as late as 1960, to question the patriotism of Catholic politicians such as John F. Kennedy. However, during the same April 2006–April 2008 period, papal infallibility was mentioned in only 6 of 997 articles about Catholicism (.6 percent), and it does not occur in a single one of more than a thousand articles about Catholic presidential candidate and eventual vice president Joe Biden. (Biden's Catholicism, in fact, is mentioned in only nineteen articles, less than 2 percent of the total). Clearly neither the press nor the American electorate continues to associate Catholics with the doctrine of papal infallibility (which the Roman Catholic Church still professes), but both persist in linking the Church of Jesus Christ of Latter-day Saints with polygamy (which has not been practiced or sanctioned for more than a century). A Gallop poll conducted in August of 2006, in fact, found that more than a quarter of all Americans agree with the statement "most Mormons favor polygamy."[5]

Romney himself understood the underlying connection between polygamy and the public's suspicion of Mormonism. The same week that *Big Love* debuted on HBO, Romney appeared on the Don Imus radio show and attempted to neutralize these suspicions with humor: "I believe," he said with an ironic sternness, "marriage should be between a man and a woman . . . and a woman . . . and a woman." This attempt at humor, which *Slate* columnist Adam Reilly aptly described as Romney's "clumsy Mormon shtick,"[6] was part of a conscious effort to diffuse the Mormon issue by joking about polygamy. By making light of it, Romney acknowledged the stereotype, showed that he knew it to be false, and demonstrated that he was comfortable enough in that knowledge to laugh at the whole thing. When pressed for a serious answer, however, Romney generally gives the standard Mormon response—much the same answer, in fact, that the church gave in a press release about *Big Love* in 2006: "Polygamy was officially discontinued by The Church of Jesus Christ of Latter-day Saints in 1890. Any Church member adopting the practice today is excommunicated. Groups that continue the practice in Utah and elsewhere have no association whatsoever with The Church of Jesus Christ of Latter-day Saints."[7]

This longstanding connection between Mormonism and polygamy owes much to American popular culture, where the fanatical polygamous patriarch has been a staple for 150 years. At first stories about Mormons and their many wives appeared primarily in pulp novels and magazines whose names barely survive. But the literary potential offered by these modern polygamists proved irresistible, and within a single generation, the trope popped up in works by some of the day's most important writers, such as Mark Twain's *Roughing It* (1872), Robert Louis Stevenson's *The Dynamiter* (1885), and Arthur Conan Doyle's *A Study in Scarlet* (1887). When the Mormons issued an official manifesto ending polygamy in 1890, the practice almost immediately became a favorite subject in such works as Zane Gray's novel *The Riders of the Purple Sage* (1912), Jerome Kern's musical *The Girl from Utah* (1914), and about a dozen early silent films with titles like *A Victim of the Mormons* (1912), *The Mormon Maid* (1917), and the irresistibly campy classic, *Trapped by the Mormons* (1922).[8]

By the middle of the 1920s, the figure of the bearded, wild-eyed Mormon polygamist had become a fixed trope in the American cultural landscape—an image that has remained remarkably consistent for the past hundred years. In my own research for a 1998 article, I examined thirty-eight true-crime and mystery novels with Mormon themes written between 1980 and 1997. About half of them featured a contemporary polygamy plot—more often than not one where an average Mormon or high church official practiced polygamy in secret and either got killed because of it or killed somebody else to cover it up.[9] The Mormon characters in these novels—no matter how respectable they may seem at first—invariably degenerate into wild-eyed fanatics whose clothing, dress, and attitudes come straight from the set of *The Riders of the Purple Sage*.

Such caricatures provide the raw clay from which more sophisticated literary images of Mormonism are shaped. In a slightly different form, the view of Mormons as cryptopolygamists persists even in scholarly literature sympathetic to Mormonism and its theology. Consider the arguments of the noted literary scholar Harold Bloom in *The American Religion:* "Who can believe that the Mormons ever would have turned away from the practice of Celestial Marriage, if it were not for federal pressure? . . . I cheerfully do prophesy that some day, not too far on in the twenty-first century, the Mormons will have enough political and financial power to sanction polygamy again. Without it, in some form or other, the complete vision of Joseph Smith never can be fulfilled."[10]

The perpetuation of the polygamous Mormon stereotype has, of course, been helped along by the indisputable facts that (1) several thousand people who call themselves Mormon fundamentalists continue to practice polygamy in Utah and other areas of the American West, and (2) these modern polygamists have a remarkable penchant for committing spectacular crimes in numbers far disproportionate to their demographic representation. The list of real-life polygamists behaving badly is as long as it is fascinating: Joel LeBaron, who once stopped traffic in Salt Lake City by doing two hundred pushups to prove that he was the "one mighty and strong" predicted by Mormon scripture; his brother, Ervil, who sent his followers to kill rival polygamous leaders, including Joel; the Lafferty brothers, who murdered their sister-in-law and her infant daughter because (they claimed) God demanded it; Addam Swapp, who blew up an LDS Church and killed a police officer in revenge for a raid that killed his polygamous father-in-law; Warren Jeffs, the head of the Fundamentalist Church of Jesus Christ of Latter-day Saints, who was convicted of child abuse in the marriages that he authorized; and, of course, Brian David Mitchell and Wanda Barzee, the homeless couple who kidnapped Elizabeth Smart and forced her into a polygamous relationship for nine months.

Nobody could make up stories this good. Of course, the LDS public-relations office always insists—and most news organizations responsibly point out—that the Church of Jesus Christ of Latter-day Saints prohibits polygamy and has no connection at all to those who practice it. But these official denials impact perceptions much less than do the stories themselves. Non-Mormons always see Mormon culture as more homogenous than Mormons see it, and no matter what adjective is applied to modern polygamists (fundamentalist, breakaway, disaffected, former, excommunicated, unaffiliated, etc.), the noun that follows is always the same. When the high-profile news cases make the inevitable move to best-selling books, movies, and TV specials, they merge with the literary stereotypes already available for depicting polygamy, ensuring that twenty-first-century Americans experience Mormonism as a cultural phenomenon in much the same way that their nineteenth-century counterparts did as historical fact.

Ironically, this increased attention to crimes committed by polygamists comes at a time when it has become difficult to defend the criminalization of polygamy. As alternative lifestyles in general have become more accepted, people from distinctively different constituencies have begun to question the exclusion of polygamy from legal and cultural definitions of "nobody else's business." Polygamist wives themselves have come forward to argue that their way of life empowers women and preserves families.[11] Nonreligious scholars have advocated a serious national rethinking of polygamy's advantages, especially for child care and female-support networks.[12] And, perhaps most importantly for the current study, libertarian and civil-rights groups—keenly aware of the legal relationship between polygamy and other kinds of nontraditional lifestyles—have taken the position that what any configuration of consenting adults do in the privacy of their own compound should be of no interest whatsoever to the state.[13]

## II.

*Big Love* marks a radical departure from pop-culture portrayals of Mormon polygamy. From early pulp novels and *The Riders of the Purple Sage* up through contemporary mystery fiction and *Under the Banner of Heaven*, polygamy has generally been portrayed as a nonconsensual relationship between controlling men and abused women. *Big Love* does include such polygamists, but the family at its center fits solidly within the progressive American mainstream in everything but the number of monograms on the towels. Bill Henrickson is a successful businessman who owns a chain of home-supply stores in the Salt Lake Valley. Bill was born on a polygamist compound called Juniper Creek and—as is often the case with surplus males—was forced out and into the streets at the age of fourteen. He married his first wife, Barb, in an LDS temple and was a pillar of the Mormon community for years. But he was unable to escape the clutches of his upbringing, and he drifted back into polygamy, eventually taking a second wife, Nicki—the daughter of Juniper Creek's current leader—and a third wife, Margene, who worked for him, fell in love with his whole family, and chose to join it, even though she had very little knowledge of either fundamentalist or mainstream Mormonism.

The Henricksons live in three adjacent houses in Sandy, Utah, a middle-class suburb of Salt Lake City. With the occasional exception of Nicki, they dress like a modern suburban family. They send their children to public schools, go to movies, watch TV, listen to music, and participate in the life of the community, all while trying to hide the true nature of their family from the world. The polygamous family dynamic allows ingenious plot twists and conflicts that can be seen nowhere else, such as a man who has to sneak around to have an affair with his own wife, a woman who is trying to steal the affections of her sister wife's mother and is disowned by her own mother, and a woman who secretly tries to convince her best friend to marry her husband so that she can have another vote in the family. I can think of no other program in the history of television where the sentence, "Our husband's dating life is none of our business," could be uttered without any trace of irony and make perfect sense.[14]

But what, if anything, does *Big Love* mean in a larger cultural context? What does it contribute to, or detract from, the debates and conversations of which it is a necessary part? The first duty of any television program, of course, is to be entertaining, and the way we choose to be entertained tells us a great deal about who we are and what we value. But trying to analyze an entire television series in the middle of its run is a risky proposition at best. At the time of this article, HBO has aired thirty-four one-hour episodes of *Big Love* over three seasons and renewed the show for a fourth season that will begin filming in the fall of 2009. These thirty-four hours of programming contain several major story arcs, a number of ongoing subplots, and the individual story lines that define each episode. To make the task of analysis manageable, the remainder of this section focuses on three individual scenes that, taken together, provide an entry point into the way that *Big Love* incorporates polygamy into the larger cultural conversations about polygamy, Mormonism, marriage, sexuality, and identity.

*Scene 1: From Episode 3, "Home Invasion," First Aired on 3/26/06*

Roman Grant (Harry Dean Stanton), the "prophet" of the polygamous compound where Bill grew up, takes a reporter on a tour and gives him a lecture on the history of Mormon polygamy. His son, Alby, reminds him, "The gays, papa . . . don't forget the homosexuals." Roman, initially flustered, regains his bearings and says, "If the Supreme Court says 'yes' to the privacy rights of homosexual persons, surely it's time to recognize our rights to live in peace, too." The well-rehearsed talking point, however, comes back to haunt the prophet. Near the end of the episode, one of his wives excitedly opens a newspaper and reads the lead paragraph aloud: "Roman Grant, prophet and patriarch of Juniper Creek, home to the second largest polygamous sect in Utah, says, 'We're just like . . . homosexuals.'"

Early in its run, several years before the LDS Church generated national headlines for helping to pass California's Proposition 8 outlawing same-sex marriage, *Big Love* made the connection between gay marriage and Mormon polygamy explicit. It was a major subtext of the show long before it aired, largely because its creators—Mark Olsen and Will Scheffer—are longtime domestic partners and Scheffer's earlier play, *Falling Man and Other Monologues,* deals largely with gay themes and was written in direct response to antigay marriage legislation in California.[15] In an interview about *Big Love* with the gay-themed magazine *The Advocate,* Olsen insisted that "we have no agenda on this show." Then he went on to explain exactly what (despite having no agenda) the creators were trying to accomplish: "There were three things we wanted to dramatize—self in marriage, self in family, and self in society: What is it like to be marginalized and deemed off the table of legitimate discussion for who and what you are? Some of the struggles of the characters are very analogous to the gay community of 15 or 20 years ago. These characters are dealing with a lot of self-loathing. And it's ingrained by a society that says you are freaks."[16] In the light of these remarks, commentators from both sides of the political debate must be forgiven for suspecting that *Big Love* may have an agenda after all.[17]

This is not to say that *Big Love* is merely, or even primarily, political allegory. It is primarily, and merely, a television program. But the connections between polygamy and gay marriage run so deep in both legal precedent and popular culture that any treatment of one necessarily has something to say about the other. This is true for both cohabitation and legally recognized marriages. The unlawful-cohabitation laws, created by the Edmunds-Tucker Act to prosecute polygamists not legally married, criminalize all homosexual relationships and many heterosexual ones as well. Many legal experts believe that the Supreme Court's 2003 *Lawrence v. Texas* decision, which struck down antisodomy laws used to prosecute homosexual behavior, will eventually lead to the decriminalization of polygamy.[18] In practice unlawful-cohabitation laws have not been used since 1960 to prosecute polygamy cases in Utah or Arizona.[19] The attitude of officials—which a fictional Utah prosecutor makes clear to Bill Henrickson in the first episode of *Big Love*'s second season—is tolerance based on a desire to keep the worms in the can: "Keep your hands off of underage girls, don't commit welfare fraud," the prosecutor tells Bill, "and we have no beef with you."[20]

Polygamy has entered into the gay-marriage debate in another way, though, as the end point of a slippery slope that, many conservatives feel, must end in its legalization. Justice Antonin Scalia makes an early form of this argument the cornerstone of his dissent in *Romer v. Evans,* which overturned a Colorado statute forbidding jurisdictions within the state from passing legislation protecting homosexuals from discrimination. "Polygamists, and those who have a polygamous 'orientation,'" he writes, "have been 'singled out' by these provisions for much more severe treatment than merely denial of favored status. . . . The Court's Disposition today suggests that these provisions are unconstitutional; and that polygamy must be permitted in these States . . . unless, of course, polygamists for some reason have fewer constitutional rights than homosexuals."[21]

As laws against sexual-orientation discrimination have created pressure to extend marriage rights, this same slippery slope has become a common argument against gay marriage. Stanley Kurtz, who has criticized *Big Love* several times in his *National Review Online* column, wrote in a 2000 article that gay marriage represents but a critical first step toward the legitimation of multipartner marriages and then, perhaps, the eventual elimination of state-sanctioned marriage as we have known it. Once gay male couples with open sexual relationships or lesbian couples with de-facto families are legally married, the way will be open to even more imaginative combinations. On what grounds, for instance, could the sperm donor and aging rock star David Crosby be denied the right to join in matrimony with both the lesbian rock singer Melissa Etheridge and her lover Julie Cypher, the "mothers" of his child?[22]

Kurtz's rhetorical strategy assumes that all right-thinking people already know how terrible it would be to allow a man and two women to "join in matrimony." All that he needs to point out is that gay marriage is the first step in that direction. *Big Love* responds to this rhetoric by challenging this assumption and asking audiences to at least consider whether David, Melissa, and Julie might not (like Bill, Barb, Nicki, and Margene) form a reasonably happy married family without hurting anyone else in the process. What better way to blunt the effectiveness of a slippery-slope argument than to show that what lies at the end of the slope is not that scary?

But Roman Grant and the Juniper Creek polygamists in *Big Love* are that scary. They represent the side of polygamy that usually appears on the news: violence, intimidation of opponents, authoritarian rule, and teenage girls forced to marry septuagenarian patriarchs. By giving Roman the speech tying gay and polygamous rights to each other—and showing the sheer horror of the community when these statements are reported in a way that emphasizes their logical conclusions—*Big Love* resists a simplistic "Why can't we all just respect each other's families?" approach to marriage rights. Olsen and Scheffer suggest that the legal fight for marriage rights creates strange collations that are likely to be difficult and distasteful for all involved.

*Scene 2: From Episode 8, "Easter," First Aired on 4/30/06*

Barb has a heart-to-heart talk with her husband's younger brother, Joey, whose wife, Wanda, has recently had a baby. Barb listens in disbelief as he tells her, "I don't know that I believe in polygamy anymore." He asks Barb to keep his secret. He is even afraid to tell his wife because she would be afraid that her husband's defection would keep them both from the celestial kingdom. When he finishes, Barb exclaims in disbelief, "You're a monogamist." "I guess so," he says, hanging his head in shame. He continues, "The only way I know what to believe in is to listen to my heart, and it says that Wanda is it for me."

The genius of this scene is that it plays a classic "coming-out" scenario with a double reversal: not only is Joey not gay, but he is also not inclined toward polygamy. The closet in this situation is heterosexual monogamy—the very lifestyle that most people in closets come out of. However, Joey is a third-generation polygamist who has had only minimal exposure to the norms of the monogamous world. His values were shaped in a polygamous culture, and, in violating the norms of that culture, he feels the same kind of guilt and shame endemic to anybody whose inclinations violate the moral precepts they were taught as children. As a closeted monogamist, Joey must also deal with a religious narrative similar to that held by sexual minorities in other conservative religious cultures. His native culture sees plural marriage as a requirement for salvation; therefore, by refusing to take additional wives, Joey places not only his own but also Wanda's soul in danger. His confession to Barb, then, is a declaration that he is willing to accept eternal punishment for the sake of a subjective feeling—much as Huckleberry Finn does when he declares his willingness to go to hell, rather than betray his friend, Jim, who is wanted as a runaway slave.

This scene also highlights the randomness of existing categories of *normal* and *aberrant*. Western society almost universally condemns polygamy as an aberration. The scene between Joey and Barb works so well as an ironic reversal precisely because viewers have such a difficult time thinking of polygamy as normal. From a biological perspective, however, there is no question that Joey is right and the rest of us are wrong: polygamy is normal. Even a cursory glance at a few human beings would tell a trained alien scientist that natural selection designed humans for polygamous relationships.[23] Almost all preindustrial societies were polygamous, and, of the 1,154 human cultures ever encountered or studied by anthropologists, 980 (85 percent) have sanctioned some form of polygamy.[24]

The Western preference for monogamy has often been ascribed to the influence of Christianity, but this gets it backward: neither the Old nor the New Testament insists upon monogamy. The former clearly supports polygamy, while the latter praises celibacy and authorizes marriage only as a kind of last resort for weak souls who would otherwise commit fornication (1 Cor. 7:1–8). Western Christianity adopted monogamy, as Augustine explains in "On the Good of Marriage," not because of the requirements of scripture but "after the usage of Rome."[25]

But the Romans, like nearly all other societies that prohibit polygamy as a form of formal bonding, did little to prevent adulterous liaisons from duplicating the sexual dynamics of polygamous marriages. There have been few societies in human history where high-status men with plentiful resources have not found ways—legally sanctioned or otherwise—to have multiple sexual relationships.

This is not to say that monogamy conquered the West through sheer dumb luck, nor is it an accident that the rise of monogamy corresponded exactly to the development of more complex social systems. As long as human beings continue to experience a male-female birth rate of one to one, monogamous pairing is the only way to make sure that everyone (or at least almost everyone) ends up with a mate. This is not a problem for ground squirrels, silverback gorillas, or even small tribes of hunter-gatherers—these populations generally follow the harsh logic of natural selection, where very few males monopolize the gene pool. As societies become more complex, however, the problem of extra men becomes much more difficult to handle. If large numbers of young males are sent off to war in each generation (a fairly standard strategy in many pre-industrial civilizations), their societies never experience the prolonged periods of peace and stability necessary to develop complex relationships. If, on the other hand, men are required to compete for multiple wives within their society, both natural and social selection favor those men who are aggressive, violent, manipulative, domineering, and homicidal. Evolutionary psychologists David Barash and Judith Eve Lipton explain that "historically, monogamy arose in Europe as in implicit trade-off. The wealthy and powerful would in effect have agreed to give up their near-monopoly on women in return for obtaining greater social involvement on the part of middle- and lower-class men, who, if reproductively excluded, might have refused to participate in the social contract necessary for the establishment of large, stable social units."[26]

But "necessary for the establishment of large . . . social units" is not quite the same thing as normal. Human biology and psychology are predisposed to polyamorous sexual relationships and polygamous pair bonds. That something is natural does not mean that it is morally acceptable, of course; human beings are also predisposed to beat each other over the head and steal each other's food. But there is no getting around the naturalness of polygamy. It is monogamy that must be learned—and most people in supposedly monogamous societies have not learned the lesson particularly well. When high divorce rates and serial dating are added to the adulterous relationships that have always been part of the human experience, very few Westerners can claim perfect adherence to the monogamous ideal of strict abstinence before marriage and unwavering fidelity thereafter. Anyone who can (and here the irony is almost unbearable) is probably a Mormon.

*Scene 3: From Episode 15, "Reunion," First Aired on 6/25/07*

Barb and a group of her friends—all women in polygamous marriages—are having a book club in Barb's living room when the discussion turns to the general perception of polygamists by the larger world. One of the women exclaims, "It's all Larry King and Anderson Cooper's fault; they make us look like retards and perverts." Another begins, "If they could show one normal plural family for a change . . . ," and a third chimes in, "The good ones are all closeted." The women express their distaste for the term closeted, which, Barb says, "rubs me the wrong way, too."

This scene echoes the crucial points of the previous two—it highlights the connection between homosexuality and polygamy and the distaste that conservative fundamentalists have for sharing language ("closeted") with those that they consider sinful. But this scene goes one step further; it presses against the invisible "fourth wall" separating the audience from the fictional characters. The major argument of the scene—that the media never portray normal polygamists—is contradicted by the scene itself, which shows polygamists acting normally. What could be more normal than a group of middle-class women sitting in a living room in the suburbs participating in a book club (the book on the table is Thomas Friedman's *The World Is Flat,* a popular best seller with a wide and generally well-educated audience) and discussing current events?

Other sympathetic portrayals of Mormon polygamists have made some inroads into popular culture, of course.[27] Perhaps the most revolutionary thing about *Big Love* is not just that it portrays polygamists sympathetically but that it treats polygamists differently—that is, it does not lump all practicing polygamists together. The different ways that polygamy is practiced in *Big Love* correspond quite accurately to what is known about the way it actually exists in Utah and the American West. Mormon historian Michael Quinn's article "Plural Marriage and Mormon Fundamentalism," based on interviews with dozens of practicing fundamentalists, gives as well documented an account of contemporary plural marriage as we are likely to get, given the notorious difficulty of collecting reliable data from people hiding from public view. Quinn's figures are now somewhat dated (the original article was written in 1993), but the basic patterns they illuminate are probably still reliable.[28]

Quinn's research suggests that the number of people actually living a polygamous lifestyle tends to be overestimated by media reports, which, in 1993, regularly claimed that between forty and sixty thousand people practiced polygamy in the western United States. Quinn estimates that, at the time he wrote the article, there were no more than twenty-one thousand practicing fundamentalists and that "many of these committed fundamentalists are living in monogamous relationships"—even though they may believe in plural marriage as a valid theological doctrine.[29] The two largest fundamentalist groups are the Fundamentalist Church of Jesus Christ of Latter-day Saints (FLDS) with its headquarters in Colorado City, Arizona, and the Apostolic United Brethren, also known as the Allred group, whose members live chiefly in Salt Lake City. As events since the publication of Quinn's article have demonstrated, the two groups occupy opposite ends of the polygamist spectrum. The FLDS live on isolated compounds, pool all of their assets into a trust administered by their leader, and practice *placing,* by which women and young girls are assigned to men (and can be reassigned to other men) by "the prophet."[30] The Allred group, on the other hand, does not practice placing or allow underage marriages. Members of the Allred group are not required to live polygamous lifestyles, and, according to its former leader, Owen Allred, only 10 to 15 percent of its members ever do.[31]

At the time of Quinn's research, both the FLDS and the Allred group had between seven and eight thousand members. He adds several smaller groups to the polygamists, the most notorious being the members of the LeBaron family, a violent sect that killed a number of polygamous rivals—including Rulon Allred—in an attempt to unite all practicing fundamentalists under their banner. Along with these fundamentalist churches, there are thousands of "independent polygamists" practicing in Utah and elsewhere in the American West. These practitioners do not believe that they have the authority to establish a church or congregation, so they practice "the principle" in their own homes and occasionally join small study groups with other independent fundamentalists. Quinn describes them as an "anti-institutional, frequently anti-authoritarian, and very pluralistic" collection of individuals whose numbers include "political liberals and conservatives, religious conservatives and ecumenicals, as well as social conservatives and liberals."[32] Both husbands and wives in these independent families often work and interact in communities without revealing that they practice polygamy. The children of independent polygamists, along with members of the Allred group, usually attend public schools, associate with mainstream

Mormons, take part in normal activities, and generally pass as monogamous members of the community.

Big Love creates its characters by fictionalizing many of the contemporary polygamous groups that actually exist. Olsen and Scheffer have
acknowledged that the characters of Roman Grant and his son, Alby,
were based in large part on FLDS leaders Rulon and Warren Jeffs.[33] The
Allred group in Salt Lake is most likely the basis of the unnamed congregation attended by Bill Henrickson's partner, Don Embry, and his wives.
The Henrickson family itself, according to the creators, is modeled
directly on an independent polygamous family featured in the first (and
only) issue of the pro-polygamy magazine Mormon Focus.[34] In the second season, the show introduced two additional characters—Hollis and
Selma Green—based directly on members of the LeBaron clan, who ter-
rorized rival polygamous groups throughout the 1970s—demonstrating
that the "bad polygamists" of Juniper Creek are only moderately insane
when compared to the genuine psychopaths that inhabit the world of
Mormon fundamentalism. Each of these groups serves as a background
for the others, and collectively they make the argument that, just as
Mormons cannot and should not be lumped together with polygamists,
polygamists cannot and should not be lumped together with each other.

*Scene 4: From Episode 26, "Empire," First Aired on 1/26/09*

> During an important meeting with a potential backer in a casino
> business, Bill's partner, Don, is visibly agitated. After the meet-
> ing, he becomes angry with Bill and himself. Believing that Don's
> first wife, Peg, is responsible for this mood, Bill confronts her and
> continues to press for the reason behind Don's behavior. Finally,
> she tells him that Vernie and Jo-Jo (Don's other two wives) "ran off
> together," taking Don's children with them. Bill expresses disbelief,
> and Peg responds, disgusted, "As of a week ago, Don and I are
> sadly monogamous."

Though Vernie and Jo-Jo are minor characters in Big Love, their relationship was established very early in the show's run. In "Viagra Blue,"
the second episode of the first season, they are shown playing footsie
with each other during a bridge game. This early scene is a subtle, but
unmistakable, reference to a key irony that became more apparent as the
series continued. Not only are homosexuality and polygamy connected
to each other by a binding set of legal precedents, but they are related
by the fact that the women in a polygamous marriage are sealed to each
other as well as to their husband—making polygamy a form of same-
sex marriage. Maxine Hanks emphasizes this aspect of the polygamous

relationship among nineteenth-century Mormons. "These women," she explains, "'courted' other wives, placed their husband's hand on the new wife's, and were present at the sealing ceremonies." A polygamous marriage, therefore, "qualifies as a same-sex covenant of eternal companionship between women who were, in effect, sealed to each other."[35]

The sexualized relationship among polygamous wives that Hanks hints at becomes explicit in the relationship between Don Embry's two wives in the beginning of the third season of *Big Love*. This same season contains a less explicit, but much more prominent, portrayal of precisely the same dynamic. Throughout the first five episodes, Bill courts a beautiful Serbian immigrant named Ana, who briefly becomes his fourth wife. Bill and Ana actually met and began dating in season two, but Ana did not learn about the Henricksons' lifestyle until Margene—who had surreptitiously become her best friend—informed her. Ana initially ran away, but in season three, she returns and agrees to be courted, not just by Bill but the entire family. What follows comes straight from Hanks's description. It is Barb, not Bill, who decides that it is time to take a "fourth" and first proposes courtship to Ana. All three of Bill's wives accompany Bill and Ana on their dates—from a rowdy trip to a drive-in movie to a quiet dinner at home. Though the same-sex relationship is not explicitly sexualized, as it is with Vernie and Jo-Jo, it becomes clear that Ana is marrying Barb, Nicki, and Margene as well as Bill. Once they all do marry—in episode 29, "For Better or Worse"—the three other wives compete over whose house Ana will live in, and, by extension, who will be her primary emotional intimate. The bickering becomes so bad that Ana asks for a divorce within days of the marriage. Jealousy destroys the marriage, as one might expect in a polygamous union, but it is jealousy among four women who are all married to each other. The husband, Bill, is reduced to a hapless spectator in his own wives' marital drama.

Season three's emphasis on the same-sex marriage dimension of polygamy follows directly on the heels of California's Proposition 8—a legal battle over same-sex marriage in which the Church of Jesus Christ of Latter-day Saints was deeply involved. Opponents of same-sex marriage placed Proposition 8 on the California general-election ballot after the California Supreme Court ruled that laws against same-sex marriages were unconstitutional. Proposition 8 amends the state constitution by adding that "only marriage between a man and a woman is recognized in California." The hierarchies of both the Catholic Church and the Church of Jesus Christ of Latter-day Saints supported the amendment, and, on June 29, 2008, all Mormon congregations in California were read a letter from the LDS First Presidency

instructing members to "do all you can to support the proposed constitutional amendment by donating of your means and time to assure
that marriage in California is legally defined as being between a man
and a woman."[36] Though LDS members comprise only a small fraction
of California voters, Mormons provided at least half of the financial
support for the measure and, according to some estimates, as much as
80 to 90 percent of the labor.[37]

When the proposition passed—effectively outlawing gay marriages
in California—opponents were furious at the LDS Church. Bloggers
and editorial writers excoriated the church, not just for interfering with
what they perceived as a fundamental civil right but for the hypocrisy
in trying to enforce the same definition of marriage (one man and one
woman) that was invoked to persecute Mormon ancestors a century earlier. Time and time again, during and after the controversy, opponents
of Proposition 8 cited the historical Mormon support of polygamy in an
effort to counter current Mormon opposition to gay marriage. In declar-
ing the Mormon Church "hypocrite of the year," GayWired magazine
columnist Duane Wells echoed the sentiments of many others with his
charge that "if there is any religious group that should have remained
mum about the issue of gay marriage, it's Mormons."[38] The story lines in
the third season of Big Love deepen this irony by portraying polygamy
not just as something comparable to gay marriage but as a literal union
between people of the same gender.

The last four episodes of season three also bring polygamy from
the margins of the Mormon world directly to its center through a Mark
Hofmann–inspired story involving a historical document. The document—a letter by early LDS Church President Wilford Woodruff (who
issued the original 1890 manifesto forbidding polygamy) authorizing
secret plural marriages in direct opposition to the church's stated position—becomes a flash point for tensions between polygamists and the
mainstream LDS Church. Without knowing what the letter contains, Bill
helps his brother-in-law, Ted, who has recently become an LDS General
Authority, purchase it. When Bill learns what is in the letter, he demands
it back, but Ted has already passed it on to the church. Eventually the
Greens get involved in the controversy and kidnap Ted's daughter to
force him to hand over the letter, but the church refuses to release it
under any circumstances. In the season finale (episode 34, "Sacrament"),
Roman Grant admits to Bill that he forged the letter himself, but this does
not diminish the critique implied by the narrative: during the time that
the LDS Church was doing everything in its power to defeat Proposition
8 in California, it was actively suppressing evidence of its own historical

acceptance of a definition of marriage that contradicted the standard that it was presenting to the world as the will of God.

## III.

In its official response to *Big Love*, the LDS Church asserts that "placing the series in Salt Lake City, the international headquarters of The Church of Jesus Christ of Latter-day Saints, is enough to blur the line between the modern Church and the program's subject matter and to reinforce old and long-outdated stereotypes."[39] This objection is especially ironic in light of the fact that the creators of *Big Love* almost obsessively *clarify* the lines among all sorts of Utahns: the "good polygamists" (the Henricksons and the Embries), the "bad polygamists" (Roman and Alby Grant and other members of the Juniper Creek Compound), the "really-scary-mega-bad-crazy polygamists" (the Greens), the "monogamous polygamists" (Bill's brother, Joey, who eventually does attempt, unsuccessfully, to take a second wife), and the mainstream Mormons. And while LDS Church spokesmen can (and should) complain that the regular Latter-day Saints in *Big Love* are almost universally portrayed as narrow minded, self-righteous, bigoted, and hypocritical, there is no possibility that anyone watching the show can miss the fact that these Mormons are not polygamous. They are, rather, irrationally hostile to polygamy and the major reason why the show's good polygamists cannot live their lives in the open.

But there is a catch. While there is no group more committed to ridding the world of polygamy than the Church of Jesus Christ of Latter-day Saints, the same cannot be said about the world to come. Current Mormon practice allows a widower (but not a widow) to remarry in the temple "for time and all eternity," a ceremony that, according to Latter-day Saints, seals the marriage relationship so that it will continue in the afterlife. The implication of this practice—which is lost on very few practicing Mormons—is that a man can have more than one wife in the afterlife, while a woman can only have one husband. *Big Love* exploits the irony of this practice in the penultimate episode of its second season, "Take Me as I Am." In this episode, Barb Henrickson crashes the wedding of her mother, Nancy, a devout Mormon who has refused to speak to her daughter since she became a polygamist. At the wedding, Barb's sister, Cindy, explains how their mother was sealed to her new husband despite having been sealed to their father earlier: "Ned wanted to be sealed, so she was unsealed to Daddy. And Ned's children don't want Ned to have to share Vera in the afterlife."[40]

Under the terms of their shared belief system, Nancy's actions are much less defensible than her daughter's. Barb has stayed with her husband despite his decision to marry polygamously. Nancy, on the other hand, has (for the afterlife at least) divorced a faithful husband to become the second eternal wife of another man and, in the process, deprived Barb and all of her other children of the stable eternal family unit that Mormons see as the cornerstone of celestial glory. Either she does not understand the theological consequences of her decision, or, more likely, she does not really believe that her actions have the eternal consequences that her religion—which she regularly uses as a weapon against her daughter—claims. Either way she becomes a metaphor for contemporary Mormonism generally, which officially denounces polygamy in one form while tacitly accepting it in another. This passing reference to obscure Mormon eschatology will barely register with most casual viewers, and the writers do very little to emphasize it even in the episode where it occurs. But most viewers will understand that the show intends for us to see the hatred that most Mormons have for polygamy as exceptionally ironic and fundamentally incompatible with their own origins.

The charge that *Big Love* perpetuates stereotypes about Mormons and polygamy is only partially accurate. Some aspects of the show do tap into existing cultural preconceptions about polygamists, but many do not. However, like most portrayals of polygamy, *Big Love* is about much more than marriage arrangements. The actual religious practice of plural marriage occurs so infrequently in American culture that it doesn't even register in demographic tables. There are fewer Mormon fundamentalists in America than practicing Taoists, Deists, Scientologists, Eckists (practitioners of Eckankar), or Sikhs.[41] But these twenty to forty thousand American polygamists exercise a cultural influence that far exceeds their numbers. Mormon polygamy has always served as a test case for much larger cultural agendas. *Big Love* is perhaps the most significant recent artifact in a larger cultural movement to change what kinds of cases polygamy tests.

In the nineteenth century, Mormon polygamy provided fertile ground for testing the limits of religious pluralism in a young democracy. Legal scholar Sarah Barringer Gordon's recent book, *The Mormon Question: Polygamy and Constitutional Conflict in Nineteenth-Century America*, explains in great detail the way the conflict over polygamy shaped the evolution of constitutional law. In the introduction to this book, Gordon writes that

The conflict of faiths pitted the laws of God against the laws of man; believers on both sides learned that their Constitution was, perhaps, not theirs after all. The instability of constitutional claims and interpretation tortured and energized the combatants. Their struggle to capture and hold the Constitution provided a unifying field of conflict; antipolygamists and Mormon defenders of polygamy alike yearned for the dignity and validity that the defeat of their enemies would bring. To win would be to acquire constitutional legitimacy, and to prove that the opposition had betrayed the legacy that was enshrined in the constitutional text.[42]

In a nation that had, since its founding, internalized the principles of both religious liberty and Puritan morality, Mormon polygamy provided just the right background for the question, "How far must overwhelmingly accepted moral principles bend to accommodate religious belief?" The legal precedents established by this conflict—especially in *Reynolds v. United States*—continue to be cited in cases where religious worship bumps up against community standards in questions such as Native Americans using peyote in sacred rituals, Hatian immigrants sacrificing chickens, and religious universities denying admission to students in interracial relationships.[43]

It has been some time, however, since polygamy has functioned this way. While contemporary morality does not accept polygamy, it does embrace so many actions and relationships that are legally indistinguishable from it that there is no longer any point in trying to enforce unlawful-cohabitation laws. There is no legal distinction between a married man who has sex with another woman and (with no authority from the state) calls her a wife and a similarly married man who calls the other woman a mistress, a friend, or a White House intern. And if there is a moral distinction, it almost certainly favors polygamists, who are at least willing to make some minimal commitment to the women they sleep with and the children they create. As anthropologists Irwin Altman and Joseph Ginat argue, "The widespread occurrences in American society of serial marriages and divorces, repeated cases of cohabitation of unmarried couples, affairs and mistresses, seem . . . less burdensome than a permanent involvement with multiple wives and families."[44]

*Big Love* does not set out to challenge laws directly (fundamentalists do not generally seek the right to marry under any authority but their own) but to change the cultural definitions upon which laws are ultimately based. Olsen is very direct about this aspect of the show: "Will and I have watched the country become divisive with an increasingly strident debate about the culture wars and what is and is not a family and what should be an accepted family," he says in an interview with *The Washington Blade*. "We want to examine it at a different level without labels. Let's take a look at people as people and find the values of family that are worth celebrating separate of who the people are and how they're doing it."[45] The purpose of *Big Love*, in other words, is to try to change what we mean when we talk about families.

And talking about families is the central activity of the American civil religion. There is no more disputed or important question in America today than "what makes a family?" This question intersects with almost all of the hot-button political issue of the past three decades: abortion, gay marriage, school choice, the right to die, and the proper role of the government in temporal welfare, to name only a few. In this conversation (and despite differences too numerous to mention), the fictional polygamist Bill Henrickson and the very-real presidential candidate Mitt Romney sit uncomfortably on the horns of the same dilemma: their comforting normalness flows from the same source as their irreducible weirdness. Perhaps the greatest paradox of the Romney campaign was how to take advantage of the candidate's image as a family man—which seemed tailor-made for conservative religious voters—without antagonizing those same voters with his unorthodox beliefs and the less savory aspects of his religious tradition. Henrickson, who embodies the most notorious aspect of that same tradition, faces the same struggle as he tries to build Henrickson's Home Plus into the corporate embodiment of Utah's conservative, family culture.

Both men, in their own way, symbolize the larger dilemma of Mormonism in America: Mormons are, in many ways, quintessentially American—they are, on the whole, honest, patriotic, hardworking, and devoted to their families. But these values stem directly from those aspects of Mormonism most at odds with American culture: Mormon industry derives directly from the communalism that placed early Mormons at odds with their Missouri and Illinois neighbors. Mormon patriotism flows from the same authoritarian impulses that turned late-nineteenth-century Utah into a strict theocracy. And the well-known Mormon emphasis on families comes from a view of the family as a sacred institution that propels men toward godhood through the creation of eternal posterity—the same ideology that supported the institution of polygamy.

The weirdly normal polygamists at the center of *Big Love* are not, as all of the politically correct disclaimers hasten to point out, affiliated with the Church of Jesus Christ of Latter-day Saints—but they aren't quite not Mormon. Standing at the fringes of Mormondom generally, they help to clarify some of the conflicting ways that the story of Mormonism—as a religion, a culture, and a historical narrative—weaves into the much larger narrative of America. And whatever one thinks about the practice of polygamy, it is an integral part of the story that the Mormons have to tell.

## Notes

1. Feldman, "What Is It about Mormonism?," 34.
2. Heilemann, "The Right Man," 21.
3. Full results of the survey can be found at http://pewforum.org/surveys/ religionviews07/.
4. As linguistic purists will no doubt point out, *polygamy* actually means more than one spouse. The correct term for the relationship between one man and more than one wife is *polygyny*, while the name for a relationship between one woman and more than one husband is *polyandry*. However, in popular culture and usage, polygamy almost always refers to the first kind of relationship.
5. Carroll, "One in Four Americans Think Most Mormons Endorse Polygamy."
6. Reilly, "Take My Wives . . . Please! Mitt Romney's Clumsy Mormon Shtick."
7. Church of Jesus Christ of Latter-day Saints, "Church Responds to Questions on HBO's *Big Love*."
8. For surveys of Mormon portrayals in early literature and film, see Arrington and Haupt, "Community and Isolation"; Arrington and Haupt, "Intolerable Zion"; Lambert, "Saints, Sinners, and Scribes"; and Nelson, "From Antagonism to Acceptance."
9. Austin, "Troped by the Mormons.
10. Bloom, *The American Religion*, 123.
11. See, for example, Elizabeth Joseph's well-known speech, "Polygamy—The Ultimate Feminist Lifestyle." See also Batchelor, Watson, and Wilde, *Voices in Harmony*.
12. See, for example, Dixon, *We Want for Our Sisters What We Want for Ourselves*; Kilbride, *Plural Marriage for Our Times*.
13. For a clear and well-argued comparison of the legal foundations of both plural marriage and same-sex marriage, see Handley, "Belonging(s)."
14. The quoted line occurs in the final episode of the second season, "Oh, Pioneers," originally broadcast on August 26, 2007.
15. Chung, "Will Scheffer's 'Falling Man and Other Monologues.'"
16. Frei, "Big Love," 66.
17. The role of *Big Love* in the debate over gay marriage is examined approvingly in Tierney, "Who's Afraid of Polygamy?"; Moylan, "Feeling the 'Love'"; and Frei, "Polygamy, Gays, and TV." The same connection is examined critically in Dennis, "The Big Problem with 'Big Love'"; Kurtz, "Big Love, from the Set"; and Marquardt, "Two Mommies and a Daddy."
18. In his dissent on *Lawrence v. Texas*, Justice Scalia declares the decision to be the end of any legislation against behavior considered immoral. He writes, "This effectively decrees the end of all morals legislation. If, as the Court asserts, the promotion of majoritarian sexual morality is not even a *legitimate* state interest, none of the above-mentioned laws [against fornication,

bigamy, adultery, adult incest, bestiality, and obscenity] can survive ratio-nal-basis review." (italics in the original.)

19. Van Wagoner, *Mormon Polygamy*. One of the charges against polygamist Tom Green in 2001 was bigamy, which was sustained by using his own statements to establish that he had entered into common-law marriages with more than one woman. This was the first antibigamy prosecution of a polygamist for more than fifty years, but it did not invoke the unlawful-cohabitation statutes. See "Mormon Polygamist 'Legally Single . . . Eter-nally Married'"; "Bigamy Conviction May Affect Thousands."

20. Episode 13, "Damage Control," first aired on June 11, 2007.

21. *Romer v. Evans*, 1996.

22. Kurtz, "What Is Wrong with Gay Marriage," 35.

23. The big tip-off is the difference in average size between males and females. In monogamous species, males are no larger than females since there is no selective advantage to a specific body size (in predation, predator avoidance, etc.). It is only when males must compete with other males of the same species that they derive an evolutionary advantage from being larger—a selection pressure that does not affect the females they compete for.

24. Wright, *The Moral Animal*, 90.

25. Augustine, *On the Holy Trinity,*, 211.

26. Barash and Lipton, *The Myth of Monogamy*, 137.

27. Generally sympathetic portrayals of polygamy during the Nauvoo and early Utah periods are found in such moderately popular works as Bailey, *Polygamy Was Better Than Monotony*; Card, *A Woman of Destiny*; and Taylor, *Family Kingdom*.

28. This is only to say that nothing has happened in the last fifteen years to increase or decrease dramatically the distribution of the polygamous popula-tion among several groups, though the actual numbers are probably higher due to higher-than-average birthrates. The most recent published version of the article, which first appeared in Marty and Appleby, *Fundamentalism and Society* (1993) is Quinn, "Plural Marriage and Mormon Fundamentalism (1998)."

29. Ibid., 6.

30. Since the publication of Quinn's article, the FLDS has come under the lead-ership of Warren Jeffs, who is currently in jail for various crimes stemming from underage marriages he performed, authorized, or entered into. Many accounts portray Jeffs's leadership as much more extreme and authoritarian than that of his father and predecessor, Rulon Jeffs. A vivid insider's account of the FLDS under Warren Jeffs can be found in Jessop and Palmer, *Escape*.

31. Quinn, "Plural Marriage and Mormon Fundamentalism," 30. One of Rulon Allred's daughters, Dorothy Allred Solomon, has written an excellent, best-selling memoir about her experiences as a member of this group, published in hardcover as *Predators, Prey, and Other Kinfolk : Growing up in Polygamy*. It was issued in paperback in 2004 under the title *Daughter of the Saints: Grow-ing Up in Polygamy*.

32. Quinn, "Plural Marriage and Mormon Fundamentalism," 22–23.

33. Lattin, "Gay Monogamous Couple Are Brains behind Polygamy Show," PK–32.

34. Adams, "The Real Sources behind Big Love."
35. Maxine Hanks in a letter to D. Michael Quinn, August 4, 1995, quoted in Quinn, *Same Sex Dynamics among Nineteenth-Century Americans*, 260n89. Quinn there urges caution about reading too much into this relationship. "While I see it as possible that some plural wives regarded themselves as joined together eternally through their shared husband, the ceremony's wording involved only the new bride and the already married groom."
36. Church of Jesus Christ of Latter-day Saints, "Preserving the Divine Institution of Marriage.".
37. McKinley and Johnson, "Mormons Tipped Scale in Ban on Gay Marriage"; Pyrah, "LDS Donate Millions to Fight Gay Marriage."
38. Wells, "Hypocrite of the Week: 5 Biggest Hypocrites of the Year."
39. Church of Jesus Christ of Latter-day Saints, "Church Responds to Questions on HBO's *Big Love.*"
40. It is extremely unlikely that the situation described would occur. The LDS Church generally does not grant a temple divorce or a sealing cancellation to a surviving spouse unless the marriage was dissolved civilly while both partners were alive.
41. See religious membership figures at http://www.adherents.com/rel_USA.html.
42. Gordon, *The Mormon Question*, 6.
43. The three Supreme Court cases referred to—each of which cites *Reynolds v. United States*—are *Employment Division v. Smith; Church of Lukumi Babalu Aye v. City of Hialeah;* and *Bob Jones University v. United States*.
44. Altman and Ginat, *Polygamous Families in Contemporary Society*, 439–40.
45. Moylan, "Feeling the 'Love.'"

## Bibliography

Adams, Brooke. "The Real Sources behind Big Love." In *The Polygamy Files, Salt Lake Tribune*, March 8, 2006. http://blogs.sltrib.com/plurallife/2006/03/real-sources-behind-big-love.htm.

Altman, Irwin, and J. Ginat. *Polygamous Families in Contemporary Society*. New York: Cambridge University Press, 1996.

Arrington, Leonard J., and Jon Haupt. "Community and Isolation: Some Aspects of 'Mormon Westerns.'" *Western American Literature* 8 (1973): 15–31.

———. "Intolerable Zion: The Image of Mormonism in Nineteenth Century American Literature." *Western Humanities Review* 22 (Summer 1968): 243–60.

Augustine. *On the Holy Trinity; Doctrinal Treatises; Moral Treatises*. Edited by Philip Schaff. Vol. 3 of *A Select Library of the Nicene and Post-Nicene Fathers of the Christian Church*. Edinburgh: T. & T. Clark, 1890.

Austin, Michael. "Troped by the Mormons: The Persistence of 19th-Century Mormon Stereotypes in Contemporary Detective Fiction." *Sunstone* 21, no. 3 (August 1998): 51–71.

Bailey, Paul. *Polygamy Was Better Than Monotony*. Los Angeles: Westernlore Press, 1972.

Barash, David P., and Judith Eve Lipton. *The Myth of Monogamy: Fidelity and Infidelity in Animals and People*. New York: W. H. Freeman and Co., 2001.

Batchelor, Mary, Marianne Watson, and Anne Wilde. *Voices in Harmony: Contemporary Women Celebrate Plural Marriage*. Salt Lake City: Principle Voices, 2000.

"Bigamy Conviction May Affect Thousands." *Toronto Star*, May 20, 2001.

Bloom, Harold. *The American Religion: The Emergence of the Post-Christian Nation*. New York: Simon & Schuster, 1992.

*Bob Jones University v. United States*, 461 U.S. 574 (1983).

Card, Orson Scott. *A Woman of Destiny*. New York: Berkley Books, 1984.

Carroll, Joseph. "One in Four Americans Think Most Mormons Endorse Polygamy: Only 2% Think Most Americans Support Polygamy." *Gallup Poll Briefing*, September 7, 2006, 4–7.

Chung, Jennifer. "Will Scheffer's 'Falling Man and Other Monologues.'" *Gay & Lesbian Times*, March 24, 2005. http://www.gaylesbiantimes.com/?id=4707&issue=900.

Church of Jesus Christ of Latter-day Saints, "Church Responds to Questions on HBO's *Big Love*." http://newsroom.lds.org/ldsnewsroom/eng/commentary/church-responds-to-questions-on-hbo-s-big-love.

———. "Preserving the Divine Institution of Marriage." http://newsroom.lds.org/ldsnewsroom/eng/commentary/california-and-same-sex-marriage.

*Church of Lukumi Babalu Aye v. City of Hialeah*, 508 U.S. 520 (1993).

Dennis, Wendy. "The Big Problem with 'Big Love.'" *Maclean's*, April 17, 2006, 66–67.

Dixon, Patricia. *We Want for Our Sisters What We Want for Ourselves: Polygyny—Co-Partnering: A Relationship, Marriage and Family Alternative*. Decatur, GA: Oji Publications, 2002.

*Employment Division v. Smith*, 485 U.S. 660 (1988).

Feldman, Noah. "What Is It about Mormonism?" *New York Times Magazine*, January 6, 2008, 34.

Flake, Kathleen. *The Politics of American Religious Identity: The Seating of Senator Reed Smoot, Mormon Apostle*. Chapel Hill: University of North Carolina Press, 2004.

Frei, Darren. "Big Love." *The Advocate*, March 14, 2006, 66.

———. "Polygamy, Gays, and TV." *The Advocate*, June 6, 2006, 1.

Gordon, Sarah Barringer. *The Mormon Question: Polygamy and Constitutional Conflict in Nineteenth-Century America*. Studies in Legal History. Chapel Hill: University of North Carolina Press, 2002.

Handley, William R. "Belonging(s): Plural Marriage, Gay Marriage and the Subversion of 'Good Order.'" *Discourse: Journal for Theoretical Studies in Media and Culture* 26, no. 3 (2004): 85–109.

Heilemann, John. "The Right Man." *New York* 40, no. 6 (2007): 20–22.

Jessop, Carolyn, and Laura Palmer. *Escape*. 1st ed. New York: Broadway Books, 2007.

Joseph, Elizabeth. "Polygamy—The Ultimate Feminist Lifestyle?" http://www.polygamy.com/articles/templates/?A=100z=3.

Kilbride, Philip Leroy. *Plural Marriage for Our Times: A Reinvented Option?* Westport, CT: Bergin & Garvey, 1994.

Kurtz, Stanley N. "Big Love, from the Set." *National Review Online,* March 13, 2005. http://www.nationalreview.com/kurtz/kurtz200603130805.asp.

———. "What Is Wrong with Gay Marriage." *Commentary* 110, no. 2 (2000): 35.

Lambert, Neal. "Saints, Sinners, and Scribes." *Utah Historical Quarterly* 36 (Winter 1968): 63–76.

Lattin, Don. "Gay Monogamous Couple Are Brains behind Polygamy Show." *San Francisco Chronicle,* June 10, 2007, PK-32.

*Lawrence v. Texas.* 539 U.S. 558 (2003).

Marquardt, Elizabeth. "Two Mommies and a Daddy." *The Christian Century,* July 25, 2006, 8–10.

Marty, Martin E., and R. Scott Appleby, eds. *Fundamentalism and Society: Reclaiming the Sciences, Education, and the Family.* Chicago: University of Chicago Press, 1993.

McKinley, Jesse, and Kirk Johnson. "Mormons Tipped Scale in Ban on Gay Marriage." *New York Times,* November 14, 2008. http://www.nytimes.com/2008/11/15/us/politics/15marriage.html?_r=3&pagewanted=1&hp&oref=slogin.

"Mormon Polygamist 'Legally Single . . . Eternally Married.'" *Globe and Mail* (Canada), May 19, 2001, A12.

Moylan, Brian. "Feeling the 'Love.'" *The Washington Blade,* March 10, 2006. http://www.washblade.com/2006/3-10/arts/television/feeling.cfm.

Nelson, Richard Alan. "From Antagonism to Acceptance: Mormons and the Silver Screen." *Dialogue: A Journal of Mormon Thought* 10, no. 3 (1977): 58–69.

Pyrah, Joe. "LDS Donate Millions to Fight Gay Marriage." *Provo Daily Herald,* September 15, 2008. http://www.heraldextra.com/news/local/article_84a8a9bf-6851-56a1-8c36-f170e8cd9f13.html.

Quinn, D. Michael. "Plural Marriage and Mormon Fundamentalism." *Dialogue: A Journal of Mormon Thought* 31, no. 2 (1998): 1–68.

———. *Same-Sex Dynamics among Nineteenth-Century Americans: A Mormon Example.* Urbana: University of Illinois Press, 1996.

Reilly, Adam. "Take My Wives . . . Please! Mitt Romney's Clumsy Mormon Shtick." *Slate,* April 26, 2006. http://www.slate.com/id/2140539/.

*Reynolds v. United States.* 98 U.S. 145 (1878).

*Romer v. Evans,* 517 U.S. 620 (1996).

Solomon, Dorothy Allred. *In My Father's House.* New York: Franklin Watts, 1984.

———. *Predators, Prey, and Other Kinfolk: Growing up in Polygamy.* 1st ed. New York: W.W. Norton & Co., 2003.

Taylor, Samuel Woolley. *Family Kingdom.* New York: McGraw-Hill, 1951.

Tierney, John. "Who's Afraid of Polygamy?" *New York Times,* March 11, 2006, A15.

Van Wagoner, Richard S. *Mormon Polygamy: A History.* Salt Lake City: Signature Books, 1986.

Wells, Duane. "Hypocrite of the Week: 5 Biggest Hypocrites of the Year." *Gay-Wired,* December 26, 2008. Archived at http://www.gaywiredmedia.com.

Wright, Robert. *The Moral Animal: The New Science of Evolutionary Psychology.* 1st ed. New York: Pantheon Books, 1994.

**3**

# Teaching *Under the Banner of Heaven*

## Testing the Limits of Tolerance in America

KEVIN KOLKMEYER

## Entry: A Unique Place by the Sea

*Walking through the halls of Kingsborough Community College we are all very used to by now, there are several female Islamic students who observe their religious right to be fully covered.*

Kingsborough Community College student paper

Kingsborough Community College in Brooklyn, New York, is bound by water on three sides. It is on a peninsula, but in some ways, it might as well be on an island. There are only two ways to enter the campus, and each is fenced and gated, with guards to check whether you are authorized to come in. Every day students ride buses that ferry them to the campus from subway stops about a mile away, past swanky ocean- and bay-front homes, but there is no other contact between students and the neighborhood surrounding the campus. A former World War II maritime training center, the campus is a sanctuary for many, a haven for students who come from cramped apartments and neighborhoods; however, most would never be welcome to own the homes they pass to get to school, much less be able to afford to do so. The students come from geographically different and sometimes-isolated neighborhoods in Brooklyn that sharply contrast with genteel Manhattan Beach, where the school is located. As long as they keep to the buses, the subway stops, and the fenced-in campus, the relationship between the students and the neighborhood works. It is not clear what would happen if that boundary was ever breached. It is the separation, the isolation, that seems to make the relationship tolerable, but at what costs?

62

During the summer I am describing, it is generally midmorning when I arrive on campus and head for the Clusters, the building that houses my office and is connected to the Marine and Academic Center (MAC) where I teach my class. I never have to step outside for the remainder of my day on campus. As I walk down the buffed and waxed hallway of the A wing, past the copy center, bookstore, and cafeteria, I can see the ocean through the bank of floor-to-ceiling windows that face south. It is the view from the dining area, a stunning panorama of Breezy Point, the Atlantic Ocean, and a nub of the Jersey Shore. In my reverie, I am actually happy to be back in such a relaxed setting for a summer-session freshman writing class, but then I hear clap! slap!—sounds of something scratching a wooden tabletop and, finally, loud voices filled with good-natured insults and invective. Even in summer session, a group of students always play dominoes, while those at other tables eat, chat, sleep, read, or do homework, often with very loud music playing. The domino players sit at a table with other students hovering over their shoulders, and they, along with everyone else in the area, appear oblivious to the landscape on the other side of the glass. All the students are engrossed in the game, a bagel, class notes, or a dream, cocooned in an air-conditioned maze of tables and chairs.

These are my students, the ones who come from more than 176 nations and speak more than ninety-five different languages; the ones who are the proverbial firsts in their families to graduate from college; the ones who will sometimes tell you that they were excited to have been accepted to the community college, even though there have been open admissions since the 1970s; the ones who come from marginal—though also gentrifying—areas of Bedford Stuyvesant, Sunset Park, and Coney Island. To call them "outsiders" or "marginal" or "at-risk" or "diverse" would be using terms that apply to and yet simplify their situations. They are too savvy to be reduced in such a way, though they often are all of these. They come to college having realized or been told that it is a way out of something or a way into something better; however, while they are earnest, they often know very little about what it means to go to college. Their understanding of their place in the society outside of their neighborhoods or boroughs is limited. For many of the students, school is the place to unwind, a relaxed DMZ of sorts between the old and the new.

My class had twenty-four students that summer, a mix that is typical for Kingsborough. In addition to the handful who were native born, there were students from Mexico, the Dominican Republic, China, Haiti, Pakistan, Trinidad and Tobago, Russia, and Argentina. Despite the global representation, most students were simply taking the course to get a general-education requirement out of the way, inching ever closer to graduation and better-paying jobs. It was not that they did not care about noninstrumental learning, but rather that they felt there was little time to waste in achieving their goals. This meant that dwelling on issues that I considered central to the class—immigration, assimilation, and place—was ancillary to doing whatever it took to get an A or B to maintain their GPAs. I understood these things. But I have always marveled at how rarely students, regardless of background, question America's reputation as "the land of opportunity." Many students seem to think there is no reason to ask whether that opportunity extends to all equally. They argue that all you have to do is work hard.

I decided to do something different, tricky even, but perhaps more compelling, to get them to address these same questions. Instead of a typical story of migration and assimilation—something like Jhumpa Lahiri's *The Namesake* or Khaled Hosseini's *The Kite Runner*—I had students read, discuss, and write about an entirely American story. The students did read other essays and articles, but the core text was Jon Krakauer's *Under the Banner of Heaven: A Story of Violent Faith*, a national best seller about the Church of Jesus Christ of Latter-day Saints' (LDS Church) experience in America.

I was betting that no students had read the book before taking the class, and I was right; no one had even heard of it. I was also fairly sure that few, if any, knew much about Mormons or Mormonism, and again I was correct; there were no Mormons in the class. In fact, only one—a student who had been raised in Tacoma, Washington—said she had even known a Mormon. A few of the others vaguely remembered Mormon missionaries visiting their homes. My hope was that reading about something unfamiliar to them and comparing it to other texts and their own experiences might enable them to appreciate what they had in common with the universal struggle to gain acceptance based on race, ethnicity, culture, or faith. I also had the idea that if I placed this text in tension with more contemporary arguments about the role of immigrants in American culture, the students could consider the issue of assimilation in a larger historical context. To be sure, other texts might have done this, too, but I chose Krakauer because I like his writing, and, having used his *Into the Wild* in other college writing classes, I knew that students generally did as well.

The hour before class began that summer, I stood alone in the empty classroom on the second floor of the MAC building. I found myself thinking that if the discussions faltered—and they certainly did at times—we could always stare out the windows at the ocean and blue sky. It would be a summer oasis from the heat and humidity. We could imagine the room as an island, I thought, a refuge much like the Great Salt Lake basin was a haven for Mormons in the mid-to-late nineteenth century, and on this island, we could read and discuss a church with a questionable beginning, a persecuted past, a rebellious spirit, a zealous and still-growing following, and, finally, an extraordinary story of assimilation into mainstream America.

As it happened, the students had lots to say. It helped, perhaps, that the book was controversial—students like scandal and debate. Given its focus on the history of violence and the connection Krakauer makes between the LDS and self-proclaimed fundamentalist sects of the faith (FLDS), the LDS Church unsurprisingly denounced the book; in contrast, the students were intrigued. To help frame what is controversial about the book, in a class the first week, the students read the church's official response in a section Krakauer provides in the back. While he claimed in that section to have "puzzled over" the negative LDS reaction to his book, my students' responses as we read it that summer might have enlightened him to the church's discomfort.[1]

When the summer began, I was apprehensive, worried that students might be so affronted by the violence in the book that they would not be able to assess it critically. And this did happen. Early on, some made comments that Mormons are "evil" or "crazy" without trying to distinguish between past and present, LDS and FLDS, or an active Saint and one who had been excommunicated. It took some time and sorting out to make those distinctions, but in the end, most of the students came to agree that the paradoxical Mormon pursuit of the American Dream paralleled their own quests, often in troubling ways. Reading how the LDS came to understand that they could only be Mormon on America's terms pushed my students to reflect on their own places in American society.[2]

My approach to teaching the class was simple. I value the jarring, but thought-provoking, cross talk between texts that discuss seemingly disparate ideas. With this in mind, the students typically came to class having read a few chapters in *Under the Banner of Heaven,* and then, in class, they were given other essays and articles to read that they compared and debated with Krakauer's point of view. Although this sometimes created tension in the classroom, these debates eventually led the students to insights about their own experiences. As a result of working with the texts in this way, they began to identify what they tolerated in others, which then became a way for them to gauge if they themselves were tolerated. Finally, they used their discoveries to support the arguments they made both in informal discussions and reading responses and in formal essay assignments.

In short, reading Krakauer's book pushed my students to grapple with the very questions that their presence in Manhattan Beach raised every day: To what extent do outsiders ever fully assimilate into mainstream America? How difficult is it for those deemed "others" by mainstream society to shed stereotypes that inhibit their acceptance into that society? To what extent should America tolerate practices judged antithetical to mainstream values? What roles do religion, race, government policy, or region play in determining the outcome of the assimilation process?

In the course of the summer, many of my students came to articulate an experience of assimilation that cultural anthropologist Renato Rosaldo neatly characterizes as "Come in, sit down, shut up. You're welcome here as long as you conform with our norms."[3] Even though many started the summer insisting that they had been assimilated into American society—after all, they were in an American classroom getting an American education that they hoped would lead to a middle- or upper-class American life—the class members found themselves discussing— in their exploration of the Mormons' experience—the ways they, like the Mormons, were also not fully accepted. Based on their own sometimes-tenuous relationships with America, my students could identify with the Mormon dilemma. They were, some realized, constrained at times by their associations to lingering stereotypes, regardless of how little or much they identified themselves by their races, ethnicities, cultures, or religions. Then, too, they debated the complexities of assimilation: What is lost, and what is gained? At one point in American history, the Mormons were a bona fide minority facing extermination. Today Mormons struggle to recapture some of the "specialness" that they think they have lost now that they have largely integrated into the mainstream.[4]

## Assessing the Landscape: The Book's Appeal and Structure

*My personal interest in the mosaic of cultures that encompass our world prevents me from seeing these matters as exclusively black and white. There is a gray area.*

Kingsborough Community College student essay

The Mormon story, as Krakauer tells it, is sensationalized and violent, and I was hoping this would spark debate among the students, that is, if it did not disgust them too much. I was not disappointed; many of the liveliest class discussions were fueled by the most gruesome details of LDS and FLDS exploits in Krakauer's book. Some commentators have complained that Krakauer's book gives only a selective view of LDS history and a flawed representation of the present church as a result. For example, Claudia L. Bushman, a Mormon scholar, wrote, "Best-selling journalist Jon Krakauer tied together several violent incidents perpetrated by fundamentalist, excommunicated Mormons to illustrate the violent potential of supposed revelations."[5] Bushman is referring to a revered LDS tenet that states that Saints can receive divine revelation directly from God. As one might assume, several of the faithful have abused this doctrine over the years, even using it to justify committing murder. Krakauer chooses one such notorious murder as a focal point for his book: the brutal 1984 slayings of Brenda and Erica Lafferty by Ron and Dan Lafferty, the victims' fundamentalist Mormon brothers-in-law and uncles. Indeed, it is through the lens of these murders that Krakauer unfolds the history of the church, thus suggesting an unbreakable link between LDS and FLDS.

That the LDS and FLDS exist on a spectrum of Mormonism seems logical to non-Mormon readers, including my students (who, indeed, had trouble understanding the distinction). Many LDS readers, however, were outraged by Krakauer's conflation of the two groups; they do not regard FLDS history as their own, for they claim that "there is no such thing as a Mormon fundamentalist" since such a person would have been excommunicated for any acts that the church deemed unacceptable.[6] In *Under the Banner of Heaven*, Krakauer explicitly disagrees with the church on this. To him the existence of the FLDS directly evolved from the rigorous indoctrination into the LDS.

No moment in the book better emphasizes this association than when Krakauer quotes Ron Lafferty's response to a judge's sentence of death by lethal injection for his part in the murders: "I've already had the lethal injection of Mormonism," meaning that his upbringing in the LDS Church was the root of his fanaticism. Clearly Krakauer wants readers to see the "dark side to religious devotion" that can develop homegrown extremists of the kind we read about in newspapers or see on television operating in Baghdad, Peshawar, or Kabul.[7] Krakauer sees the Mormon story as a broader parable of religious extremism globally, a topic of great interest to the public, whose curiosity made his book a best seller.

Indeed, the book's very appearance suggests that emphasizing the violent aspects of the religion's history that Krakauer tells was central to the publisher's marketing strategy. Its provocative cover accentuates the sensational: a picture of what appears to be a Mormon settlement in the American West is framed by a *San Francisco Chronicle* blurb announcing that the book is on a par with Truman Capote's *In Cold Blood* and Norman Mailer's *The Executioner's Song*, and the opening lines of a narrative of the Lafferty murders appear. On the back, three additional blurbs plug the book as a tale of thrilling violence. The *New York Times Book Review* states that the book is an "arresting portrait of depravity." Another excerpt, from the *New York Post*, adds that it is "a white-knuckle mix of true-crime reporting and provocative history." Finally, *Newsweek* declares, "It is also the creepiest book anyone has written in a long time—and that's meant as the highest possible praise." Obviously Krakauer touched a nerve with the sensationalized elements of the book.[8]

A brief overview illustrates why *Under the Banner of Heaven* garnered such intriguing praise. Krakauer begins the book with two epigraphs that illuminate the content and structure of what follows. In the first, John Taylor, the LDS president, prophet, seer, and revelator who succeeded Brigham Young in 1877, defiantly defends polygamy in a phrase that gave Krakauer his title: "God is greater than the United States," Taylor wrote, "and when the Government conflicts with heaven, we will be ranged under the banner of heaven and against the Government. . . . I defy the United States; I will obey God."[9] The second epigraph reflects a more contemporary assessment. In this quote, literary critic Harold Bloom states that America is a "religion-soaked" nation and "doom-eager society" whose collective fear of death can inspire passionate devotion.[10]

Taylor and Bloom constitute an important pairing. As well as setting the ominous tone for the book—a kind of doomsday showdown—the juxtaposition of historical and current commentators illustrates Krakauer's habit of shuttling readers between past and present, suggesting causal and thematic links between them. Taylor's epigraph is clearly meant to provide an example of the extremist mindset of the then-still-young LDS Church, while Bloom hints at the present potential for homegrown terrorism, suggesting that since there are more people who believe in God in the United States per capita than anywhere else in the world, inevitably some will be attracted to radically destructive forms of faith.

In the prologue that follows the epigraphs, Krakauer invokes an array of historical sources to tell the tale of the grisly Lafferty murders, the subsequent manhunt for the brothers, and their conversion to fundamentalism. The murders are a parable for LDS history, as Krakauer sees it, because the incident illuminates the link between religious devotion and violence, his book's central theme. The four main parts of the book then move between LDS history, beginning in the early 1800s, and the present. Anchoring and framing these sections are Krakauer's interviews with DeLoy Bateman, an apostate who was excommunicated from the FLDS Church in Colorado City, Arizona, and the narrative of the Lafferty brothers' change from devout Mormons and devoted family men to FLDS members bent on blood atonement, a long-abandoned LDS doctrine that advocates revenge.

In class we spent time discussing the structure of the book because I wanted students to understand that Krakauer was drawing parallels and connections between past and present. I also wanted them to be aware of the criticism that LDS officials leveled at him for this. In the back of the book, Krakauer includes the full text of what he calls Richard E. Turley's "screed" that "excoriated [his] book as 'a decidedly one-sided and negative view of Mormon history.'"[11] In addition, we read what Mike Otterson, LDS director of media relations in 2006, wrote on the LDS Web site: "This book is not history, and Krakauer is no historian. He is a storyteller who cuts corners to make the story sound good."[12] Many historians might agree, contending, perhaps, that Krakauer plays too fast and loose with the parallels between past and present.

However, Krakauer's response is that the parallels, "however disquieting," are necessary for understanding "the actions of the murderous Lafferty brothers, or any other Mormon Fundamentalist."[13] It was these links, moreover, that roused the students from their summer-school malaise; the unfamiliar material actually invited them to take sides on issues and make connections to their own experiences to justify their positions. Reading about religious fundamentalism, it turns out, is good for provoking discussion in the classroom because it presents students with challenges to their often-complacent notions of themselves and the relationships they have with history and place.

## Traversing the Landscape: Students' Responses to the Book's Controversies

*It is difficult to know when to tolerate something and when not to, but these choices and decisions must be made.*

Kingsborough Community College student essay

The students focused on three aspects of the book: the episodes of violence in the history of the LDS Church, the lingering perception that the LDS Church is racist, and the controversy over polygamy, which is arguably the issue that brought the FLDS into existence. After their initial outrage over all these issues subsided, the students generated additional questions about these specific aspects of the book to add to our larger questions about outsiders/insiders, tolerance, assimilation into the mainstream, and place: Does the emphasis on violence in the book paint an unfair picture of the church? In the outsiders' struggle for acceptance, is violence ever justified? Should the LDS Church's actions to fix its racist image be viewed any differently from attempts by the nation as a whole to come to terms with its history of slavery and civil-rights abuses? Is polygamy such a threat to the moral fabric of society that it needs to be banned? And finally, what, if anything, did any of these questions about the Mormon story—playing out in this foreign, western landscape—have to do with them, today, in Brooklyn?

From Haun's Mill to the Mountain Meadows Massacre to the grue-somely detailed account of the Lafferty murders, the book is one violent tale after another. A key moment in the text that the class took time to discuss comes in the middle chapters. In chapter twelve, Krakauer describes Joseph Smith's assassination at the hands of an unruly mob of Warsaw Dragoons, an Illinois militia. Four chapters later, Dan Lafferty gives his *In Cold Blood*-style narrative of the murders of Brenda and Erica. At one chilling point, Dan says, famously, "I told [Erica], I'm not sure what this is all about, but apparently it's God's will that you leave this world; perhaps we can talk about it later" only seconds before he used a ten-inch boning knife to nearly decapitate her. Krakauer writes, "Afterward, all that held the baby's head to her tiny body were a few thin shreds of skeleton and tendon." The three chapters in between reveal the factors contributing to the brothers' conversion to Mormon fundamentalism. Without overtly saying so, Krakauer stresses the fanat-icism: Joseph Smith's martyrdom has spawned the Laffertys; past and present are one; the LDS story is one that charts the making of a funda-mentalist. In his jail interview with Krakauer, Dan voices the author's own idea about religious faiths in general: "Organized religion is hate masquerading as love. Which inevitably leads you back to the religion as it originally existed, before it was corrupted. It leads you to become a fundamentalist."[14]

My students were astounded by the brutality of the Lafferty murders and the LDS Church's history of battling with the state militias in Missouri and Illinois that were intent on preventing the Mormons from establishing their Zion within the United States. They had no idea that recent American history included a conflict of such magnitude with a religious group within its own borders, and they were not aware of current tensions between law enforcement and FLDS groups. In the course of the arguments they had about these issues, I asked them if they thought Krakauer made a convincing case for the connection between LDS history and contemporary FLDS activities and the threat posed by homegrown religious fundamentalists. I was worried that they might accept his story wholesale without questioning whether he overstated the link and the resulting violence and dangers.[15] Ultimately some students used their own sense of outsiderness to argue a very different perspective from Krakauer's. They felt we needed to distinguish between the violent history of the LDS Church in the nineteenth century that related to the Mormons trying to find a permanent place to worship and isolated incidents such as the Lafferty murders. The early Mormons, they said, were generally fighting back against being pushed around, while the Lafferty brothers were misguided individuals who had grown up in a violent home.

Furthermore, others in the class rejected Krakauer's idea that clannishness in the LDS Church means it is grooming future fanatics in the same fashion as Al Qaeda or the Taliban. They saw his use of the word *shadowy* to describe FLDS activities as analogous to the populist use of the term by government officials to propagate the war efforts in Afghanistan and Iraq, problematizing the link Krakauer makes to the LDS Church. Since 9/11 and the passing of the Patriot Act, tensions have run high in some of my students' neighborhoods. An immigrant Muslim student who lived in a predominantly Muslim section of downtown Brooklyn said that he was now suspicious of the government that purported to accept him after watching armed National Guardsmen caravan up and down the streets in his community in the weeks following the World Trade Center attacks. Ostensibly the government was protecting his community from harassment by people who linked them to the parties who orchestrated the attacks, but in class he explained that the community could not help but feel besieged as well.

Reflecting on the Haun's Mill chapter in the book, the student added that he could understand how some Mormons felt the urge to fight back, but that doing so did not make someone a terrorist. In that chapter, Krakauer describes the events leading up to the 1838 Haun's Mill massacre in northwestern Missouri, where the Missouri militia shot and killed eighteen Mormons of that settlement, including some children, as they sought safety inside a blacksmith's shop. In one example of the incessant harassment experienced by the Mormons, Krakauer writes that "in July 1833 an armed mob of five hundred Missourians tarred and feathered two Latter-day Saints and destroyed a printing office because an LDS newspaper had published an article deemed overly sympathetic to the antislavery viewpoint." Just prior to the massacre, the Mormons had finally begun to fight back. This, the student pointed out, was different from the motivation behind the actions of the Lafferty brothers, and Krakauer's long footnote in the middle of the chapter on connections some have made between the violent aspects of Mormonism that make it "akin to Islam" bothered him.[16]

When threatened, people can react violently, many students contended. The class spent a long time debating an incident Krakauer describes in great detail. Ironically, it happened on September 11 but in the year 1857: the Mountain Meadows Massacre. Only 17 very young children in a wagon train of approximately 137 emigrants heading for California were spared by the Mormons and Paiute Indians who attacked them.[17] Today few scholars dispute that Mormons took part in the massacre, but there is ongoing controversy about its causes and the degree of LDS culpability. Some students pointed it out as an example of the way a siege mentality can lead to tragedy. Utah was still only a territory at the time of the massacre, and the Mormons had been labeled as one of the "'twin relics of barbarism,'" that is, a threat equivalent to the antiabolitionist southern states.[18] Mormons justifiably feared that federal troops were coming to exterminate them, a concern exacerbated by the taunts from members of passing wagon trains and the history of persecution that had forced them to migrate west.[19] Although my students were not defending LDS actions, they did recognize the confluence of extenuating circumstances leading up to the massacre, the danger of judging the church based on events that occurred 150 years ago, and the problem with placing contemporary extremist activity of FLDS members in the same context.

I decided that this was a good time to discuss the article "The Cult of Ethnicity" by Arthur Schlesinger Jr., a classic critique of the dangers of multiculturalism. In the piece, Schlesinger claimed that "people of different origins, speaking different languages and professing different religions, inhabit[ing] the same locality and liv[ing] under the same political sovereignty . . . is the explosive problem of our times." Writing in 1991, Schlesinger saw ethnicity as a cause of instability around the world. If the United States did not want to "break up" as other nations— like the Balkans—had, it should, he argued, return to a melting-pot mentality that creates "a brand-new national identity." Basically Schlesinger is warning readers of an uncertain future in America if ethnic and racial groups are allowed the unrestricted freedom that conflicts with traditional notions of assimilation. He claimed, finally, that "if separatist tendencies go unchecked, the result can only be the fragmentation, reseg-regation and tribalization of American life."[20]

Once the students could unpack Schlesinger's argument to under-stand the attack it directed toward many of them, they were able to see themselves through the eyes of an LDS Church that is categorized by its past. Just as they contested Schlesinger's logic about connecting ethnic identity to the undoing of nations—citing instead economic disparity and social injustice—so they saw the limitations in Krakauer's presen-tation of violent incidents to speak for the current LDS Church. They were unwilling to admit that their own ethnic affiliations interfered with identifying themselves as Americans, even as they were becoming more aware that some people perceive them as dangerous outsiders.

If the Mormons were outsiders in fundamental ways that the stu-dents identified and sympathized with, however, this perception was complicated by the matter of race. Mormons had long been perceived as dangerous religious freaks, to be sure, but *white* ones at a time when race was the most crucial division in the nation. Indeed, with its settlements in the Midwest, and especially Missouri, the early LDS Church was forced to take a stand on the issue of race, a position that the class discussed at length because Krakauer emphasizes it at important moments in the book. Early on, he writes that "Uncle Rulon" Jeffs, the FLDS sect leader in Colorado City when Krakauer researched his book, used "Brigham's warning that for those who commit such unspeakable sins as homosexu-ality, or having sexual intercourse with a member of the African race, 'the penalty, under the law of God, is death on the spot'" to intimidate followers to be obedient. Later, in a footnote, Krakauer adds that ". . . Brigham Young was an unapologetic racist (as were a great many other nineteenth century Americans) whose interpretations of scripture insti-tutionalized racism within the LDS Church. Upon his leadership, Utah became a slave territory, and the Mormon Church supported the aims of the Confederacy during the Civil War."[21]

Krakauer makes a connection to the present, too, when he uses DeLoy Bateman to provide a final scathing indictment of the LDS Church in the book's last chapter. Bateman says he was taught that "Negroes were terri-ble, that they weren't even human" as a child, adding that as an adult he could not watch Oprah on television "because she was black." Although he knew it was wrong, Bateman claims that "it's surprisingly hard to shake something that's so deeply ingrained." These moments culminate in the book's final words, a footnote on the last page where Krakauer writes, "A horror of miscegenation is something Mormon Fundamentalists have in common with their Mormon brethren: even after LDS President Spencer

W. Kimball's 1978 revelation reversing the church doctrine that banned blacks from the priesthood, official LDS policy has continued to strongly admonish white Saints not to marry blacks."[22]

Race was a vexing topic for our class, dividing white students from others and immigrants from African Americans. Respecting how incendiary the subject can be, they at first seemed apprehensive to discuss it in depth. Clearly some were continuing to experience racism, and all of them knew it was a sensitive issue. After all, they were reminded of the divide each day when they rode the bus into Kingsborough's oceanfront campus. Students of color at Kingsborough are in a sea, so to speak, of a white neighborhood, adding to the difficulty of talking about race. However, Fawn Brodie's *No Man Knows My History: The Life of Joseph Smith,* her exhaustive biography, sections of which I gave them to read, provided the class with an access point. In her book, Brodie questions the church's authenticity; however, she does provide historical contexts for some of its most controversial aspects, one being the initial reasons why the LDS Church established antiabolitionist doctrines. She writes that Smith was conflicted in his attitude toward blacks, so he used the Bible's "Book of Abraham," which "dispatched the problem of the Negro" as justification—a tactic common among believers of many faiths, the students noted. More significant, however, is Brodie's statement that "perhaps [Smith's] attitude was merely a concession to Missouri," a slave state at the time Smith and his followers resided there in the 1830s. As Brodie points out, abolitionist sentiments were far from popular at the time, either in the South *or* North, however reprehensible we may find that fact.[23]

Brodie's insights encouraged the students to venture their opinions. I explained to them that Brodie was an active Mormon when she wrote her book. She was critical of her own people prior to her excommunication, something the students decided was an act of courage. It gave her credibility in their eyes. They understood that it was not easy to be honest, but disloyal—that it was difficult, as one student put it, to "out" those to whom you are closest. In contrast to Krakauer, many students read Bateman's statements and viewed the church's long-overdue change to its official policies on race as not atypical. Of course nothing Brodie wrote and the students said condones the LDS Church's inertia. The students were merely pointing out that they understood that real change for divisive issues does not occur overnight and that it was important to place the Mormon experience with racial prejudice in the context of the historical evolution of race issues in the nation as a whole.[24]

They came to these conclusions with the help of Mortimer B. Zuckerman's 2002 article "Our Rainbow Underclass." In his piece, Zuckerman, a real-estate and publishing magnate with conservative views, focuses on immigration, especially what happens to immigrant cultures after they establish themselves in America. While Zuckerman argues against "clos[ing] the door" to immigration following 9/11, he quickly follows this with the claim that "immigration has been out of control since 1965" when the Immigration Reform Act "upset 'the ethnic mix in this country.'" What this means to him is that "traditional immigrants from northern and western Europe were discriminated against in favor of Third World immigrants."[25]

Zuckerman's arguments struck the students as xenophobic because they understood that he was saying that today's immigration laws unfairly favor people of color—people like them. Ostensibly he is speaking out of benevolence toward the nation's newcomers by claiming that assimilation is no longer "swift" for new immigrants because the economy is weak; however, the students noted the warning he issues by using the example of Mexican immigrants, who, Zuckerman says, do not learn English rapidly and form a self-sufficient "subnation" that does not interact with the mainstream. The result, he claims, is a "rainbow underclass, caught in a cycle of downward assimilation, poverty combined with racial segregation." To the students, his suggestion that America "slow down the process [of immigration] until we can thoroughly assess how the children of today's immigrants will fare as adults" was insulting since many *were* those children, and they thought they were faring just fine.[26]

The implications of Zuckerman's attitude for their own lives registered with them. Racism, they asserted, was alive and well, even in multicultural Brooklyn. The Trinidadian student, for example, recalled being unable to rent an apartment when, she suspected, the landlord realized that the British-accented caller now in front of her was black. In addition, some of the students' experiences of living in recently undesirable sections of the borough that are now hotbeds of gentrification enabled them to speak at length about what it feels like to watch as developers claim neighborhoods, knock down and rebuild apartments, and raise rents that force once-thriving minority communities to relocate. The children of today's immigrants would be fine, they declared, as long as they were not made the scapegoat for race problems in America. They resented the ugly connotation that safer neighborhoods and higher property values are possible only when lower- and middle-income minority populations are pushed out of their homes and neighborhoods by speculators.

Without question racism is an unseemly side of LDS history, and Krakauer is not out of line to make this known, but, by pointing out Zuckerman's xenophobia, the students illustrated that racism is a pervasive problem in America, not one unique to Mormons. In addition, the fact that Zuckerman's piece was first published in 2002, only a few years before our class met that summer, in a widely read news magazine— *U.S. News & World Report*—was further evidence to them that racism is still rampant and acceptable to many; therefore, they determined that the LDS Church should not be singled out for criticism for its struggle to overcome racial prejudices. Finally, egregiously late as it may have been in coming, some students felt that the LDS Church's 1978 policy change was an open admission of guilt. It was an important first step—to paraphrase one student's essay—toward real change in race issues, even though my student was aware that theory and practice are not always the same thing.

The issue the students found most interesting in Krakauer's book— and what is perhaps the most difficult challenge the LDS Church faces—is its relationship with polygamy. In 1890 LDS President Wilford Woodruff issued what is known as the Manifesto, which officially ended polygamy, a requirement for Utah's statehood. Some scholars cite this as the moment when fundamentalists began to separate themselves from the LDS Church, and, indeed, it is *the* key issue dividing FLDS and LDS people today.[27] This sharp division helps explain why the LDS Church takes issue with Krakauer's insistence that the church's past and today's FLDS activities are linked. Again, whenever associated with the FLDS, the LDS Church asserts, "No members of the Church today can enter into polygamy without being excommunicated."[28] Krakauer, though, while acknowledging the church's claim, provides a salacious, soap-opera-like account of the LDS history of what is known as "living the principle." At one point in the book, he describes Smith's clandestine celestial marriages for himself and others in the LDS hierarchy as leading to hubris and recklessness, which resulted in "a scandal of Monica Lewinsky-like proportions" only months before his death.[29]

Today the LDS must contend with the current stigma attached to polygamy due to scandalous headlines about FLDS groups accused of marrying underage girls to much older men and otherwise abusing women. Krakauer contends that the LDS Church tries to downplay its history of polygamy as "a quaint, long-abandoned idiosyncrasy practiced by a mere handful of nineteenth-century Mormons," when, in fact, it remains part of "Section 132 of *The Doctrine and Covenants*, one of Mormonism's primary scriptural texts." Krakauer focuses on the abusive practices of polygamists in large FLDS clans. According to him, FLDS women are held captive in communities that "[bear] more than a passing resemblance to life in Kabul under the Taliban." Early on, for example, he describes one former polygamist wife's complicated family tree and her eventual escape from the Blackmore clan in Bountiful, Canada. At age fifteen, Debbie Palmer was married to fifty-seven-year-old Ray Blackmore. "As his sixth wife," Krakauer writes, "Debbie became a stepmother to Blackmore's thirty-one kids, most of whom were older than she was. And because he happened to be the father of Debbie's own stepmother, Mem, she unwittingly became a stepmother to her stepmother, and thus a stepgrandmother to herself." After more abuse led to drug addiction, Palmer set fire to her home, with her family still inside, before finally fleeing altogether.[30]

Palmer's story shocked students, and although Krakauer says that legalized polygamy will not become a reality because the LDS Church is not going to risk its lucrative standing in society to back it, some in the class were alarmed simply at the prospect. After all, they read in *Under the Banner of Heaven* that Mormonism is one of the fastest-growing religions in the world, and the FLDS draws its followers from LDS members who are not pleased that the church has become so "ordinary."[31] In class we considered what this meant for Mormons. To the students, it seemed that the church is in a no-win situation: if it maintains its stance on excommunicating polygamists, the FLDS ranks will grow, and unwanted notoriety will come back to haunt the LDS Church; however, if the church relaxes its stance, it equally risks its good standing in American society. Students could see that compromise either way would come with great costs.

Students also brought up broader issues of sexual practice and the law. Krakauer writes that Joseph Smith had "disregard for every article of the United States Constitution except those that assured Mormons the freedom to worship as they saw fit."[32] After debating Smith's contradictory interpretation of the Constitution, most still had too much respect for the idea of the civil liberties it protects to say that Smith's antics warranted suppression. Indeed, some of their families had emigrated from places in the world where practicing faith openly was a privilege, not a right. They may have thought that Mormonism was strange and the abuses of polygamists Tom Green, Brian David Mitchell, and Warren Jeffs were abhorrent, but they eventually decided that it was important to distinguish polygamy that is religiously inspired and involves consenting adults from the crimes of statutory rape and incest. There would always be abuse, but the students asked if it would be extensive enough to merit closer scrutiny in general. They also wondered how prosecuting polygamists might threaten their own freedom. If polygamists were forced to abandon their lifestyle, they asked, what did it say about the limits of the nation's tolerance for people like themselves?

To help them further debate that question, I gave them John Tierney's *New York Times* opinion piece "Who's Afraid of Polygamy?" which was published on the eve of the debut of HBO's *Big Love*. Tierney tells everyone to relax, making the argument that "[polygamy] looks more like what it really is: an arrangement that can make sense for some people in some circumstances, but not one that could ever be a dangerous trend in America." While he agrees that coercion into polygamous relationships is wrong, one reason he is not worried is simply that American women do not need to choose it. With modernization, he says, women become better educated and economically self-sufficient—a reality, Tierney notes, that does not exist in other places in the world where polygamy is more common. If American women do choose it, they may do so because—as Elizabeth Joseph, the wife of a polygamist cited in the article, said to a National Organization for Women's audience—they think that polygamy "offers an independent woman a real chance to have it all' and represented 'the ultimate feminist lifestyle.'"[33]

The students found Joseph's comments especially interesting, and though they could imagine Krakauer responding that women in polygamous FLDS communities are too often victims of abuse—the very antithesis of Joseph's liberated womanhood—they noted that polygamy was not the only means by which women were abused in America. After reading Krakauer's portraits of victims such as Debbie Palmer and Elizabeth Smart, students were not as dismissive of the dangers as Tierney seemed to be in his piece; they did see, though, that telling the history of the LDS Church concurrently with FLDS abuses encouraged a harmful association that made it seem that all Mormons are lurid polygamists. Such stereotyping, they said, can criminalize the innocent.

The students grappled with this idea after reading "Creating a Criminal" by Michael Kingston.[34] Kingston wrote about a change to the California Penal Code that made selling dogs and cats for the purpose of eating them illegal. The amendment appealed to many people, Kingston wrote, because it implied that it was protecting dogs and cats from abuse, but he argued it was a racist amendment that punished innocent Vietnamese Americans by suddenly criminalizing them for their ethnic diet. Kingston critiqued the amendment's "racial intolerance" and illogic, claiming that it overlooked other forms of animal abuse, took away his freedom to choose, and, finally, labeled good people as savages.

Most students agreed with Kingston, and they were able to relate what he wrote to the "barbaric" designation given to Mormons in the nineteenth century in large part because of polygamy. Outlawing polygamy might have made Utah's statehood possible, but at that time, it did little to change the stereotypical images of Mormons.

We then explored the logic and consequences of taking legal action to deal with sensitive cultural or religious practices that are outside the mainstream by comparing Kingston's essay with Krakauer's chapter on the Short Creek Raid in 1953, when Arizona National Guardsmen arrested "122 polygamous men and women," making "263 children from these families . . . wards of the state."[35] Although the raid backfired on authorities, fundamentalist Mormons moved deeper into secrecy after it, which creates a problem for law enforcement today when dealing with FLDS communities.[36] Eventually the students debated whether pursuing legal avenues in such circumstances is a good idea. In fact, they asked, do you create more problems than existed in the first place? With this question in mind, one student wrote an essay on the limits of tolerance in which she referenced an article about the backlash some European countries were confronting because they had made wearing *hijabs* and burkas illegal in certain public places.

Just as Kingston was concerned with being labeled and losing his freedom to choose, the students said that, although they might not want to become polygamists, they neither wanted to be targeted in certain ways nor have their freedom restricted. In their final papers, they made connections to what such perceptions and restrictions meant to them: an African American male wrote of police harassment on a recent outing with friends on the boardwalk in Brighton Beach; a female West Indian student explained that Americans did not, and probably never would, understand how cockfighting was a spectator sport in her country; an Arab student discussed the apprehension women in her community have about wearing head scarves in certain places because the stares associating them with jihads and terrorism have become too discomforting.

In a similar way, some students thought polygamy should not be a reason automatically to label someone a miscreant.[37] In one essay, a student cited the fact that DeLoy Bateman is still a practicing polygamist—and "a good husband and father"—even though he has been excommunicated from the FLDS. Polygamists, the writer was implying, may be no different from the rest of us. Another student suggested that legalizing polygamy might actually do more to help women in these relationships because it would at least recognize them, give them court-upheld rights to their well-being and property, and encourage victims to expose abusers. Regardless of where students stood on the issue of polygamy at the summer session's end—and their opinions varied—they did agree in principle with what a female African American student wrote: "We need to understand the practices of others rather than blindly condemn without merit. Furthermore, we must stop trying to exploit the law just to protect delicate sensibilities."

## Exit:
## A Unique Paradox of Place

*Although many believe that America is a tolerant country and that Americans are a tolerant people, the evidence overwhelmingly shows otherwise.*

Kingsborough Community College student essay

My students identified an interesting irony that summer: once the Mormons established a place—real and symbolic—in America, they became alienated in another way. In noting this, the students were expressing in their own way what several scholars have argued, namely that the Mormons have long experienced an identity crisis that stems from their simultaneous and contradictory needs to be both an insider and outsider community, that is, a church that is assimilated into mainstream America and is, at the same time, distinct from it. For many Mormons, an urgent problem today is that when they look back, they realize what has been lost: they are no longer considered a "special" or "peculiar" people staunchly defending what they believe is the true Christian church; for others the problem is that the church is too slow or altogether resistant to making alterations to core doctrines and policies that acknowledge societal changes, such as the advances made in minority, gay, and women's rights. And as LDS membership increases worldwide to include more people who do not have familial or historical ties to Mormonism and the church's bureaucracy burgeons and leaders become increasingly detached from members, the challenge of maintaining core doctrines and policies in ways that placate the leadership's efforts to control the image and direction of the church is exacerbated.[38]

This delicate balancing act creates tension in the LDS Church that is experienced at all levels. Mormon "retrenchment," the conservative policies adopted since the 1950s aimed at preserving a particular version of the church's history as timeless, has thus resulted in its share of scrutiny from the outside and duress on the inside. For example, several sources note the ongoing issue of excommunications of followers. Forced out most notably have been feminists and scholars whose progressive ideas and inquiry into the church's history have rankled LDS authorities.[39] Through its reactionary responses, the LDS Church at times has looked anti-intellectual and secretive to both outsiders and insiders, and as Mormon leaders strive to "find the optimum balance between sectarian refuge and worldly participation," they risk losing more members to excommunications and defections to FLDS by Saints no longer willing to bear the costs of compromise.[40] Indeed, the LDS Church curiously draws attention to its suspect past by attempting to silence those who want to talk about it or cutting off ties to those who want to relive it fully. The threat to Mormonism, then, is as much internal as external.

All of this provided interesting fodder for discussion with my students, who explored their own literal and figurative connections to the Mormon identity crisis. Several students were either first- or second-generation immigrants who had come from developing countries in the Caribbean and southern Asia. They could understand what it meant to be caught between two places. Success in America made returning to their homelands to live nearly impossible; abandoning their native identities for that success made not returning equally difficult to imagine. Just as the utopian dream of the early LDS Church will never be realized fully, immigrants often find that the American Dream has its limitations. Excommunication from the LDS Church or merely identity confusion leaves many former Saints feeling alienated or adrift.[41]

Similarly some students in the class noted that, even though their standards of living had improved in America, they sometimes felt lost in the transition. And like Mormons, they experienced pressure as coming more from the inside, from those closest to them who perhaps unknowingly presented them with a similar conundrum to one that the LDS Church faces today: prosper in the American system but do not fully become members of it. Such a contradictory pressure can cause divided allegiances that one student—using a term she had learned in a psychology class the semester before—said was an example of *cognitive dissonance:* people battling to balance the pressures of two worlds at the same time. As a result, they are never completely able to find a place that they accept and accepts them.

The LDS and FLDS have become somewhat ubiquitous in the national consciousness since the class that summer: *Big Love* has had a successful run on HBO; the PBS *American Experience* documentary *The Mormons* has aired; FLDS leader Warren Jeffs was captured and imprisoned; Mitt Romney's run for the Republican nomination for president ended; the fifteenth LDS president, prophet, seer, and revelator, Gordon

B. Hinckley, died, and Thomas S. Monson assumed his mantle; the FLDS compound in Eldorado, Texas, was raided by federal authorities, reminiscent of previous ill-advised raids on fundamentalist settlements; and since the fall of 2008, the church has been attacked for its support of Proposition 8 in California, which restricts marriage to heterosexual couples. It will take more time, however, to determine whether the forebodings of Krakauer and others will be validated as the LDS Church continues to negotiate its place in America.

As for my students, probably little has changed tangibly in their lives, and I doubt that they often think about Mormons. However, I still see students from that summer class riding the bus to and from the campus. When I do, I wonder whether they think about Kingsborough's location, a place often far from their neighborhoods. Interestingly the City University of New York proposed other sites for Kingsborough when it was a new community college in the system in the early 1960s. The Atlantic Terminal area in downtown Brooklyn, where the NBA Nets are soon to have a new arena, and the hallowed ground in Crown Heights, where the Brooklyn Dodgers had played only a few years earlier, were two places that received consideration. Either option would have been far more central to the students' lives, to *their* realities. But maybe traveling to Kingsborough—and the place itself—will help students reflect on these realities more than they would otherwise because it is a place apart from most other things in their lives. And perhaps the students from the class who still ride the bus saw media images of what happened in Eldorado, remembered Krakauer's description of the Short Creek Raid in 1953, and looked out of the bus windows with widened eyes.

## Notes

Sincere thanks to my friend and colleague Libby Garland for reading multiple drafts of this paper and providing invaluable feedback. This paper would not have been possible without the time and effort she put into her thoughtful criticism. Also, for their support and encouragement throughout the process, I would like to thank Ann-Marie Henry-Stephens, Rick Armstrong, and Even Wood.

1.   Krakauer, *Under the Banner of Heaven*, 343. Subsequent citations to this work include just the author's name and the page number.
2.   Leone, *Roots of Modern Mormonism*. Leone writes, "Having been hounded to the edge of existence as an institution, it had to realize, as it never had to before, that it could not be American on its own terms, but only on America's," 27.
3.   Rosaldo, *Culture and Truth*, x.

4. Mauss, *The Angel and the Beehive*, 1–45. Mauss writes, "If in its quest for acceptance and respectability, a movement allows itself to be pulled too far toward assimilation, it will lose its unique identity altogether," 5.

5. Bushman, *Contemporary Mormonism*, 17. For a more nuanced response to Krakauer's book, see Burton's "The Province of the Extreme," 194–98. Burton argues that although "Krakauer relies heavily on overstatement," *Under the Banner of Heaven* is a serious work that asks important questions such as, "Why has fundamentalism survived into the twenty-first century?" In addition, see the following contrasting reviews: Mathis, "A Story of Violent Defensiveness," 45–46, 48–49; and Driggs, "Krakauer's Fundamentalists," 47.

6. *The Mormons*, produced and directed by Helen Whitney, DVD. At the end of part I, act 6, "Polygamy," LDS President Gordon B. Hinckley is shown making this statement to the LDS General Conference in 1998.

7. Krakauer, 311, xxi. See also where Krakauer writes, "To comprehend Brian David Mitchell—or to comprehend Dan Lafferty, or Tom Green, or the polygamous inhabitants of Bountiful and Colorado City—one must first understand the faith these people have in common, a faith that gives shape and purpose to every facet of their lives. And any such understanding must begin with the aforementioned Joseph Smith Jr., the founder of the [LDS Church]," 55.

8. Wright, "Thou Shalt Kill." Adding to the list of provocative blurbs, Wright states, "[Krakauer] mentions Osama bin Laden near the beginning and end of the book and leaves it for readers to draw their own conclusions, with some help from the book jacket's reference to 'Taliban-like theocracies in the American heartland.'"

9. Krakauer, ix.

10. Bloom, *The American Religion*, 15–111. Bloom writes, "Where there is overwhelming religious desire, there must also be religious anxiety, for which the pragmatic name is Fundamentalism, the great curse of all American religion, and of all religion in this American century," 39.

11. Krakauer, 343.

12. Otterson, "Church Response to Jon Krakauer's *Under the Banner of Heaven*."

13. Krakauer, 363.

14. Ibid., 188, 316.

15. Maslin, "The Mormon Image, from Alien to Human." Maslin sums up the concern I had when she states, "But 'Under the Banner of Heaven' understands [the] freakishness rather than the fervor. Echoing Mark Twain's opinion that 'The Book of Mormon' is 'chloroform in print,' this book provides more voyeuristic astonishment than curiosity or understanding."

16. Krakauer, 18, 45, 97–106, 102n. In this footnote, Krakauer writes, "George Arbaugh nevertheless went on to assert, 'Mormonism is one of the most boldly innovating developments in the history of religions. Its aggressive theocratic claims, political aspirations, and use of force, make it akin to Islam.'"

17. Ibid., 225.

18. Leone, *Roots of Modern Mormonism*. Leone captures the nation's perception of Mormons when he writes, "In their 1856 party platform, Republicans had denounced both slavery and polygamy as 'twin relics of barbarism,'" 26.

19. Brooks, *The Mountain Meadows Massacre*.

20. Schlesinger, "The Cult of Ethnicity," 62–65. This article was originally published in *Time* magazine in 1991.
21. Krakauer, 12, 209n.
22. Ibid., 333–34.
23. Brodie, *No Man Knows My History*, 172–73.
24. Hansen, *Mormonism and the American Experience*. See pages 179–204 for a discussion of the evolution of the LDS policies on race.
25. Zuckerman, "Our Rainbow Underclass," 43–45.
26. Ibid.
27. *The Mormons*, produced and directed by Helen Whitney, DVD. In part I, act 6, "Polygamy," historian B. Carmon Hardy states, "In my own view, the largest consequence of the [manifesto] fed into the development of fundamentalism. . . ." See also Ostling and Ostling, *Mormon America*, 56–75. The Ostlings quote D. Michael Quinn, who states, "The murkiness and ambiguities of these authorized polygamous marriages after 1890 (and especially after 1904) guaranteed the growth of a polygamous underground that continues today in opposition to church policy . . . ," 73.
28. Official LDS response to *USA Today* headline: "30,000 Mormon Polygamists" at http://www.lds.org.
29. Krakauer, 124.
30. Krakauer, 6, 11, 31–42.
31. Krakauer, 3–4.
32. Krakauer, 130.
33. Tierney, "Who's Afraid of Polygamy?" A15.
34. Kingston, "Creating a Criminal."
35. Krakauer, 16.
36. Johnson, "Polygamy Raid in West Texas May Pose a Risk for the Authorities Elsewhere," A12. In this article, Mark Shurtleff, Utah's attorney general, said, "[Polygamist groups] were opening up, . . . Now they've kind of pulled back" as a result of the raid on the Eldorado compound, a reminder, it was noted, of what happened following the Short Creek Raid in 1953.
37. Mojtabai, "Polygamy," 128–132. This article was used to discuss Muslim polygamy. After visiting her Iranian father-in-law, Mojtabai states, "I saw a polygamous marriage work, and work well," 131.
38. Ostling and Ostling, 372–85. In this chapter, "Mormonism in the Twenty-first Century," the authors point out that the internal struggles of the LDS Church are akin to the efforts of other religious denominations to stem the influence of radical and liberal theological thought. They write, "Many leading analysts of the LDS Church agree that the hierarchal defensiveness, disciplining, and 'correlation' are natural responses to exponential growth," 382. However, they add that because of this stance "some of the church's best and brightest have become alienated," including the "brilliant analyst" D. Michael Quinn, who argues that "the leadership of the church basically writes off North American liberals as disloyal," 383.
39. Ostling and Ostling, 351–71. The authors write about the high-profile excommunications and disfellowship of six prominent Mormon scholars, the "so-called 'September Six,'" in 1993, indicating that the LDS "will tolerate no deviations from stated public policies and no public questioning of General Authorities," 355.

40. Mauss, "Refuge and Retrenchment," 24. Mauss adds, "Some retrenchment toward authentic Mormon traditions might make an important contribution to the reconstruction of a truly Mormon special identity, but beyond that lies the risk of fundamentalist excess and a loss of the intellectual expansiveness for a truly universal religion," 38.

41. Ibid. Mauss makes the point that it is not just the excommunicated Saints who feel unmoored, noting that "In the face of such ambiguity and dissonance about their identity, some Mormons have sought resolution by defecting from the religion, but they almost always become religiously inactive instead of joining another religion," 37.

## Bibliography

Bloom, Harold. *The American Religion: The Emergence of the Post-Christian Nation.* New York: Simon & Schuster, 1992, 15–111.

Brodie, Fawn. *No Man Knows My History: The Life of Joseph Smith.* 2d ed. New York: Vintage Books, 1995.

Brooks, Juanita. *The Mountain Meadows Massacre.* Norman: University of Oklahoma Press, 1950.

Burton, Stacy. "The Province of the Extreme." Review of *Under the Banner of Heaven: A Story of Violent Faith,* by Jon Krakauer. *Dialogue: A Journal of Mormon Thought* 37, no. 4 (Winter 2004): 194–98.

Bushman, Claudia. *Contemporary Mormonism: Latter-day Saints in Modern America.* Westport, CT: Praeger, 2006.

Driggs, Ken. "Krakauer's Fundamentalists." Review of *Under the Banner of Heaven: A Story of Violent Faith,* by Jon Krakauer. *Sunstone,* July 2004, 47. http://www.sunstonemagazine.com/pdf/133-45-51.pdf.

Hansen, Klaus. *Mormonism and the American Experience.* Chicago: University of Chicago Press, 1981.

Johnson, Kirk. "Polygamy Raid in West Texas May Pose a Risk for the Authorities Elsewhere." *New York Times,* April 12, 2008, A12.

Kingston, Michael. "Creating a Criminal." In *Everything's an Argument,* edited by Andrea A. Lunsford, John J. Ruszkiewicz, and Keith Walters. Boston: Bedford/St. Martin's, 2001: 129–31.

Krakauer, Jon. *Under the Banner of Heaven: A Story of Violent Faith.* New York: Anchor Books, 2004.

Leone, Mark P. *Roots of Modern Mormonism.* Cambridge, MA: Harvard University Press, 1979.

Maslin, Janet. "The Mormon Image, from Alien to Human." Review of *Under the Banner of Heaven: A Story of Violent Faith,* by Jon Krakauer. *New York Times,* July 17, 2003. http://www.nytimes.com.

Mathis, Greg. "A Story of Violent Defensiveness." Review of *Under the Banner of Heaven: A Story of Violent Faith,* by Jon Krakauer. *Sunstone,* July 2004, 45–46, 48–49. http://www.sunstonemagazine.com/pdf/133-45-51.pdf .

Mauss, Armand L. *The Angel and the Beehive: The Mormon Struggle with Assimilation.* Urbana: University of Illinois Press, 1994, 1–45.

———. "Refuge and Retrenchment: The Mormon Quest for Identity." In *Contemporary Mormonism: Social Science Perspectives,* edited by Marie

Cornwall, Tim B. Heaton, and Lawrence A. Young, 24–42. Urbana: University of Illinois Press, 1994.

Mojtabai, Ann Grace. "Polygamy." In *The New World Reader: Thinking and Writing about the Global Community,* edited by Gilbert H. Muller, 128–32. Boston: Houghton Mifflin, 2005.

*The Mormons,* produced and directed by Helen Whitney. PBS Home Video, 2007. DVD.

Ostling, Richard N., and Joan K. Ostling. *Mormon America: The Power and the Promise.* New York: HarperCollins: 1999.

Otterson, Mike. "Church Response to Jon Krakauer's *Under the Banner of Heaven.*" Newsroom.LDS.org., June 27, 2003: http://www.lds.org/newsroom/mistakes/ 0,15331,3885-1-17125,00.html.

Rosaldo, Renato. *Culture and Truth: The Remaking of Social Analysis.* Boston: Beacon Press, 1993.

Schlesinger, Arthur, Jr. "The Cult of Ethnicity." In *The New World Reader: Thinking and Writing about the Global Community,* 62–65.

Shipps, Jan. *Mormonism: The Story of a New Religious Tradition.* Urbana: University of Illinois Press, 1985.

"30,000 Mormon Polygamists." Newsroom.LDS.org.: http://www.lds.org/newsroom/mistakes/ 0,15331,3885-1-9077,00.html.

Tierney, John. "Who's Afraid of Polygamy?" *New York Times,* March 11, 2006, A15.

Wright, Robert. "Thou Shalt Kill." Review of *Under the Banner of Heaven: A Story of Violent Faith,* by Jon Krakauer. *New York Times,* August 3, 2003. http://www.nytimes.com.

Zuckerman, Mortimer B. "Our Rainbow Underclass." In *The New World Reader: Thinking and Writing about the Global Community,* 43–45.

# 4

# Avenging Angels

*The Nephi Archetype and Blood Atonement in Neil LaBute,*
*Brian Evenson, and Levi Peterson, and the Making*
*of the Mormon American Writer*

J. Aaron Sanders

## I. Prologue:
## Heroes and Righteous Murder

On July 24, 1984, in American Fork, Utah, Dan Lafferty and his brother Ron paid a visit to their sister-in-law, Brenda, while their youngest brother, Allen, was at work. "[Dan] found his fifteen-month old niece, Erica, standing in her crib, smiling up at him. 'I spoke to her for a minute,' Lafferty recalls. 'I told her, I'm not sure what this is all about, but apparently it's God's will that you leave this world; perhaps we can talk about it later.' And then he ended her life with a ten-inch boning knife. After dispatching Erica, he calmly walked into the kitchen and used the same knife to kill the baby's mother."[1]

These heinous murders are the impetus for Jon Krakauer's 2003 book *Under the Banner of Heaven*. In it Krakauer delves into Mormon history and doctrine in an attempt to understand what motivated the Lafferty brothers. "There is a dark side to religious devotion that is too often ignored or denied," Krakauer writes. "As a means of motivating people to be cruel or inhumane—as a means of inciting evil, to borrow the vocabulary of the devout—there may be no more potent force than religion."[2] One of Krakauer's specific discoveries is that the ritualistic details of the Lafferty murders (the slitting of the throat), along with Don's motivation to murder (God told me to), evoke the controversial nineteenth-century Mormon doctrine of blood atonement.

Blood atonement is the ritual killing of apostates, sinners, or gentiles. Historically blood atonement takes two forms: (1) blood atonement
as self-atonement. "Joseph Smith taught that certain grievous sins put
sinners 'beyond the atoning blood of Christ.' Their 'only hope [was]
to have their own blood shed to atone'";[3] and (2) blood atonement as
enforcement. Brigham Young once asked the members of his congregation if they loved their neighbors "enough to shed their blood. This is
loving our neighbor as ourselves," he said. "If he wants salvation and it
is necessary to spill his blood on the earth in order that he may be saved,
spill it."[4]

The first instance of blood atonement in the Mormon mythos appears
in Joseph Smith's 1830 religious narrative, the Book of Mormon.[5] The
story opens in 600 BC when God commands Lehi to leave Jerusalem.
Days before Lehi and his family are to set sail to the Americas, God sends
Lehi's sons—Nephi, Laman, Lemuel, and Sam—back to Jerusalem for a
set of historical records on brass plates because his family "could not
keep the commandments of the Lord according to the law of Moses, save
they should have the law. And [he] also knew that the law was engraven
upon the plates of brass."[6]

In Jerusalem Nephi and his brothers make three attempts to get
the plates. First, they ask Laban, and he refuses. Second, they attempt
to barter for the plates, but Laban steals their possessions, then tries to
kill them. On the third attempt, Nephi's brothers have had enough, so
Nephi sneaks into Laban's house alone, where he finds Laban drunk and
passed out.

> And it came to pass that I was constrained by the Spirit that I
> should kill Laban; but I said in my heart: Never at any time have
> I shed the blood of man. And I shrunk and would that I might not
> slay him.
>   And the Spirit said unto me again: Behold the Lord hath deliv-
> ered him into thy hands. Yea, and I also knew that he had sought to
> take away mine own life; yea and he would not hearken unto the
> commandments of the Lord; and he also had taken our property.
>   And it came to pass that the Spirit said unto me again: Slay him,
> for the Lord hath delivered him into thy hands;
>   Behold the Lord slayeth the wicked to bring forth his righteous
> purposes. It is better that one man should perish than that a nation
> should dwindle and perish in unbelief.[7]

The rhetoric in this passage is clear: Nephi has given Laban an opportunity to do the right thing, but Laban chooses "not [to] hearken unto the
commandments of the Lord." Nephi still needs the plates, and Laban

stands in the way, so the Spirit argues that "it is better that one man should perish than that a nation should dwindle and perish in unbelief." With this realization, Nephi acts: "I did obey the voice of the Spirit, and took Laban by the hair of the head, and I smote off his head with his own sword."[8] The story of Nephi killing Laban contributed three key elements to the Mormon mythos: (1) Nephi as archetypal Mormon hero; (2) righteous murder committed by that hero, or blood atonement; and (3) the rhetorical justification for blood atonement.

More than 150 years later, we see the Nephi archetype appear not only in the horrific Lafferty murders but in Mormon literature as well—specifically in three contemporary works by Neil LaBute, Brian Evenson, and Levi Peterson. In LaBute's *bash: latter-day plays*, John beats a gay man to death in a Central Park bathroom; in *The Open Curtain*, Evenson's Rudd Theurer develops an obsession with blood atonement that leads to bizarre campsite murders; and Levi Peterson's protagonist in *The Backslider*, Frank Windham, contemplates suicide as self-atonement for his sins. This essay discusses how these three contemporary representations of blood atonement are rooted in the real nineteenth-century expectation that Mormons perform ritualized murder on sinners, apostates, or gentiles. These literary portraits suggest that the Mormon Church's attempt to bury its own history has failed—its past is always present, whether the church acknowledges it or not, and has found its way into these three writers' work.

The larger significance of *bash: latter-day plays*, *The Backslider*, and *The Open Curtain* lies in the shortage of critical discourse about Mormon literature. Many Mormon intellectuals write literary criticism exclusively for Mormon audiences, criticism that reflects essential Mormonism and shuts out non-Mormons. In the context of such exclusive literary analysis, these creative works become the critical discourse as they translate insider secrets and cultural memory into narratives for outsiders, a starting point for a discussion that may grow into a serious study of Mormon literature.

## II. The Mormon Hero

Joseph Smith created his archetypal Mormon hero, Nephi, in the context of what Joseph Campbell calls the "vast and amazingly constant statement of basic truths" that comprise "myths and folk tales from every corner of the world."[9] Put another way, the story of Nephi is a typical hero narrative: "A hero ventures forth from the world of common day into a region of supernatural wonder: fabulous forces are there encountered and a decisive victory is won: the hero comes back from this mysterious adventure with the power to bestow boons on his fellow man."[10] Nephi ventures to Jerusalem for the brass plates, encounters three stages of obstacles, speaks with God, kills a man, and returns with the plates. What is unique about the Mormon hero is not its archetypal form; it is in the way the Mormon experience activated that archetype.

Carl Jung writes that when a situation that corresponds to a given archetype occurs, that archetype becomes activated, and "a compulsiveness appears, which like an instinctual drive, gains its way against all reason and will, or else produces a conflict of pathological dimension, that is to say, a neurosis."[11] When Joseph Smith wrote the Book of Mormon, he replicated the hero archetype he inherited from biblical myths and American history, but that hero archetype had to be activated to accumulate its specific meaning.[12]

At least two major situations activated the Nephi archetype. The first has been mentioned already: the publication and distribution of the Book of Mormon, where God tells the first Mormon fictional character, Nephi, to kill Laban. This murder introduced blood atonement into the Mormon mythos and triggered an "instinctual drive" in early members of the Mormon Church to be heroic like Nephi. Joseph Smith understood that to create a new religion, he needed what Richard Slotkin calls "a complex of narratives that dramatizes the world vision and historical sense of a people or culture, reducing centuries of experience into a constellation of compelling metaphors."[13] The Nephi archetype, which appears repeatedly in the Book of Mormon, gave the new religion both a historical sense of itself and a constellation of metaphors.

The second situation that activated the Nephi archetype was Joseph Smith's own murder in 1844. Before discussing the murder, however, it is useful to go back a few years to the origins of blood atonement. Understanding this helps us see how Joseph Smith's murder helped shape the Nephi archetype. When Smith's hold on his fledgling church began to slip in 1838, "Sampson Avard, who considered himself an ultraloyal Mormon, proposed organizing the 'Danites'. . . a civil appendage of Mormon power . . . [that] developed an infamous reputation for its intimidation of Mormon dissenters and its warfare against anti-Mormon militia units."[14] These loyalists "would become the most legendarily feared bands in frontier America."[15] It was only a short distance between this kind of frontier vigilantism and blood atonement, which was based on an overly aggressive interpretation of the New Testament doctrine, "Almost all things are purified in blood, and without the shedding of blood there is no remission."[16]

John D. Lee, a Danite himself, described the inner workings of the organization in his deathbed confession:

> The members of this order were placed under the most sacred obligations that language could invent. They were sworn to stand by and sustain each other. *Sustain, protect, defend,* and *obey* the leaders of the Church, under any and *all circumstances unto death;* and to disobey the orders the leaders of the Church, or to divulge the name of a Danite to an outsider, or to make public any of the secrets of the order of the Danites, was to be punished with death. And I can say of a truth, many have paid the penalty for failing to keep their covenants.[17]

Both the Danites and blood atonement were conceived as a way of protecting the church from apostates and gentiles, and after Joseph Smith's murder, Brigham Young reinvigorated blood atonement to galvanize the Mormons against their enemies.

Smith's murder was the "overwhelming catastrophe" that sent Mormons looking for a scapegoat. As René Girard argues, "any community that has fallen prey to violence or has been stricken by some overwhelming catastrophe hurls itself blindly into the search for a scapegoat. Its members instinctively seek an immediate and violent cure for the onslaught of unbearable violence, and strive desperately to convince themselves that all of their ills are the fault of a lone individual who can be easily disposed of."[18] The Mormons were devastated by losing their prophet, and when the trial for Smith's murder produced no guilty verdict, the new prophet, Brigham Young, "proclaimed that 'it belongs to God and his people to avenge the blood [of His] servants.' Towards this end, he instructed church authorities to issue a formal 'Oath of Vengeance,' which was immediately made part of the temple endowment ceremony, one of the church's most sacred rituals." Mormons recited, "I will pray, and never cease to pray, and never cease to importune high heaven to avenge the blood of the Prophets on this nation, and I will teach this to my children, and my children's children unto the third and fourth generations."[19] Righteous murder was now a commandment of God, a constant search for a scapegoat, and a heroic act any Mormon should feel honored to carry out. The Nephi archetype embodied what all Mormons aspired to be—one who enforces this warning from Joseph Smith written in the voice of Nephi: "He that fighteth against Zion, both Jew and Gentile, both bond and free, both male and female, shall perish."[20]

In his comprehensive study of the frontier narrative, Richard Slotkin describes the conditions that nourished an American mythology, a situation applicable to the Mormons: "Their new circumstances forced new perspectives, new self-concepts, and new world concepts on the [Mormons] and made them see their cultural heritage from angles of vision that [non-Mormons] would find peculiar."[21] From the church's inception in 1830, stability was difficult to achieve, and the Mormons encountered new circumstances repeatedly. They moved from New York to Ohio to Missouri to Illinois; then, after their prophet's murder, they went west, where they set about establishing the Kingdom of God in the Salt Lake Valley, only to come under attack by the U.S. government for their practice of plural marriage.

During this time, often called the Mormon Reformation, Mormons united in a defensive posture against the rest of the United States. "Mormons followed a lesson, already by their time well established in American experience," writes R. Laurence Moore, "that one way of becoming American was to invent oneself out of the sense of opposition."[22] In Utah obedience and loyalty became paramount, and blood atonement was a way for Brigham Young to keep church members in check. "The cultural system thus becomes a self-reinforcing, self-perpetuating structure of using 'violence to prevent violence,' writes Barbara Whitmer. "The culture is able to subsume violence and destructive conflict under the rubric of cultural security and the protection of its citizens against themselves, in the name of cultural survival."[23] While the blood-atonement ritual was uniquely Mormon, its structural function was typical of other cultures in crisis, where nonmembers or outsiders were fair game insofar as they posed a threat to the culture.[24]

But the threat can come from within, too. According to Sally Denton, "Hundreds of Saints were aghast, as [the blood atonement] doctrine had never been published or openly acknowledged before, and many schemed to leave the territory . . . [but] those who dared to flee Zion were hunted down and killed."[25] "Perhaps the most troubling aspect of the Reformation was the Mormon leadership's obsession with blood," writes Will Bagley. "Of all the beliefs that laid the foundation of Utah's culture of violence, none would have more devastating consequences."[26] In Utah, under these circumstances, the Mormon mythology continued to take shape, and at its core was the Nephi archetype: one who, according to Brigham Young, loved his neighbor enough to spill his blood.[27]

As the Mormon Church has pushed toward the mainstream in recent years, the unsavory details of blood atonement rituals have been dismissed as the practice of a few radical Mormons in the earliest days of the church and not official doctrine. The Mormon Church's tight grip on its own history has resulted in an exceptionalist view of that history[28]—a *metanarrative* that "organizes [historical narratives] into an ideological edifice."[29] Sandra Gustafson uses the term *ideological edifice* in reference to "the 'official nationalism' of the cold war," but the term also describes the way the Mormon Church has created a version of history that omits or modifies controversial events and practices.[30] Scholars who uncover historical facts that run counter to that Mormon ideological edifice are either dismissed as anti-Mormon sensationalists (if they are outsiders) or excommunicated as apostates (if they are insiders). Indeed, the manner in which the Mormon Church manages its own doctrine and history calls to mind the motivation for blood atonement itself, which protected the early church from apostates, sinners, and gentiles.[31]

In their creative work, Neil LaBute, Brian Evenson, and Levi Peterson bring the contradictions and barbarities of blood atonement to the surface as a conscious act of criticism of Mormonism and its history.[32] Perry Kerry Powers argues that fiction "can textualize the ethnic cultural memories that are elsewhere ritualized, embodied, disciplined, and maintained through religious traditions. Fictions provide a discursive space wherein the counter-memories of ethnic religious practices can be articulated and can resist the universalizing and rationalizing impulse of enlightenment."[33] LaBute, Evenson, and Peterson textualize both cultural memories and countermemories of blood atonement and erode the underpinnings of that ritual: violence as a means of cultural survival.

## III. Sacrificing the Outsider in *a gaggle of saints*

Neil LaBute's short play, *a gaggle of saints*, features two Mormon characters, John and Sue, as they recap their trip to New York City from Boston with two couples from their church group (Tim and Patrice; David and Karen).[34] In New York, the three couples plan to attend a Mormon-sponsored dance at the Plaza Hotel. On their way to the dance, they decide to take a walk through Central Park, where, John tells us, they hear a rustling sound from the woods: "I'm not scared but it's night, city all around . . . what else can you do, girls with you? So we walk along. (BEAT) and two guys, middle aged guys, l.l. bean shirts on and the whole thing . . . come out of the dark. smiling. and I don't need a map to tell me what's been going on . . . *pause* . . . I don't."[35]

From the start, John is portrayed as the protective hero—"what else can you do, girls with you?"—and the two gay men are described as the dragon in need of slaying. "The warrior-kings of antiquity regarded their work in the spirit of the monster-slayer," Joseph Campbell writes.

"This formula, indeed, of the shining hero going against the dragon has been the great device of self-justification for all crusades."[36] As Mormon priesthood holders, the male characters have the responsibility to protect and provide for the female characters, who do not hold the priesthood. In the Mormon faith, the priesthood allows men to hold leadership positions in the church, be head of households, and give priesthood blessings. The three men, with John in the lead, escort their dates away from the dragon.[37]

The evening proceeds as planned, but the men do not forget. After the dance, they leave the women at the hotel and return to Central Park, where they encounter the men again:

> Both of them. Those guys. . . . they were saying "goodnight . . ." well, not saying it exactly. But kissing. Two men, grown men, standing in this park, public park in the middle of new york and kissing like something out of a clark gable film. Tongues out, and the arms around each other, and nothing else in the world matters to these two . . . just finishing off the date, big night at the symphony, or some foreign film, who knows? But it's this "see you soon" and "thanks so much" and hands all where they shouldn't be. I mean, come on, I know the scriptures, know 'em pretty well, and this is wrong.[38]

The invocation of scripture, and by extension sin, sets up what happens next. The first scene portrays the two gay men as a threat. Here that threat is spelled out: the two men are dangerous because they are sinners, and the sin is significant. Like many religions, the Mormon Church singles out homosexuality as patently unacceptable. The two men function as the outsider, the other by which these Mormons will define themselves. "The outsider is the *illegitimate* excluded model of challenges to the social order," writes Barbara Whitmer. "Behavior may be evaluated according to these models and labeled acceptable or unacceptable accordingly. Persons may be labeled and justifiably harmed or killed when categorized as 'mere animals.'"[39]

That instinct, which is present in the Nephi archetype, has been passed down to John, Tim, and David in Mormon scripture and history. John's reaction to the two men calls to mind the avenging angels and blood atonement. If the setting were the nineteenth century, his obligation as a priesthood holder would be to save the two men by killing them. What LaBute's play suggests is that the Central Park situation activates the Nephi archetype in John's cultural memory—a memory comprised of lifelong church attendance, scripture study, and secret temple rituals (of which blood atonement was an integral part until 1990, a few years after the Lafferty murders).[40] He assumes the role of Mormon hero, and like Nephi, the Danites, and the avenging angels before him, John decides to take action.

John, Tim, and David watch as the two men say good-bye—one man leaves the park; the other goes into a public bathroom. John tells Tim and David to wait outside for his signal while he flushes the man out. Inside the bathroom is "like another world."[41] He spots the man's legs in one of the stalls and slips into the booth next to him. The man reaches under into John's stall and gives a signal: "I lay my open palm in his and two minutes later we're standing near the mirrors." We learn the man's name, Chet. John lets Chet kiss him and touch his crotch; he waits to whistle until Chet trusts him. Tim and David rush inside the restroom, and despite Chet's pleading—"He's babbling and wetting himself like an infant . . . he even got down on his knees and the pleading. Begging"[42]—the three men initiate a beating that will end Chet's life.

The beating scene is divided into three movements. In the first, the three men hit and kick Chet until he is unconscious: "My first shot catches him against the cheek, just under the eye and he slams into a sink. All snot and blood running down. With so many of us hitting, tearing at him, it's hard to get off a clean punch but I know I connect a few more times. I feel his head, the back of it, softening as we go, but I just find a new spot and move on. Tim kicking him long after he's blacked out. . . ."[43] When Tim breaks Chet's nose the first phase ends.

Here John and Tim worry about David, whom they do not know well, and whether he will "stand by and sustain" them in what they have done—the start of the second phase: "Us together, Tim, myself, that's one thing, it's unspoken, our bond, but we don't know David. Don't really know him . . . what's he thinking?" This moment hearkens back to the oath each Danite took that every member would uphold the secrecy of the group and its actions at the penalty of death. "And right then, and if to answer us through revelation . . . [David] grabs up the nearest trash can, big wire mesh thing, raises it above his head as he whispers, 'fag.'. . . And brings that can down right on the spine of the guy, who just sort of shudders a bit."[44] David's actions are the equivalent of an oath of secrecy.

The third movement turns the beating into a ritual. If there was any doubt about their actions' relationship to blood atonement, the priesthood blessing Tim gives Chet erases it. "There, with the three of us over this guy's body, he pulls out his key chain, opens the little cylinder he's got dangling on the end of it, and dumps the last of his oil, consecrated oil, on this dude's forehead! I'm not kidding . . . dumps it and starts offering up a short blessing."[45] Such a blessing is not uncommon in Mormon culture, where men carry consecrated oil in tiny vials often attached to their key chains; indeed, administering to the sick is one of the duties of the Mormon priesthood holder. Chet is obviously ill—they've injured him to the point of death—but the blessing is meant to heal his spiritual illness, and the oil consecrates the blood-atonement ritual in the same way the victim's blood did in the nineteenth century.[46]

After the blessing, the three men "slip out, one by one, running back toward the plaza in the dark and whooping it up like Indians. War cries, and running with just a trace of moonlight dancing off the pond as we go. . . ."[47] This last sentence brings us full circle to the impetus behind violence in the frontier narrative: *"Progress depends on the exclusion/extermination of a congenitally regressive type of humanity."*[48] The violence in *a gaggle of saints*, at least from the hero's perspective, is what Marilyn Wesley calls *constructive violence*, "enacted by the young male protagonist who is seeking a 'power' that confirms community values."[49] But the audience sees it differently. It is difficult to imagine anyone condoning what John and his two friends do to Chet, and LaBute's relentlessly violent portrayal leaves no doubt about the way we are to interpret it. *a gaggle of saints* investigates John's assumption that the violence he and his friends commit is constructive, and in so doing shows how destructive it is.[50]

Neil LaBute has recreated blood atonement in a way that questions its place in the contemporary Mormon identity. The dramatic situation—encountering the two gay men—corresponds to the Nephi archetype and activates that archetype. What happens next is, in Jung's words, "a conflict of pathological dimension."[51] But the parallel between LaBute's play and the Matthew Shepherd murder (see note 50) suggests that the impulses behind blood atonement—fear and xenophobia—are as typical as the Nephi archetype—a sobering reminder that "the voluminous reports of presidential commissions on violence, racism, and civil order have recently begun to say what artists like Melville and Faulkner had earlier prophesied: that myths reach out of the past to cripple, incapacitate, or strike down the living."[52]

## IV. The Burden of History in *The Open Curtain*

In Brian Evenson's novel, *The Open Curtain*, blood atonement reaches out of the past to "strike down" the protagonist, Rudd Theurer, when he discovers a box containing letters and books that belonged to his dead father. In the letters, Rudd learns both of his father's affair and a possible child from that affair; and in the books, he finds marginalia that highlight his father's obsession with blood atonement. The letters and books also help Rudd understand the reasons his father committed suicide—his father slit his throat to atone for his infidelity—and inspires Rudd to search for his half brother.

Soon after Rudd finds his half-brother, Lael, "things [begin] to go odd."[53] One day Lael takes Rudd to the top of a mountain, asks Rudd if he trusts him, then pushes him down the hill, breaking his arm. "He saw Lael once a week after that. He knew immediately something was different, yet it took days for him to realize Lael had started making a game out of everything, testing him. Lael offered the oddest appeals to brotherhood, at the oddest moments. Outside of these moments he did not mention their being brothers at all—as if brotherhood were a kind of bond activated only *in extremis.*"[54] The words "brotherhood" and "bond" suggest that Rudd and Lael's relationship is similar to the one between John, Tim, and David, or the nineteenth-century Danite brotherhood, a "bond activated only *in extremis.*" Lael is preparing Rudd for something big.

Rudd's discovery of his father's letters and books, and subsequent friendship with Lael, dovetails with a school research assignment for history class. In the Brigham Young University library, Rudd discovers a *New York Times* article about William Hooper Young's trial for the murder of Mrs. Anna Nilsen Pulitzer. "In New York in 1902, William Hooper Young, [Brigham Young's] grandson, slit the abdomen of an alleged prostitute and wrote the words 'Blood Atonement' in his father's apartment."[55] In the same *Times* article, Rudd finds a definition for the doctrine of blood atonement: "[it] teaches that the soul of any Mormon who has gone back on his or her faith may be saved by the shedding of blood."[56]

Rudd uncovers other real-life examples of blood atonement, and the burden of this knowledge weighs him down. The more he delves into his father's suicide, the Hooper Young murder, temple rituals, and blood atonement—and the more time he spends with Lael—the more he loses touch with reality. Then, in a pivotal scene, we learn that Rudd has "reached a point where he had begun to see some value—strictly theoretical, or course—in blood sacrifice." The passage goes on,

> It was perhaps Lael's voice, dim and quiet as they sat on a large iron-rich slab up the canyon, speaking slowly of the Lafferty brothers who had sacrificed their wives, of Ervil LeBaron, of a man in Salt Lake City who had slit his child's throat and then hung the child from the laundry line by its feet to let the blood drain out.
> "Morbid," said Rudd.

"Sure," said Lael. "But that doesn't make the act any less powerful. You do something like that and it takes you completely outside
of the world."

"Seems to me digging up a coffin does the same."

Lael shrugged. "It's not a bad start."

Rudd did not respond, but kept listening as Lael kept talking.
There were people, Lael claimed, who had sinned so greatly it was
a mercy to kill them. Killing them did them a favor.[57]

Lael preaches straight from the transcripts of nineteenth-century
Mormon leaders, whose "obsession with blood" led to numerous murders committed as blood atonement. That history—and its doctrinal
connection to his father's suicide as self-atonement—suffocates Rudd
until he complies with the Nephi archetype within him and acts out that
history in the campsite murders.

One day Lael takes Rudd to a campground and points out a family
setting up their tent next to their station wagon. "They're the ones," he
says. Rudd watches the family as they play frisbee, while next to him,
Lael plays with his knife. Then, the narrator tells us, Rudd blacks out:
"He took a deep breath, felt his vision grow dim. He felt himself crowded
out of his senses and into oblivion."[58] The campsite murders happen off
the page—in the gap between Rudd's third-person section of the novel
(part one) and Lyndi's narrative (part two). This narrative break retains
some ambiguity about who committed the murders—temporarily any-
way—until we later learn that Lael is nothing more than an alter ego for
Rudd—his journey back into his own history, which activated the Nephi
archetype, has parsed him into two characters.

Lyndi's narrative opens as she hears about the murders on the news:

Four bodies, not yet identified, a campsite, vicious slaying, three
long and careful cuts across throat, breasts, hips. Each body
arranged on the ground to form a pattern: a V, a right angle, each
next to each. And then, a little downslope, midway between the
V'd body and the right-angled body, a corpse spread straight with
hands to sides, a horizontal line; and another body, beneath the
right angle but farther down the mountainside, spread straight as
well: so that from the air (according to the artist's graphic representation) it looked like:

V        L

—

—

Suspiciously resembling, the reporter went on to say, if you cared for an instant to block out the river disrupting the pattern, the distinctive markings of the Mormon temple garment.[59]

As the facts of the murder become known, we learn that Rudd murdered Lyndi's mother, father, and sister, then arranged the bodies in the upper-three shapes of the symbols on Mormon temple garments. Rudd then slit his own throat and took his place as the lower fourth body and temple-garment symbol (at the knee). As the only survivor, he escapes suspicion—at least for a while—and he himself does not remember what happened. Lyndi and Rudd meet when she goes to see the only survivor of the murder in the hospital.

The significance of the temple garment in the murder scene is based on something Evenson writes in the afterword to *The Open Curtain*: "that any book that spoke in any detail about the relationship of Mormon culture to violence needed to acknowledge the connection of the temple ceremony to violence."[60] Earlier this essay described the way Brigham Young integrated the "Oath of Vengeance" into the temple ceremony. It also mentioned the oath taken by the Danites, where they swore to *"sustain, protect, defend,* and *obey* the leaders of the Church, under any and *all circumstances unto death."*[61] The early Mormon leaders' "obsession with blood," as evidenced by these oaths, evolved into the controversial penalty phase of the temple ceremony, where Mormons mimicked their own deaths as the penalty for breaking temple covenants.[62]

Later in *The Open Curtain*, during Rudd's temple marriage to Lyndi, the narrator describes this penalty ritual:

> They moved from signs and tokens to the penalties—promises that one would never reveal the signs and tokens, even at the peril of one's own life. If you were put in a position where you were forced to reveal the signs, you were apparently supposed to kill yourself. [The bride] was made to draw her hand across her throat as if it were a knife. She was made to pull her hand across her chest and then let both hands fall, as if she had opened her chest to let blood spill down her ribs. Later still, the back of her thumb traveled symbolically from one hip to another, slitting open her loins.[63]

Evenson's novel depicts the campsite murders as a contemporary blood-atonement ritual transmitted to Rudd "through [the] myths and psychology of [his] cultural ancestors."[64] His father killed himself based on the knowledge he gained from reading the history discussed earlier in this essay. Rudd's discovery of the details leading to his father's suicide, his relationship with Lael, and his school history project activate the Nephi archetype in him, too, but to a different end: the campsite murders.[65]

The implication in *The Open Curtain* is clear: when an institution — in this case, the Mormon religion — disassociates itself from its past, that past rears its head in one way or another. Evenson also writes that "the undercurrent of violence in Mormon culture really hasn't changed, that the conditions that made violence well up in earlier Mormon culture are still very much present today."[66] These conditions — or "situations," as Jung calls them — activate the Nephi archetype that lies dormant in Mormon culture. LaBute's hero punishes the sinner in *a gaggle of saints*, while Evenson's hero fights off history as it has traveled down through temple rituals. Both heroes commit murder as did the first Mormon hero, Nephi, in the Book of Mormon.

## V. Self-Atonement in The Backslider

Levi Peterson's protagonist, Frank Windham, has more in common with Rudd's father, who self-atoned by slitting his own throat, than with Rudd. Frank's impulse to harm himself as atonement for his sins comes from his repeated failure to live a Mormon life. Frank, a twenty-one-year-old Mormon cowboy living in small-town Utah, cannot measure up to his religion's standards, cannot keep himself from sinning, and believes that these sins are beyond the power of Christ's atonement. Frank's guilt and shame activate a slightly different version of the Nephi archetype than LaBute's John and Evenson's Rudd do, but one that still fits into Campbell's hero archetype:

> Stated in direct terms: the work of the hero is to slay the tenacious aspect of the father (dragon, tester, ogre king) and release from its ban the vital energies that will feed the universe. This can be done either in accordance with the Father's will or against his will; he [the Father] may 'choose death for his children's sake,' or it may be that the Gods impose the passion upon him, making him their sacrificial victim . . . The hero of yesterday becomes the tyrant of tomorrow, unless he crucifies *himself* today.[67]

Frank's dilemma is even better understood in the context of René Girard's argument in *Violence and the Sacred:* "any community that has fallen prey to violence or has been stricken by some overwhelming catastrophe hurls itself blindly into the search for a scapegoat."[68] In this case, that search turns inward, and Frank convinces himself that he is the "lone individual" at fault for all his problems. He believes that God has designated him as the sacrificial victim because he cannot live a righteous life. He must slay the dragon within to prevent it from getting out and harming the other members of his community. His heroic quest is to cleanse himself, and if that does not work, then to have the courage to sacrifice himself to save the community.

As *The Backslider* progresses, so, too, does Frank's inability to measure up to Mormon standards. He nearly kills a man, he impregnates a Lutheran girl, he masturbates obsessively, and he drinks alcohol. More important than the details is his constant failure to live up to the standard he sets, then resets, for himself. Along the way, he meets Bertha Chittenden, a polygamist, who tells him about Ross, her former fiancé, who initiated his own blood-atonement ritual:

> He atoned himself. It turned out he sometimes went to bed with men. Every time he went to Salt Lake, he did it. He had lived in hell's fire for many years. He had a black witness, knew he was damned, asked to be cleansed by his own blood. They took him out, I'm not saying who; they dug a grave, prayed together, then somebody held him by the hair, cut his throat, pointed the spurt of blood into the grave. He wanted to be cleansed by his own blood. It's the only way if you've had a black witness.[69]

Ross's blood atonement plays into Frank's self-atonement fantasy. His sins, he believes, are on par with Ross's, and his course of action is clear. If he cannot live God's laws, then he will have to atone, just as Ross did.

Frank recommits himself one more time to live the way he believes God wants him to. To him this means no sex in his marriage with Marianne (the Lutheran), no masturbation (Frank constructs an anti-masturbation device that prevents him from accidentally touching himself while sleeping), no coffee or alcohol, no meat, and no good-tasting foods. In other words, Frank eliminates all pleasure from his life. But he fails again, and after a sexual encounter with his wife, he harms himself:

> He stood, swayed, looked around. A vegetable grater lay on the sink counter. He walked toward it, pondered, took it up with his left hand. Suddenly he extended his right hand and forced the grater across his fingers and knuckles like a rasp, back and forth, one, two, three, four, five times, and more. Skin curled into tiny shreds; flesh lumped and clogged; blood welled, flowed, dripped.
>
> Marianne screamed, rolled off the bed, ran across the room, tore the bloody grater from his hand, and flung it to the floor. "My God, Frank!" she moaned. "My God, my God, my God!"
>
> He stood stupidly in the center of the floor, his arm dangling,

blood dripping. She pulled on her robe, found a roll of gauze, and wrapped his hand, his arm tucked under hers. He could feel her breast and big belly and for the moment he was very calm, very comforted.[70]

The calm and comfort he feels after cutting himself are the euphoria of self-atonement, as if hurting himself offsets the pleasure of sex—a kind of spiritual masochism.

Near the end of the novel, Frank must choose whether or not to go all the way and self-atone for his failure to live God's laws. He believes he has given his best effort to no avail and contemplates his next move. About this time, he has another conversation with Bertha; he wants to know if Ross really requested his own blood atonement:

> "Yes, [Ross] asked for it himself. He had a black witness, a testimony of damnation, sealed and sure. He asked to be cleansed by his own blood. It's the only way if you've had a black witness."
> "Who said blood would wash clean?"
> "Who said? God said!"
> "Where did he say it?"
> "I'll show you where," she declared. She disappeared into the hall, reappearing quickly with an old leather bound book. "This is the *Journal of Discourses* for 1856. Sermons by Brigham Young, George A. Smith, Heber C. Kimball, a bunch of other early apostles and prophets." She wet a thumb and leafed through the pages, peering closely at the dense, brown print. She pushed the book in front of Frank. There was a sermon by Jedidiah M. Grant, delivered on September 21, 1856 in the Bowery in Great Salt Lake City. It was titled "Rebuking Iniquity."
> I say, that there are men and women that I would advise to go to the President immediately, and ask him to appoint a committee to attend to their case; and then let a place be selected, and let that committee shed their blood. We have those amongst us that are full of all manner of abominations, those who need to have their blood shed, for water will not do, their sins are of too deep a dye.
> As he pushed the book aside, Bertha whispered, "have you got feelings of hell?"[71]

What is strange about this passage is Bertha's stance on blood atonement. She does not seem fazed at all by what happened to Ross and wonders if Frank needs blood atonement, too. She grounds her understanding of blood atonement in the words of Mormon church leaders in the *Journal of Discourses*,[72] and both Bertha and Frank believe that blood atonement is Mormon doctrine.[73]

*The Backslider* builds to the moment when Frank will either kill himself or change course altogether. If Peterson chooses blood-atonement suicide for his hero, then his novel will, like *a gaggle of saints* and *The Open Curtain*, suggest that the legacy these heroes inherit from Mormon culture is too much for them to bear. John, from *a gaggle of saints*, believes he has demolished the dragon in killing Chet, but LaBute's play shows us how destructive his worldview is. Rudd, from *The Open Curtain*, loses himself when he enacts blood atonement on an innocent family in the campsite murders—Evenson's novel suggests that the burden of the past, when buried, may also bury those in the present.

*The Backslider* takes another turn. Frank does not kill himself; instead, he sees a vision that reconfigures his understanding of Christianity. Moments after Frank baptizes his Lutheran wife, Marianne, into the Mormon Church, he is alone in the men's bathroom.

> He heard the soft plod of a horse's feet. Beneath the juniper boughs he saw a horse's legs. The animal emerged, a shiny roan mounted by a rider. The cowboy had a beard and he wore boots, ancient chaps, a denim shirt, a creased, sweat-stained Stetson. Touching spurs lightly to his mount, he reined toward Frank. Coming close, he halted and lifted a hand. It was Jesus, his face as kind as an August dawn.
> "You're lost," he said.
> Ashamed, Frank cast his eyes downward. "I expect I am."[74]

The two men proceed to have a conversation where Frank confesses he enjoys sex; loves to eat, hunt, and fish; and hates God. He also explains his urge to self-atone for these sins: "It's in my mind to do the same thing Jeremy did. Except when I cut myself off, there won't be anybody around to stop the bleeding."[75] Jesus listens sympathetically—never shocked or surprised at Frank's confessions—and even smokes a cigarette during their conversation. When Frank confronts him about smoking, Jesus shrugs it off: "I suppose it's a little habit I've gotten into. I hope you won't take it up." This version of Jesus, which Peterson calls the Cowboy Jesus, is the opposite of what Frank expects—instead of a vengeful god bent on punishing him for his sins, Jesus is a good listener and a laid-back cowboy who smokes.

When Frank finishes, Jesus asks, "Why can't you believe my blood was enough? . . . Why do you have to shed yours too?" He also suggests that Frank should enjoy his wife, who is "one hell of a good woman"; eat food that "tastes good," and "work on that crap about hating God."[76] By the time Jesus rides off into the sunset, we believe that Frank will not follow the Nephi archetype; instead, he will become simply a follower of Christ.

The Cowboy Jesus scene in *The Backslider* has become an iconic moment in Mormon literature for at least two reasons. The first is that Frank's shame and guilt are exposed as gratuitous spiritual masochism. All through *The Backslider,* Frank believes that the onus is on him to live a perfect life, and if he cannot, to atone for his own sins. Ironically, while trying to be a good Christian, he has overlooked the basic tenet of Christianity: Christ offered up his own life to atone for the sins of others. In the Cowboy Jesus scene, Peterson attempts to undo the theological underpinnings that led to blood atonement in the first place. Followers of Christ should not take the responsibility of atoning for anyone—themselves or others. They should instead believe that Christ's blood was enough.

Where the first reason is theological, the second is practical. What one person calls Christianity in the Cowboy Jesus scene, another may call cognitive dissonance. Jesus tells Frank to lighten up and to get over the notion that he should be perfect. To illustrate his point, Jesus smokes—a clear violation of Mormon doctrine—but remains committed to his religion. The counterpoint to Jesus is Frank himself, who, without any cognitive dissonance, is ready to kill himself for his sins. Readers of LaBute, Evenson, and Peterson may imagine Mormons as people who stand ready to kill others or themselves for their religion—indeed, such a view of Mormonism is tantalizing. The reality is that, like many Mormons, Frank must find a way to maintain conflicting Mormon principles to live his religion. He represents the average contemporary Mormon, who, when confronted with the details of his own cultural history and imperfection, finds a way to reconcile things enough within himself to stay in the religion without killing himself or others.

## VI. Epilogue: The Mormon American Writer

The motivation for this study came out of a desire to understand the pervasive violence in contemporary fiction (and drama) by Mormon American men. The bubbly, squeaky-clean public persona of the contemporary Mormon runs in stark contrast to the Nephi archetype we find on the pages of LaBute, Evenson, and Peterson. In fact, these authors have created heroes more like ones from Hebrew scripture—Samson, Abraham, King David, to name a few—who kill for their God.[77] In his study of violence in contemporary fiction by Jewish American men, Warren Rosenberg writes that he "intended to focus exclusively on twentieth-century Jewish American culture, seeing violence as a distinctly modern component of Jewish masculinity. As [he] read more and reflected on [his] own, upbringing, however, [he] realized that the narratives of violence [he] identified in Mailer, Doctorow, and Mamet were present in the foundational stories of Judaism."[78] My experience was similar. I had thought that the violence in fiction by these contemporary Mormon authors had more to do with rebelling against that pristine image, a way of projecting a more complicated Mormon identity to a non-Mormon audience, but what I found was that these authors are writing from within a Mormon tradition drenched in violence, one rooted in both Mormon scripture and history.

What further motivated this study is how American these three Mormon authors are. Harold Bloom argues that Mormonism is one of a few distinctly American religions and writes this about Joseph Smith: "I myself can think of not another American, except for Emerson and Whitman, who so moves and alters my own imagination. For someone who is not Mormon, what matters most about Joseph Smith is how American both the man and his religion have proved to be."[79] He also posits, "Some time in the future [a major American poet] will write their early story as the epic it was."[80] It appears that the American religion has already produced authors who are telling the Mormon story but not in quite the manner Bloom describes. The textual violence in LaBute, Evenson, and Peterson makes their work typically American and should place them in the conversation about contemporary American literature. They are like other "American writers [who] have persistently, almost obsessively, turned violence (and I refer here to depictions of physical violence or pain and its aftermath, not psychological violence or examples of metaphorical, 'discursive' violence) into an imaginative resource."[81]

The current Mormon Church is as mainstream, and as high profile, as it has ever been. The 2002 Winter Olympics in Salt Lake City created an international platform for Mormons, and their carefully constructed image as a patriotic, industrious, and friendly people helped broaden its appeal. More recently Mitt Romney's presidential campaign brought, as Mike Allen writes, "attention and credibility to the Church of Jesus Christ of Latter-day Saints (LDS), as the Mormons are formally known, and gives them a chance to demystify their theology and customs." At the same time, however, this attention reminds everyone else "just how different Mormonism is."[82]

Jon Krakauer's best-selling *Under the Banner of Heaven* is one example of the scrutiny that has resulted from Mormonism's more visible presence in American culture. Another less-successful example is Christopher

Cain's 2007 film *September Dawn*, which depicts the Mountain Meadows Massacre—the mass murder of 120 men, women, and children in 1857 by a local Mormon militia. While the film captures the blood-atonement-era Mormons well and grounds its depictions in many of the same historical accounts I uncovered in my research, the film relies too much on exploitation and melodrama to believably dramatize the dangers of religious fanaticism. What could have been an important addition to the small collection of blood-atonement representations in film and literature instead comes off as a schlocky B-movie. The most disappointing thing about the film is that it doesn't trust the historical events themselves to provide the drama. Instead, the filmmakers tell us how to feel about them.

Even so, *September Dawn*, which was released close to the 150th anniversary of the Mountain Meadows Massacre, inspired an official Mormon account of the event that was published in the church-owned magazine *Ensign* and could still be found on the LDS Web site almost a year after the film's release.[83] While far from perfect—the writer, Richard Turley, never mentions blood atonement and carefully navigates his way around any detail that suggests Mormon culpability—the article is significant progress for an institution that has been reluctant even to mention the event in a public forum. Such an exchange between a film and an institution helps to illustrate the significance of the books in this study.

The creative works of Neil LaBute, Brian Evenson, and Levi Peterson paint the picture of a powerful religion still coming to terms with its violent past, an insular culture bent on protecting its secrets, and the individual Mormon who struggles to reconcile that violent past with the present.[84] Together these three books have initiated a critical discourse that will hopefully grow into a more comprehensive study of Mormon literature for (and by) insiders and outsiders alike.

## Notes

1. Krakauer, *Under the Banner of Heaven*, xx–xxi.
2. Ibid.
3. Bagley, *Blood of the Prophets*, 50.
4. Brigham Young, February 8, 1857, in *Journal of Discourses* 4:219–20.
5. According to Joseph Smith, he translated the Book of Mormon from a set of gold plates given to him by an angel called Moroni. He wrote in the book's introduction, p.i, that "the Book of Mormon is a volume of holy scripture comparable to the Bible. It is a record of God's dealings with the ancient inhabitants of the Americas and contains, as does the Bible the fullness of the everlasting gospel."
6. Smith, Book of Mormon, 1 Nephi 4:15–16.

7. Ibid., 1 Nephi 4:10–13.
8. Ibid., 1 Nephi 4:18.
9. Campbell, *The Hero with a Thousand Faces*, viii.
10. Ibid., 30.
11. Jung and Hull, *The Archetypes and the Collective Unconscious*, 48.
12. I am not arguing for an essentialist view of Jung's theory—that archetypes are empty forms that then fill with cultural content. What I find useful about Jung's theory is the way archetypes are specifically activated.
13. Slotkin, *Regeneration through Violence*, 6.
14. Quinn, *The Mormon Hierarchy*, 93. The Danite organization remains a controversial part of Mormon history—not so much its existence as Joseph Smith's role, if any, in the organization. Some think that scholars like D. Michael Quinn have exaggerated the importance of the Danites, given the paucity of the historical record. Pro-Danite scholars explain this lack by pointing out that the Danites were ordered not to keep records.
15. Denton, *American Massacre*, 16.
16. Hebrews 9:22 (21st century King James version).
17. Lee, *Mormonism Unveiled*, 59 (italics in the original). John D. Lee was the local Mormon leader in charge of the Mountain Meadows Massacre on September 11, 1857, when at least 120 men, women, and children were murdered. Lee claimed that he received orders from higher-ups in the Mormon Church, but he was the only person charged in the murders and was executed by firing squad on March 23, 1877.
18. Girard, *Violence and the Sacred*, 79–80. For early Mormons, the scapegoat was the outsider (sinners, apostates, and gentiles).
19. Bagley, *Blood of the Prophets*, 21.
20. Smith, Book of Mormon, 2 Nephi 10:16.
21. Slotkin, *Regeneration through Violence*, 15.
22. Moore, *Religious Outsiders and the Making of Americans*, 45.
23. Whitmer, *The Violence Mythos*, 1.
24. Ibid.
25. Denton, *American Massacre*, 106. See also Stenhouse, *The Rocky Mountain Saints*, 408: "When the first blood atonement murder case went to trial John Cradlebaugh, a judge in the Utah territory, battled with the jurors who refused to convict the defendant. In the end he dismissed both jury and prisoner, but before he did he spoke out in frustration about his experience in Utah: 'Men are murdered here,' he said. 'Coolly, deliberately, premeditatedly murdered—their murder is deliberated and determined upon church council-meetings, and that, too, for no other reason than that they had apostatized from your Church, and were striving to leave the Territory.'"
26. Bagley, *Blood of the Prophets*, 50.
27. Brigham Young, February 8, 1857, *Journal of Discourses* 4:219.
28. For more on the way the Mormon Church manages its history, see David Brion Davis's *From Homocide to Slavery*; Jon Krakauer's *Under the Banner of Heaven*; and Harold Bloom's *The American Religion*.
29. Gustafson, "Histories of Democracy and Empire," 110. Gustafson derives her term *ideological edifice* from Donald Pease's discussion of metanarratives in "New Perspectives on U.S. Culture and Imperialism."

30. Blood atonement, the Mountain Meadows Massacre, and polygamy to name a few.

31. See the afterword to Jon Krakauer's *Under the Banner of Heaven* for an account of the way the Mormon Church attempted to dismiss his book. For more about the way the church treats insiders, see Lavina Fielding Anderson's "The LDS Intellectual Community and Church Leadership: A Contemporary Chronology" and "The Church and Its Scholars: Ten Years After." Anderson was one of the September Six, six Mormon intellectuals—the other five are D. Michael Quinn, Maxine Hanks, Paul Toscano, Avraham Gileadi, and Lynne Kinavel Whitesides—who were punished for their scholarly work (five were excommunicated; one was disfellowshipped, a formal probation). With these excommunications, the Mormon Church sent a strong warning to other Mormon scholars that still impacts Mormon studies. In addition to the painstaking work of research, up-and-coming Mormon scholars have to ask themselves if their research is worth losing their church membership. This is one reason why many Mormon intellectuals write exclusively for Mormon audiences.

32. For more on the way these authors feel about the Mormon Church and its doctrine, see Christopher Kimball Bigelow's *Conversations with Mormon Authors;* the afterword to the Bison Books edition of Brian Evenson's *Altmann's Tongue;* Levi Peterson's *A Rascal by Nature, A Christian by Yearning: A Mormon Autobiography;* and Rosalynde Welch's 2005 interview with Neil LaBute in *Times and Seasons.* Both Evenson and LaBute have resigned from the Mormon Church; Levi Peterson describes himself as a Mormon who doesn't believe in God.

33. Powers, *Recalling Religions,* 12.

34. *bash: latter-day plays* is a trilogy of one-act plays: *iphigenia in orem, a gaggle of saints,* and *medea redux.*

35. LaBute, *bash,* 57.

36. Campbell, *The Hero with a Thousand Faces,* 341.

37. The three men in the play comprise a bishopric, the basic leadership structure for a Mormon congregation—John is the bishop, and Tim and David are his first and second counselors.

38. LaBute, *bash,* 62.

39. Whitmer, *The Violence Mythos,* 56 (italics in the original).

40. See note 62.

41. LaBute, *bash,* 64.

42. Ibid.

43. Ibid., 65.

44. Ibid.

45. Ibid., 66.

46. While slitting the throat was the most common way to kill the victim in blood atonement, that model varied as soon as it began. What remained constant was the impetus behind the killing, the same one that appears in *a gaggle of saints:* kill the sinner, the apostate, or the gentile—the one who stands in the way of God's work.

47. LaBute, *bash,* 66.

48. Slotkin, *Gunfighter Nation,* 21.

49. Wesley, *Violent Adventure*, 5. Wesley borrows the terms *constructive* and *destructive* violence from Rollo May's *Power and Innocence: A Search for the Sources of Violence*.

50. The play bears a chilling resemblance to the real 1998 murder of Matthew Shepherd, who was tied to a post and beaten to death because, according to the two men who murdered him, he made a pass at them. Aaron James McKinney and Russell Henderson (a Mormon), like John, pretended to be gay to gain Shepherd's trust. When Shepherd asked for a ride home, McKinney and Henderson took him outside of town, tied him to a post, and *bashed* him.

51. Jung and Hull, *The Archetypes and the Collective Unconscious*, 48.

52. Slotkin, *Regeneration Through Violence*, 5.

53. Evenson, *The Open Curtain*, 27.

54. Ibid., 29.

55. Bagley, *Blood of the Prophets*, 379.

56. Evenson, *The Open Curtain*, 38.

57. Ibid., 71.

58. Ibid., 86.

59. Ibid., 91.

60. Ibid., 216.

61. Lee, *Mormonism Unveiled*, 59 (italics in the original).

62. Evenson, *The Open Curtain*, 216. The temple ceremony penalty phase was discontinued in 1990, six years after the Lafferty brothers murdered their sister-in-law and niece in a style that reenacted it. About this change, Evenson writes, "Many temple-going Mormons saw this as a positive step: I tend rather to see it as a further repression or Mormonism's relation to violence. Changing the ceremony hasn't changed Mormonism's underlying violence; it has only hidden it," 216.

63. Ibid., 145.

64. Slotkin, *Regeneration through Violence*, 3.

65. In part three, Rudd develops a third personality—that of Hooper Young—and travels back and forth between the nineteenth and twentieth centuries. As Hooper Young, he must dispose of the prostitute's body, and as Rudd, he marries Lyndi, the only member of the family he did not murder at the campsite. Their married life together becomes increasingly strange as he withdraws first to his bedroom and then to a shed in the backyard. The final pages of the novel revolve around whether or not Rudd will kill Lyndi as he did her family. In part three, past and present become one, clearly showing that history—in this case blood atonement—cannot be buried.

66. Evenson, *The Open Curtain*, 216.

67. Campbell, *The Hero with a Thousand Faces*, 353 (italics in the original).

68. Girard, *Violence and the Sacred*, 79–80.

69. Peterson, *The Backslider*, 306–7. Petersen coins the phrase "black witness" to parody the moment when a believer becomes a witness for Jesus Christ. In a black witness, individuals receive spiritual confirmation that their sins have placed them outside the saving grace of Jesus Christ and to be forgiven they must self-atone through the blood-atonement ritual.

70. Ibid., 331–32.

71. Ibid., 334–35.

72. Grant, September 21, 1856, *Journal of Discourses* 4:49. Jedidiah Grant's
    speech is but one example of many of this kind of rhetoric from the Mor-
    mon Reformation I discussed earlier in this essay.
73. For a broader understanding of Levi Peterson's interpretation of Mormon
    history, see his biography, *Juanita Brooks: Mormon Woman Historian.*
74. Peterson, *The Backslider*, 353–54.
75. Ibid., 355. Early in the novel, Frank's brother, Jeremy, castrates himself
    to suppress sexual desire. This act serves as model for Frank as his own
    shame and guilt build.
76. Ibid., 355–56.
77. That Nephi, Joseph Smith's hero from the Book of Mormon, resembles Old
    Testament heroes is not surprising given that "Joseph Smith absorbed the
    Bible, and he understood implicitly the burden of Jewish history: the reli-
    gion preceded, and produced, the peculiar or set-apart people." See Bloom,
    *The American Religion*, 88–89.
78. Rosenberg, *Legacy of Rage*, 30.
79. Bloom, *The American Religion*, 127.
80. Ibid., 79.
81. Kowalewski, *Deadly Musings*, 4.
82. Allen, "A Mormon as President?"
83. Turley, "The Mountain Meadows Massacre."
84. After reading this essay, my non-Mormon colleagues were not surprised at all
    by the Nephi archetype or the church's refusal to discuss blood atonement. In
    this respect, blood atonement reminds them of the Mormon Church's stance
    toward its practice of polygamy. When asked about polygamy on CNN's
    *Larry King Live* (1998), the late prophet and president of the church, Gordon B.
    Hinckley, said, "That's 118 years ago. It's behind us." Hinckley conceded that
    the Mormon Church practiced polygamy but ignored the pretext of King's
    question: that polygamy still affects Utah's economic and social policy (many
    western states other than Utah have also been impacted by polygamy—for
    example, Arizona and Texas), national and international views of Mormon-
    ism, and even current Mormon doctrine. Many outside the Mormon Church
    are surprised to learn, for example, that polygamy is still official church doc-
    trine and practiced in Mormon temples. A Mormon man, for example, may
    marry a second wife in the temple after his first wife dies. In Mormon theol-
    ogy, he is sealed to both women and will have both of them as wives in the
    hereafter—where polygamy is once again the rule.

# Bibliography

Allen, Mike. "A Mormon as President?" *Time*, November 26, 2006. http://www.
      time.com/time/magazine/article/0,9171,1562941-1,00.html.
Anderson, Lavina Fielding. "The Church and Its Scholars: Ten Years After."
      *Sunstone*, July 2003, 13–19.
———. "The LDS Intellectual Community and Church Leadership: A Con-
      temporary Chronology." *Dialogue: A Journal of Mormon Thought* 26, no. 1
      (Spring 1993): 7–64.

Bagley, Will. *Blood of the Prophets: Brigham Young and the Massacre at Mountain Meadows.* Norman: University of Oklahoma Press, 2002.

Bigelow, Christopher Kimball. *Conversations with Mormon Authors.* New York: Mormon Arts and Letters, 2007

Bloom, Harold. *The American Religion: The Emergence of the Post-Christian Nation.* New York: Simon & Schuster, 1992.

Campbell, Joseph. *The Hero with a Thousand Faces.* 2d ed. Bollingen Series 17. Princeton, NJ: Princeton University Press, 1968.

Church of Jesus Christ of Latter-Day Saints. *Journal of Discourses.* 26 vols. London and Liverpool: Latter-day Saints Book Depot, 1854–86.

Davis, David Brion. *From Homicide to Slavery: Studies in American Culture.* New York: Oxford University Press, 1986.

Denton, Sally. *American Massacre: The Tragedy at Mountain Meadows, September 1857.* 1st ed. New York: Alfred A. Knopf, 2003.

Evenson, Brian. *Altmann's Tongue.* Lincoln, NE: Bison Books, 2002.———. *The Open Curtain: A Novel.* 1st ed. Minneapolis: Coffee House Press, 2006.

Girard, René. *Violence and the Sacred.* Baltimore: Johns Hopkins University Press, 1977.

Gustafson, Sandra M. "Histories of Democracy and Empire." *American Quarterly* 59, no. 1 (2007): 107–33.

Hinckley, Gordon. Interview on *Larry King Live,* September 9, 1998, CNN television.

Holy Bible. 21st century King James version. Gary, SD: 21st Century King James Bible Publishers, 1991.

Jung, C. G., and R. F. C. Hull. *The Archetypes and the Collective Unconscious.* Vol. 9, part 1, *Collected Works of C. G. Jung.* 2d ed. Princeton, NJ: Princeton University Press, 1980.

Kowalewski, Michael. *Deadly Musings: Violence and Verbal Form in American Fiction.* Princeton, NJ: Princeton University Press, 1993.

Krakauer, Jon. *Under the Banner of Heaven: A Story of Violent Faith.* New York: Anchor Books, 2004.

LaBute, Neil. *bash: three plays.* Woodstock, NY: Overlook Press, 1999.

Lee, John Doyle. *Mormonism Unveiled, or Life and Confession of John D. Lee.* Albuquerque: Fierra Blanca Publications, 2001.

May, Rollo. *Power and Innocence: A Search for the Sources of Violence.* New York: W.W. Norton & Company, Inc., 1972.

Moore, R. Laurence. *Religious Outsiders and the Making of Americans.* New York: Oxford University Press, 1986.

Pease, Donald E. "New Perspectives on U.S. Culture and Imperialism." In *Cultures of United States Imperialism,* edited by Donald E. Pease and Amy Kaplan, 22–37. Durham, NC: Duke University Press, 1993.

Peterson, Levi S. *The Backslider.* Salt Lake City: Signature Books, 1986.

———. *Juanita Brooks: Mormon Woman Historian.* Salt Lake City: University of Utah Press, 1988.

———. *A Rascal by Nature, A Christian by Yearning: A Mormon Autobiography.* Salt Lake City: University of Utah Press, 2006.

Powers, Perry Kerry. *Recalling Religions: Resistance, Memory, and Cultural Revision in Ethnic Women's Literature.* Knoxville: University of Tennessee Press, 2001.

Quinn, D. Michael. *The Mormon Hierarchy: Origins of Power.* Salt Lake City: Signature Books in association with Smith Research Associates, 1994.

Rosenberg, Warren. *Legacy of Rage: Jewish Masculinity, Violence, and Culture.* Amherst: University of Massachusetts Press, 2001.

*September Dawn,* directed by Christopher Cain. Sony Pictures Home Entertainment, 2008. DVD.

Slotkin, Richard. *Gunfighter Nation: The Myth of the Frontier in Twentieth-Century America.* New York, Toronto: Atheneum; Maxwell Macmillan Canada; Maxwell Macmillan International, 1992.

———. *Regeneration through Violence: The Mythology of the American Frontier, 1600–1860.* Norman: University of Oklahoma Press, 2000.

Smith, Joseph, Jr., and Church of Jesus Christ of Latter-Day Saints. The Book of Mormon: An Account. Salt Lake City: Church of Jesus Christ of Latter-day Saints, 1982.

Stenhouse, T. B. H. *The Rocky Mountain Saints: A Full and Complete History of the Mormons.* New York: D. Appleton and Company, 1873.

Turley, Richard E., Jr. "The Mountain Meadows Massacre." *Ensign,* September 2007, 14–21.

Welch, Rosalynde. "An Interview with Neil LaBute." *Times & Seasons,* January 19, 2005. http://timesandseasons.org/index.php/2005/01/an-interview-with-neil-labute/.

Wesley, Marilyn C. *Violent Adventure: Contemporary Fiction by American Men.* Charlottesville: University of Virginia Press, 2003.

Whitmer, Barbara. *The Violence Mythos.* Albany: State University of New York Press, 1997.

# 5

# Elders on the Big Screen

*Film and the Globalized Circulation of Mormon Missionary Images*

J O H N - C H A R L E S  D U F F Y

Since the late-twentieth century, the Church of Jesus Christ of Latter-day Saints has maintained a widely recognized standard image for the young men who constitute the bulk of its fifty-to-sixty-thousand-strong missionary force.[1] As a result, Mormon missionaries—or more precisely, with attention to gender, Mormon elders—have become a widely recognized presence in social landscapes around the globe. People who know little about Mormonism may nevertheless recognize Mormon missionaries, much as they recognize black-habited Catholic nuns, orange-robed Krishna devotees, or buggy-riding Amish. One indication of how widely Mormon missionaries are recognized is their appearance as stock characters in film. Proselytizing characters in movies and television are often patterned after Mormon elders: young men in pairs, clean shaven, wearing white shirts and ties. This pattern occurs even in cases when the characters are not specifically depicted as Mormons but instead appear as generic evangelists.

The use of Mormon missionary images in film exemplifies a dynamic identified by Manuel Vásquez and Marie Friedmann Marquardt in connection with the globalization of religious goods; David Morgan describes the same dynamic in his study of religion and visual culture. As images and other religious goods circulate, they are often used in ways their distributors did not intend. To use Morgan's term, religious images are subject to *expropriation*. A hotline set up by American Pentecostals so that counselors can walk callers through the process of accepting Jesus as their personal savior may instead be used by Guatemalan Catholics as a kind of phone-in confessional. Protestant artist Warner Sallman's widely distributed painting of Christ standing behind a young white man at the helm of a ship can be redrawn by the followers of a Nigerian prophet to depict Christ standing behind their black leader.[2] In a similar dynamic, as Mormon missionaries circulate through public spaces around the globe, filmmakers can adapt their carefully cultivated and readily recognized image and embed it in their own projects. The filmmakers' images then also circulate, evoking meanings and performing cultural work not intended by the LDS Church.

In this essay, I analyze Mormon missionary images in seven films produced over a period of ten years (1997–2007) in different parts of the Anglophone world: the United States, the United Kingdom, and Australia. I identify the material means by which the Mormon missionary image is produced, circulated, and expropriated and explore the meanings that filmmakers attach to that image. My argument, in brief, is that through metonymy and hybridity, images of Mormon missionaries are made to represent conservative strains of religion generally and Christianity specifically. Filmmakers use these images to reinforce negative judgments about conservative religion. However, the disparity between the meanings that the LDS Church attaches to its missionaries' image and those that filmmakers create is not always as great as one expects. For example, filmmakers have evidently been persuaded to accept Mormonism as a form of Christianity, consistent with LDS claims and contrary to evangelical polemics. In conclusion, I indicate ways that theoretical frames I adopted for this study—the materiality and globalization of religion—can nuance interpretations of Mormon media images and enrich our understanding of Mormonism as an international religion.

Past discussions of images of Mormons in film have been preoccupied with whether or not the films "treat the Church fairly and positively," to quote from one recent survey. Commentators have tended to map cinematic images of Mormons in bifurcated fashion: portrayals are either accurate, sympathetic, kind, and complex, or stereotypical, two dimensional, sensationalist, and prejudiced. In other words, images of Mormons in films have typically been read as a gauge of attitudes toward Mormonism, with LDS commentators going so far as to brand negative portrayals as "anti-Mormon," "Mormon-exploitation films," or "screen persecution."[3] While I acknowledge the question of whether or not these images are "good for Mormons," my focus on the globalization and expropriation of the missionary image attempts to escape the antagonism-or-acceptance frame that dominates the literature. That is, images of missionaries are not interpreted as mirrors into which Mormons look to decide if they are being fairly and positively reflected. Instead, I analyze these images as creative borrowings and reworkings of a product—a brand—initially created by Mormons but one that, because of its wide circulation, Mormons are unable to control. Why are non-Mormon filmmakers interested in the missionary image, and how do they use it? These are questions that differ from asking how well informed filmmakers are about Mormons or whether or not they reveal anti-Mormon prejudices.

My selection of films is hardly comprehensive (it is, in fact, largely serendipitous), and their distribution varies greatly, but together they demonstrate the multiple, complex uses of recent Mormon missionary images. Because I am interested in the way non-LDS filmmakers use these missionary images, films by LDS-affiliated directors, such as *God's Army* (2000), *The Other Side of Heaven* (2001), or *The Best Two Years* (2003), are not included.[4] The seven films I examine are the following:

*Orgazmo* (directed by Trey Parker, U.S.A., 1997), a characteristically lowbrow feature film by the creator of *South Park*. The protagonist is a Mormon missionary working in Los Angeles who becomes a reluctant porn star to pay for his upcoming temple wedding.

*California Sunshine* (directed by David Mackenzie, U.K., 1997), a comedic short produced by a then-fledgling company that has since become a significant presence in the Scottish film scene. Two small-time drug dealers are visited by evangelists, whom they mistake for hired goons.

*Me Myself I* (directed by Pip Karmel, Australia, 1999), a feature film in which a thirtysomething single woman enters a parallel reality to see how her life would have unfolded had she married a former love interest. A missionary appears briefly at a pivotal moment.

*Could Be Worse* (directed by Zack Stratis, U.S.A., 2000), a low-budget independent film, fusing documentary with musical comedy, made by a Greek American director and his family. An encounter with missionaries prompts the director/protagonist to assert his gay identity more publicly.

*Latter Days* (directed by C. Jay Cox, U.S.A., 2003), a feature film about a gay Mormon missionary written and directed by a gay former Mormon missionary. While serving in Los Angeles, the missionary falls in love with a party-boy neighbor.

*Buckleroos* (directed by Jerry Douglas and John Rutherford, U.S.A., 2004), a pornographic film that attracted unusual notice within the gay adult film industry and became the subject of a "making of" documentary. One sequence features the sexual initiation of two missionaries.

*The Saviour* (directed by Peter Templeman, Australia, 2005), a short nominated for an Academy Award in 2007. A conflicted missionary having an affair with a married woman discovers that she has used him and exacts a subtle, complicated revenge.

## (Re)manufacturing the Missionary Image

Following David Morgan, I treat missionary images as artifacts of material culture. That is, they are approached not only as representations with an abstract existence but also as objects occupying physical space.[5] As such, missionary images must be manufactured. This is true not only of representations of missionaries in the media but also of the standardized image that missionaries themselves project by their regimented dress and grooming, an image that circulates as missionaries move through the locales where they are assigned to work. Conceptualizing missionary images as material goods avoids a disembodied discussion of missionary representations. It keeps us from losing sight of the material processes that produce and circulate these images. Remaining aware of those material processes generates a more concrete discussion of Mormon media images and sheds light on the dynamics of Mormonism's international expansion.

### Manufacturing the Image:
### Regulating Missionaries' Dress and Grooming

The material production of the missionary image begins with written instructions about dress and grooming that elders receive from church leaders. These instructions became progressively more specific during the twentieth century as leaders tried to ensure a consistent, favorable image. In the 1930s and 1940s, elders were instructed simply to dress "in a conservative manner—dark shoes, dark suit, quiet hat." A few decades later, the 1973 *Missionary Handbook* became more specific, instructing that shirts should be white, requiring elders to keep their hair "off the neck, collar, and ears," and banning mustaches, beards, and sideburns. An even longer set of regulations introduced to missionaries in 1986 added that "sideburns should not extend below the middle of the ear" and clarified that missionaries should wear "business suits in conservative colors."[6] In 1975 the Quorum of the Twelve Apostles distributed black-and-white photographs of an acceptable missionary haircut in a circular to local church leaders. A similar illustration later became part of the information packet that was mailed to elders with their mission calls.[7]

In 1995 the church created a two-sided color handout with photographs of acceptable missionary dress; a revised version appeared in 1998. This handout contained the most precise dress and grooming regulations yet issued to elders. It listed the range of acceptable colors for suits and shoes; directed that elders could wear "a dark, single-color V-neck sweater under your suit jacket in cooler climates, but never without a jacket"; required that if missionaries in cold climates wore boots, "the part of the boot that shows beneath the pant leg should look like a traditional business shoe";[8] forbade missionaries to roll up their shirt sleeves; and specified a number of other unacceptable clothing choices, including sports coats; "baggy, pegged, or other casual-cut pants"; "casual fabrics like cotton twill or denim"; "light-colored or tan pants"; string or bow ties; and shoes "made of suede, canvas, or any other soft material," as well as country and hiking boots. Hair styles identified as "unacceptable" were "bowl cuts," "crew cuts," "wet look styles," and "bleached hair."[9] The specificity of the instructions not only attests to the importance church leaders place on creating a uniform image but probably also reveals the variety of ways that elders have tried to maneuver within the regulations to accommodate their own sense of style and comfort.

Some adjustments to the uniform image are authorized for climate. At the discretion of mission presidents, elders may dispense with suit coats during the summer or year-round if they serve in tropical or desert locales. Also, elders in hot climates may wear short-sleeved white shirts in place of long. Hardly any adaptations to local culture are permitted, however. A notable exception is that elders in Tonga wear *ta'ovalas* (woven mats) in place of trousers, though they still wear white shirts and ties.[10] A *Culture for Missionaries* manual produced in 1980 for those working in Guatemalan indigenous communities explained at some length that missionaries should not "wear sandals and poor clothing" as some had done in the past "in an effort to identify with the people." To assure missionaries that their business-style dress would not create barriers, the manual quoted a Cakchiquel convert who related that "all the people in [his] town admired that the distinguished, spiffed-up gringos with ties were carrying [the body of] a poor, simple Indian" at a funeral. "Dress like a missionary," the manual insisted.[11]

Although name badges are a widely used and quickly recognizable feature of the missionary uniform, several editions of the handbook for mission presidents have indicated that they are optional.[12] In fact, missionaries may be instructed not to wear badges—for instance, in areas where the church is still obtaining legal recognition.[13] Black badges with white lettering, shorter than the badges used today, were used at the Language Training Mission and some mission fields by the end of the 1960s. Around 1980 the Missionary Training Center (MTC) began manufacturing badges of the now-familiar size bearing the official church logo. Mission presidents could opt to use the MTC's badges in the field or not, but they were forbidden to create different ones.[14] Starting in the late 1990s, church headquarters manufactured blank badges with the church logo, onto which mission presidents could engrave missionaries' names according to meticulous instructions about what font to choose (Helvetica Condensed Medium) and where to place the text (measured to the millimeter).[15]

Periodic inspections for compliance to dress and grooming regulations maintain the standard image. A 1975 circular from the Quorum of the Twelve Apostles announced that "mission presidents have been given instructions to carefully check each missionary concerning his personal appearance."[16] The church film *Called to Serve* (1991) depicts an inspection ritual familiar to thousands of elders: checking their haircuts when they enter the MTC. When I reached the MTC to begin my missionary service in the early 1990s, most of the dozen or so missionaries in my district failed this initial inspection and were immediately sent to the MTC barber.

A few months into my mission in the Dominican Republic, an annual tour by a visiting General Authority offered an occasion to tighten missionaries' adherence to the approved image. The visiting official instructed the mission president that missionaries should do a better job of keeping their shoes shined, should not wear sunglasses, and should discontinue a fashion some elders had adopted of wearing their already-short sleeves rolled up an inch or two higher. When the mission president forwarded these directives to missionaries, he acknowledged that keeping shoes shined would be difficult for those who worked where we regularly had to walk through mud, but he urged compliance so that we could merit God's blessings through our obedience. The 1998 *Dress and Grooming Guidelines for Elders* similarly invokes the divine authority of the church hierarchy to urge compliance: "You are to maintain the standards established by the First Presidency and the Quorum of the Twelve," the introduction declares. The appeal to authority is reiterated at the end of the document: "Follow these standards of dress and grooming, which the General Authorities have set."[17]

What impression do church leaders intend the uniform missionary image to communicate? The word *conservative* recurs prominently in dress and grooming regulations from the 1930s to the 1990s. A certain class identification is implied; hence, a mission president's handbook from the early 1960s instructed missionaries to wear hats "if the conservative gentlemen of the area wear hats."[18] Three decades later missionaries no longer wore hats, but they were still enjoined to emulate conservative fashion. The 1998 *Dress and Grooming Guidelines for Elders* instructed them to eschew "any local, traditional attire that is not in harmony with a conservative, business-like dress appearance."[19] In setting "business-like dress" against and above "local, traditional attire," this statement reflects the dynamics of a globalized corporate culture whose norms, activities, and influence cut across regional boundaries and often subordinate local practice.

The purpose of dressing in a conservative business style, church leaders told missionaries in 1995, is "so that you will be clearly recognized as an ambassador of the Lord." Missionaries were receiving a similar message as early as the 1930s: the 1937 *Missionary's Hand Book* explained that while LDS clergy have no "distinguishing costume" like ministers from other religions, dressing "in a conservative manner" signals "the dignity of [missionaries'] work." The need for a dignified as well as unified image is likewise invoked to explain why missionaries should wear standardized name tags.[20] Given how self-consciously church image makers take their cues from corporate culture, it is neither metaphoric nor ironic to call the Mormon missionary image a brand—with the understanding that church leaders intend this brand to communicate the sacred character of a missionary's calling. That is, missionaries' businesslike image should not be interpreted as crossing into the realm of the profane. Rather, the missionary image sacralizes a corporate one.

*Remanufacturing the Image for Film:*
*Imitation, Adaptation, Distribution*

Filmmakers who expropriate the Mormon missionary image must materially recreate it through costuming and props. Depending on how thoroughly a filmmaker wants to reproduce the image, this may require obtaining artifacts of LDS material culture, such as copies of the Book of Mormon, or manufacturing imitations in the case of badges. Once captured on film, these recreations of the missionary image circulate—some more widely than others—as the films are screened at festivals or in commercial theaters, viewed on video or DVD, or distributed via Internet. Television is another potential mode of distributing these images, though I am not aware that any of the seven films analyzed here has been broadcast this way.

Every film in this study can make some claim to relative significance, such as commercial release, awards, or screening at a major film festival. Nevertheless, their circulation has been relatively limited. Where a Hollywood blockbuster plays in a few thousand theaters at a time, the

widest U.S. release enjoyed by any of these films was ninety-four theaters, the figure for *Orgazmo*.[21] Of course, video/DVD rental and sales
allow feature films like *Orgazmo, Me Myself I, Could Be Worse,* and *Latter
Days* to reach viewers beyond commercial theatergoers. Film shorts face
special difficulties with circulation since they are not distributed indi-
vidually. However, *The Saviour* made the rounds as part of a DVD collection of Academy Award–nominated shorts, while *California Sunshine,*
also a short, was available for free online viewing at Atom.com. As a
pornographic film, *Buckleroos* is subject to legal restrictions on its distribution that do not affect the other films here.

Five of the films in this study *(California Sunshine, Me Myself I,
Could Be Worse, Latter Days,* and *The Saviour)* have screened at festivals
in locations ranging from the United States and Canada to Australia,
Scotland, Portugal, and Croatia. All five of these films have won festival awards, a measure of the attention they have received from the
cinematic elite. Analogously *Buckleroos* garnered a record number
of GayVN awards, indicating that it received considerable attention
within its niche market; one of those awards went to the sequence featuring the missionary characters.[22]

How, precisely, do filmmakers reproduce the Mormon missionary
image? What features do they employ as signals to viewers that these
characters are, if not Mormon missionaries specifically, then similar
evangelists? In every film analyzed, the missionaries are white males,
clean shaven, and dressed in white shirts and ties. In *California Sunshine,*
they wear suits. Almost always the missionaries appear to be in their late
teens or early twenties, and they work in pairs. Exceptions are *California
Sunshine,* where one of the evangelists is played by an actor who is
nearly forty, and *Me Myself I,* where a missionary works alone, making street contacts. The fact that missionary rules require companions to
stay together is incorporated into the story line of *The Saviour* when the
protagonist, Malcolm, is reprimanded for visiting an investigator alone.

In four of the films *(Orgazmo, Could Be Worse, Latter Days,* and *The
Saviour),* the missionaries wear name badges. In *Orgazmo* and *Latter
Days,* the filmmakers have taken some trouble to approximate the
design, color, layout, and font of an actual LDS missionary badge—
including the church logo, albeit with a slight change, probably to avoid
legal liability: in *Orgazmo* "Saints" becomes "Aints," while in *Latter Days,*
"Latter-day" becomes "Ladder-day" (figure 1). Other missionary acces-
sories that appear inconsistently across the films are scriptures and pam-
phlets, backpacks or side satchels, and bicycles and helmets (figure 2).
Publications or artwork produced by the LDS Church become props in

Figure 1. Missionary name badge as recreated for *Latter Days*. Note that "Latter-day" has become "Ladder-day."

*Orgazmo, Latter Days,* and *California Sunshine.* In *Orgazmo* the elders carry blue paperback editions of the Book of Mormon. In *Latter Days,* missionaries teach with an approximation of a 1970s-era flipchart: a three-ring binder containing artwork reproduced by the church, including Simon Dewey's *Fishers of Men* and John Scott's *The First Vision.* In *California Sunshine,* one of the missionaries briefly displays a pamphlet about Christ's visit to America as narrated in the Book of Mormon. It appears that the filmmakers may have pasted over the pamphlet's original title, but the cover artwork—a detail of John Scott's painting *Jesus Christ Visits the Americas*—is still visible.

Apropos the globalized circulation of Mormon missionaries, it is noteworthy that in the three films made outside the U.S.A. *(California Sunshine, Me Myself I,* and *The Saviour),* missionary characters speak with local—i.e., Scottish or Australian—accents. The fact that these characters are clearly inspired by Mormon missionaries and yet are not American may imply that the filmmakers are accustomed to seeing local missionaries in their countries and therefore do not think of Mormon missionaries as a foreign presence. Indeed, if Mormon missionaries were perceived as foreign, it would be harder to draft them as generic evangelists, which is the role they play in these particular films. At the same time, two missionary characters who play secondary roles in *The Saviour* do have American accents; evidently, then, writer/director Peter Templeman is aware of the Mormons' U.S. connection and assumes that viewers will also know it, even though he makes his two principal missionary characters Australian.

Of the films analyzed here, *Orgazmo* and *Latter Days* make the most concerted efforts to reproduce LDS missionaries' appearance and teaching methods. *(Orgazmo* is less concerned than *Latter Days* for reasons

Figure 2. Missionary characters from the pornographic film *Buckleroos*.

discussed below, under "Missionaries as Christians.") Not coinciden-
tally, *Orgazmo* and *Latter Days* are also the only two films where the missionary characters are explicitly identified as LDS. In addition to repro-
ducing missionary badges, the filmmakers' efforts at verisimilitude
include showing missionaries reading aloud from the Book of Mormon
with a contact *(Orgazmo)* or teaching a lesson on the restoration of the
church *(Latter Days)*. The realism of the depiction extends even to the
temple garment. It appears that *Orgazmo* merely approximates the garment with an unmarked white undershirt during a scene where an elder
undresses in a changing room. *Latter Days,* however, displays an actual
two-piece nylon-mesh temple garment. The garment first appears when
missionary protagonist Aaron is lying in bed. Later, we watch Aaron
strip off the garment at the beginning of a lengthy sex scene. The garment in the film must have come ultimately from the church-owned
manufacturer, Beehive Clothing, through one of the church's distribution centers.[23] It would have been relatively simple to obtain a garment
when *Latter Days* was made. In 2004, the year *Latter Days* was released,
the church implemented a new policy that, for the first time, restricted
the sale of temple garments to those with a temple recommend.[24]

The verisimilitude of *Latter Days* is explained largely by the fact that
writer/director C. Jay Cox is a former Mormon missionary. Though not
Mormon himself, Trey Parker, writer/director of *Orgazmo*, evidenced his
knowledge of Mormonism in a 2003 *South Park* episode, "All about the
Mormons?" The show depicts a family home evening (an LDS tradition of reserving Monday nights for family) and recounts in some detail
events from early Mormon history: Joseph Smith's "first vision" of the
Father and the Son, the discovery of the golden plates from which the

Book of Mormon was allegedly translated, and the loss of the first 116 pages of the manuscript by Smith's scribe, Martin Harris.[25]

None of the other filmmakers whose works were analyzed are as concerned about accuracy as Cox or Parker. However, Peter Templeman *(The Saviour)* and Zack Stratis *(Could Be Worse)* have alluded to interactions with Mormon elders that became the basis for the depictions of missionaries in their films. In a brief interview that appeared on the Academy Awards Web site in connection with the nomination of *The Saviour,* Templeman referred to "interviewing several Mormon missionaries for research."[26] The scene with Mormon missionaries in *Could Be Worse* reenacts a real exchange that writer/director Zack Stratis had with two LDS missionaries who happened to knock on his door while he was working on the script; Stratis decided to incorporate the conversation into the film to advance the plot.[27] Stratis's serendipitous encounter dramatically illustrates the way the circulation of LDS missionaries through public space makes their image available as a resource for filmmakers.

## Uses of the Missionary Image

Having reproduced the Mormon missionary image, how do filmmakers use it? In other words, what is the point of using missionary characters in these films? What meanings are attached to them? What functions do they serve in these stories?

### Missionaries as Christians

Missionary characters in most of these films function metonymically as representatives for Christianity generally. This is most obviously true in the films where the Mormon-like characters are generic evangelists. In *Me Myself I,* the character who resembles a Mormon missionary is identified in the credits as Young Christian. Although dressed like an LDS missionary (white shirt, tie, backpack), he asks the protagonist a more characteristically Protestant question: "Do you have faith in our Lord Jesus Christ?" Similarly the evangelists in *California Sunshine* frequently quote the Bible in a manner that recalls evangelical Protestants. Explicitly not intended to be Mormons, despite the visual similarity, these evangelists identify themselves as representatives of the Church of the Resurrection. Zack Stratis, in the DVD audio commentary accompanying *Could Be Worse,* refers to his LDS-inspired missionary characters generically as "the church guys." In the film itself, Stratis's missionaries identify themselves as representatives of The Only Church of Truth.

Figure 3. The cross engraved on missionary name badges in *The Saviour* exemplifies hybridization.

In some films, the use of Mormon missionary images to represent Christianity in general involves hybridization, where symbols associated with other Christian groups are grafted onto the Mormon image. In *The Saviour*, the missionaries' black badges feature a cross, rather than the name of the LDS Church (figure 3). Instead of the Book of Mormon, missionaries in *The Saviour* distribute softcover editions of the Bible (not the LDS edition), and the character who resembles a mission president is called a pastor. The most blatant—and playful—hybridization occurs in *Orgazmo*, when the missionary Joe kneels to pray before a statue of the Sacred Heart of Jesus he keeps in his apartment (figure 4). What follows is a satire of self-serving prayer: Joe asks God to give him a sign if he shouldn't act in a porn film; an earthquake rocks the apartment, shattering dishes and toppling the statue of Jesus so that its head breaks off; as the earthquake subsides, Joe, unfazed, prays again, "Any sign at all." Another instance of hybridization occurs later in the film, when we follow Joe's Mormon fiancée, Lisa, to the Christian section of a video-rental store, where she peruses titles such as *Jesus Scissorhands* and *Pulp Jesus*. At these moments in the film, Trey Parker combines the Mormon missionary image with artifacts evoking Catholic and evangelical material cultures to take broader satirical swipes.

While these images are plainly not realistic, the use of Mormon missionaries to represent Christians generally ought, in one sense, to please Latter-day Saints because it indicates a measure of success for LDS efforts to persuade outsiders that they are Christian. That intent has been a major focus of LDS proselytizing and public relations since the 1980s, following a rise in anti-Mormon countercult activity that began in the late 1970s. During that period, increased visibility of Mormons

Figure 4. *Orgazmo*'s Elder Young prays before a statue of the Sacred Heart of Jesus.

outside the Intermountain West and the discovery that Mormons shared many social and political concerns with conservative Protestants (such as alarm about the undermining of traditional gender roles) prompted evangelicals and fundamentalists to reassert the boundaries between "authentic" Christianity and the Mormon "cult." The 1982 film *The God Makers* exemplifies this surge in countercult activity.[28]

One way Mormons reacted to evangelical boundary maintenance was to deploy a conspicuously Christ-centered discourse that called attention to what Mormons have in common with other Christians. Landmarks in the increase of Christ-centered LDS discourse include subtitling the Book of Mormon, "Another Testament of Jesus Christ" (1982); adding many Christ-centered songs to the LDS hymnal (1985); adopting more overtly Christ-centered missionary discussions (1986); summarizing the threefold mission of the church as inviting all to come to Christ (1987–88); redesigning the church logo to give greater prominence to the name Jesus Christ (1995); issuing a joint statement by the First Presidency and the Quorum of the Twelve Apostles, "The Living Christ" (2001); requesting that journalists refer to the church as the Church of Jesus Christ (2001); distributing the missionary film, *Finding Faith in Christ* (2003); and launching the Web site jesuschrist.lds.org (2008).

My analysis of missionary images in these films suggests that the LDS Church's efforts to persuade the public that Mormons are Christian have borne fruit. Granted, many evangelicals continue to insist that Mormons differ definitively from other Christians. (Witness the polemics that surrounded Mitt Romney's campaign for the Republican presidential nomination.) Nevertheless, filmmakers who use Mormon missionaries as a metonym for Christians evidently do not regard the differences as significant. These filmmakers take for granted that Mormons represent a variety of Christianity. Indeed, mingling Mormon and evangelical Protestant attributes in *California Sunshine, Me Myself I,* and *Orgazmo* exemplifies precisely the blurring of boundaries that evangelicals have been keen to prevent.

### Missionaries as Sectarians

The kind of Christianity that Mormon missionaries represent is sectarian: intent on conversion, exclusive in its truth claims, and requiring a moral stringency enacted through various forms of abstinence—from sex, from profanity, from alcohol and other beverages. These sectarian attributes set missionaries apart from what filmmakers apparently expect audiences to accept as the cultural norm. Zack Stratis satirically underscores the exclusivity of the missionaries' religion by having them announce that they are from The Only Church of Truth; that designation even appears on their name badges. Missionaries' abstinence from green tea is emphasized in *California Sunshine* and *The Saviour,* the first made in Scotland the second in Australia. The missionaries in *California Sunshine* explain that they drink only herbal or decaffeinated tea since they abstain from stimulants to preserve their bodies as temples. When Malcolm, the missionary protagonist of *The Saviour,* is invited into someone's home for tea, the camera reveals that his teacup contains only water.

Geography is another way that these films signal sectarians' cultural marginality. The missionary characters in *Buckleroos* speak with a strong country twang suggestive of the Bible Belt ("We've come to help you find your soul!"). Twice in *Orgazmo,* the announcement that a character is from Utah prompts somber commiseration—as if the Mormons had announced they suffer from a life-threatening illness. The first exchange occurs when Joe wonders aloud to some of his fellow porn actors why the police don't intervene when gangsters extort money from a small business owner.

> Joe:     Shouldn't we call the police or something? [All laugh.]
> Saffi:   Joe, the police can't help. Jeez, where are you from, Iowa or something?
> Joe:     No, Utah. [Laughter dies.]
> Saffi:   Oh . . . I'm sorry.

Note that while being from Utah is an especially sad fate, the heartland (Iowa) also scores low on the scale of sophistication.

The missionaries' sectarian desire to convert others is greeted with annoyance, even hostility. *Orgazmo, Latter Days, Buckleroos,* and *The Saviour* all include scenes or image montages of missionaries having doors shut in their faces by irritated residents or trying to make street contacts with apathetic passersby. (Such scenes have become a cinematic cliché, employed also in films by LDS directors, such as *God's Army* or *The Best Two Years.*) One of the protagonists in *California Sunshine* begs her boyfriend not to leave her alone with the evangelists. "They're happy fucking clappers," she complains, adding that they've been "spouting the Bible at me for the last ten minutes." Pamela, the protagonist of *Me Myself I,* lashes out at an evangelist who approaches her on the street to ask if she is happy: "Probably a lot happier than you, you patronizing little prick. Now piss off." A character in *The Saviour* kicks a missionary who tries to help her carry groceries.

At the same time, the films mine missionaries' piety, equated with naïveté, for its comedic potential. A recurring gag in *Orgazmo* is that because Joe doesn't use profanity, he vents his anger with impassioned expressions like "gosh darn it" or "ah, heck" and interprets other characters' expletives literally: "Jesus!" "Where?" In addition, he tries to bowdlerize the lines in the porn film he's making, unable even to say "sex" (preferring instead "intercourse"). Missionaries' inexperience with drugs is central to the comedic situation of *California Sunshine,* in which two small-time drug dealers, believing the missionaries are goons sent by their supplier to collect money they don't have, serve the missionaries herbal tea laced with Ecstasy and LSD to put them out of commission. Although the ensuing trip has some dark moments (at one point a howling missionary has to be restrained), the audience is invited to relish the incongruity of the missionaries beginning their first acid trip within minutes of explaining that they don't drink caffeinated tea because they don't believe in taking stimulants. The missionaries' comedic behavior includes bewildered looks as the drugs kick in; an incoherent, heated conversation with each other; fascination with objects like a balloon and an artificial fish; and rapt admiration of the postmodern art pieces that fill their hosts' apartment (figure 5).

A certain ambiguity attends some sectarian images of missionaries. At the same time that Mormon missionaries represent a peculiar, marginal religious group, they also emblematize this group's ability to blend into the social mainstream. The Mormon missionary uniform is distinctive—hence, its use in all these films—but it is simultaneously familiar as the uniform of professionals. *Latter Days* uses the resemblance between Elder Aaron Davis's missionary garb and the white shirt and

Figure 5. An evangelist in *California Sunshine*, patterned after a Mormon
missionary, unwittingly ingests LSD, with comical results.

tie worn by his male love interest while he waits tables at an upscale res-
taurant to create a visual connection when the two first meet: as director
C. Jay Cox explains, they wear the same uniform.[29] In *California Sunshine*
and *Me Myself I*, the use of missionary images turns on the fact that the
uniform may actually prevent missionaries from being recognized. The
drug-dealing couple in *California Sunshine* aren't sure if the two men
in suits who show up at their door have come to break their thumbs
or invite them to church. The protagonist of *Me Myself I* doesn't realize
at first that the young man in white shirt, tie, and backpack who asks
her to complete a survey is in fact an evangelist looking for a convert.
(figure 6). Precisely because of their businesslike image, Mormon missionaries represent stealth sectarians: outsiders who can pass as insiders,
at least at first glance.

### Missionaries and Sexuality

One feature of the sectarianism Mormon missionaries embody
recurs so frequently in these films, and is so thematically prominent, that
it merits separate discussion: conservative sexual mores, especially their
transgression. *The Saviour* is the story of a missionary having an affair
with a woman he claims to be teaching. *Orgazmo* is about a Mormon missionary reluctantly turned porn star. *Latter Days* focuses on a Mormon
missionary coming out as gay. Indeed, a relationship between missionaries and homosexuality is key to three of the seven films in this study. The
pornographic film *Buckleroos* includes a sequence where two Mormon
missionaries, under the spell of a magical belt buckle, are initiated into

Figure 6. Stealth sectarian: This character in *Me Myself I* is not immediately recognizable as a missionary.

the joys of gay sex. *Could Be Worse* draws a different kind of connection to homosexuality by bringing in missionaries to provide a disapproving foil for the protagonist, who proudly asserts his gay identity.

Why are sexual themes so prominent in these films? It is not surprising that *Could Be Worse*'s Zack Stratis would latch onto Mormon missionaries as symbols of religious opposition to homosexuality, considering the publicity surrounding Latter-day Saints' support of campaigns against same-sex marriage (which predated by a decade the particularly fierce controversy over California's Proposition 8 in 2008).[30] At the same time, the fact that missionaries have same-sex companionships opens a possibility for subversive irony: missionaries can simultaneously represent opposition to homosexuality and homosexual potential. Stratis slyly incorporates that irony at the close of the scene that reenacts an actual conversation he had with LDS missionaries about the church's stance on homosexuality. After admitting that their church does not accept homosexuals, the missionaries turn to walk away. An iris-in transition follows them, but instead of the familiar device of narrowing the image with a circular iris while the rest of the screen goes black (like a diminishing spotlight), Stratis encloses the missionaries in a heart-shaped iris and has the screen turn pink—the kind of transition you expect to see in a cheesy wedding video (figure 7). Where Stratis playfully hints at the potential for missionary homosexuality, *Latter Days* and *Buckleroos* fully exploit that possibility to create narratives about missionaries' homosexual awakening.

Even when it's assumed they are heterosexual, Mormon missionaries represent a form of sexual deviance. Mormon elders as sexual deviants

Figure 7. *Could Be Worse* playfully gestures to the potential for missionary homosexuality.

have a long history in film, going back to early-twentieth-century antipolygamy narratives such as *The Mormon Maid* (U.S.A., 1917) and *Trapped by the Mormons* (U.K., 1922), in which lecherous missionaries lure away vulnerable young women.[31] By the turn of the twenty-first century, Mormon missionaries had come to stand for a very different notion of sexual deviance: celibacy, reflecting a shift in surrounding cultural values prompted by the sexual revolution.[32] The idea that young men in their late teens and early twenties would forgo sexual activity is treated as incredible. As a cynical missionary in *Latter Days* marvels, "We're nineteen, twenty years old, and we're not even allowed to beat off!" In an online interview, Peter Templeman reported that the "most amusing moment working on this movie" was "interviewing several Mormon missionaries for research and being told by them all that they never thought about sex." Templeman evidently did not believe the missionaries because he persisted: in the same interview, he identified "the hardest challenge/obstacle on the movie" as "trying to get those Mormon missionaries to talk about sex."[33]

Because of his conspicuously unrealized sexuality, the nineteen-year-old, celibate Mormon elder fits well into stories about repression, hypocrisy, loss of innocence, and sexual discovery. Some filmmakers are attracted to the possibility for dramatic role reversal: the missionary who becomes a convert from naïveté to experience. The reversal unfolds differently in various films. *Orgazmo* plays with it for farcical effect as Elder Joe Young is transformed from zealous, bright-eyed naïf to superhero porn star fighting corruption. In *The Saviour* and *Latter Days*, the missionary's journey into sexual experience coincides with loss of faith. The character arc for *The Saviour*'s Elder Malcolm is quite complicated and will be discussed in the next section.

In *Latter Days*, the arc is more straightforward: missionary Aaron Davis moves from guilt and inner conflict, culminating in a botched suicide attempt, to embracing his homosexuality, denouncing church leaders as hypocritical during a confrontational disciplinary council, and relocating from Idaho to Los Angeles, where he joins a surrogate family of accepting non-Mormon friends. In a less tragic vein, Jerry Douglas, writer of *Buckleroos*, explains that he wrote the sexual initiation of "the two little Mormon boys" into his film because he was attracted to the motif of "a journey of discovery." Apparently in earnest, Douglas enthuses that his fictional missionaries' participation in a homosexual three-way "opens doors . . . they never dreamed existed."[34]

Turning the missionary into a convert through sexual awakening reinforces a sense that religious conservatism is something from which its adherents need to be liberated. As represented by these missionary characters, sectarians are portrayed as naïve, repressed, prejudiced against homosexuals, and closed off to world-opening experiences. But, as we are about to see, this is only half the story.

### Missionaries as Moral Grounding or Agents of Transformation

Narratives about the missionary as naïf or the missionary as convert coincide with a very different trend. In all the films in my pool, with the single exception of the pornographic *Buckleroos*, missionaries are sources of moral grounding or agents of transformation—catalysts for other characters' epiphanies. In that sense, missionaries play in these films the role that LDS leaders want them to be perceived as playing, albeit in ways other than making converts to the LDS Church.

The clearest example of a missionary as agent of transformation occurs in *Latter Days*. The story is built around symmetrical transformations in its two protagonists: Aaron the closeted missionary and Christian the superficial hedonist. As a result of their romance, Aaron experiences sexual awakening that leads him out of the church into a new, accepting community. At the same time, Christian discovers the deeper satisfactions of committed intimacy in contrast to sexual promiscuity; he also begins to take spirituality seriously, becoming involved in a volunteer program to visit shut-ins with AIDS. Thus, although the LDS Church is presented as a homophobic institution from which Aaron needs to be liberated, Aaron's missionary service simultaneously provides a model of spiritual commitment that inspires Christian to change his life.

The type of exchange we see in *Latter Days*—where the missionary learns to be less sectarian while imparting spiritual values to others—appears also in *California Sunshine* and *Orgazmo*, despite these films' much-less-earnest tone. *California Sunshine* involves a conversion-of-the-missionary narrative in which the evangelists undergo an accidental acid trip, which one character describes to them as "a kind of spiritual experience." Supporting this view of the trip, we see the drugged evangelists at one point in a prayerful or meditative pose, kneeling with clasped hands in front of an art installation resembling a home altar. As the evangelists come down from their trip, hired goons suddenly enter, threatening violence. The evangelists save the day, first, by pulling a gun ("The Lord protects those who protect themselves," one of them explains) and then by writing a check for the amount that small-time drug dealer Andy owes his supplier. Impressed by this gun-toting charity, the two goons ask the evangelists how they can join their outfit, and as the film closes, we see the four of them having a discussion about learning "to share with people rather than take from them." Meanwhile, Andy slips out of the apartment with his girlfriend, vowing that he will never do drugs again. The tone is tongue-in-cheek but not entirely parodic: the evangelists' intervention resolves a highly tense climax, and Andy's vow to give up drugs finishes a character arc that began with him lamenting that he became a dealer when all he really wanted to do was be an artist. Thus, while at one level the film acknowledges the silliness of its premise, at another, more serious level, the missionaries provide the moral grounding that allows the plot to be resolved happily.

A similar interplay between the absurd and the serious occurs in *Orgazmo*, though it is tilted more heavily toward the absurd. By the end of the film, Elder Joe Young has become the center of a little group—composed of his Mormon fiancée, some of his fellow porn actors, and the owner of their favorite sushi bar—who bow their heads in prayer in the final scene to dedicate themselves to fighting corruption in Los Angeles (figure 8). Their chief weapon will be the Orgazmorator, a gunlike device that incapacitates villains by giving them paralyzing orgasms. Farcical as this is, it is also true that Joe, who leads the group in prayer in this scene, functions throughout *Orgazmo* as the film's moral center. His idealism, despite being a target for satire, is also the impetus that turns porn actors into crime fighters. Furthermore, Joe provides pastoring for his sidekick, Ben Chapleski, by helping him resolve an existential drama centered on Ben's feelings of rejection by his father. All of this, I hasten to reiterate, overflows with burlesque. But underneath, the film demonstrates that Joe's idealism and moral high-mindedness have redeeming social value.

Filmmaker Trey Parker made the same point explicitly some years later in the episode "All about the Mormons?" for his Comedy Central

Figure 8. Elder Young leads crimefighting porn actors in prayer at the conclusion of *Orgazmo*.

series *South Park*. After having great fun at Mormons' expense, the episode gives the final word to one of the Mormon characters, who declares that while Mormons may "believe in crazy stories that make absolutely no sense," the LDS Church also teaches the importance of "loving your family, being nice, and helping people" and therefore deserves respect. *Orgazmo* conveys something of the same idea.[35]

In *Latter Days, California Sunshine,* and *Orgazmo,* missionaries inspire others by their example of service, charity, or idealism. In *Could Be Worse* and *Me Myself I,* the missionaries become catalysts of other characters' transformations in more complicated ways. Zack Stratis's encounter with missionaries midway through *Could Be Worse* comes at a moment when he (as a character in the film) is conflicted over how open to be about his homosexuality because he knows that it makes his family uncomfortable. When the missionaries arrive at his door, Stratis asks whether homosexuals are allowed in their church. The missionaries respond that the church welcomes everyone, including homosexuals, but that to become a member, he would need to stop "practicing it." Stratis objects that not allowing him to be what he is doesn't seem very welcoming. Taking this epiphany to heart, he appears in the next scene hanging a rainbow flag outside his parents' home over his father's protest that he shouldn't be "that gay." The missionaries thus serve as unintentional catalysts for Stratis's gay pride.

*Me Myself I* offers another instance of a missionary whose brief appearance unintentionally contributes to the protagonist's transformation. Pamela Drury is deeply unhappy about still being single and wonders if she made a mistake in not marrying Robert Dickson, a love interest nearly fifteen years earlier. She is so unhappy that, early in the film, she attempts to commit suicide by immersing a hair dryer in the bathtub but is saved at the last second by a providential power outage. In the very next scene, Pamela encounters a missionary on the street who asks if she considers herself happy—and then, seeing her hesitation, seizes the moment to ask if she has faith in Jesus Christ. Pamela lashes out at the missionary, insisting that she's probably happier than he is. She then steps into the street, is hit by a car, and wakes up in a parallel reality where, for the past thirteen years, she has been married to Dickson. Through the rest of the film, Pamela discovers that marriage is no guarantee of happiness. Lesson learned, she is mysteriously transported back to her own reality, prepared to enjoy her singleness even as she anticipates the potential for a new relationship. Because Pamela's encounter with the missionary is the apparent trigger propelling her into the parallel reality, the encounter takes on an uncanny aspect. It is possible to read the missionary as a rough analogue to the angel who ushers George Bailey into a parallel world in Frank Capra's *It's a Wonderful Life* (1946). Be that as it may, filmmaker Pip Karmel certainly incorporates Pamela's encounter with the missionary into the mysterious events that ultimately lead her to accept her life as it is. Thus, as in *Could Be Worse*—though now with a twist of magic realism—the missionary character functions as a catalyst for an unintended epiphany.

When *The Saviour*'s Elder Malcolm acts to change the lives of other characters, his intervention proves morally ambiguous. The short film reaches its climax when Malcolm, after being rebuffed by Carmel, the married woman with whom he has been sleeping, confronts Carmel's husband Tony at their home. Malcolm intends to inform Tony of the adultery so that he will end the marriage, which Malcolm imagines will free Carmel to marry him. Before he can make his revelation, however, Malcolm learns two things: first, that Carmel is, in Tony's words, a "passionate atheist" who despises missionaries (Malcolm sees her kick his companion when he offers to help her carry groceries into the house); second, that Carmel has just become pregnant, even though doctors have told Tony he is sterile. Tony, more credulous than Carmel, asks Malcolm if he believes her pregnancy may be "a bona fide miracle." Realizing how Carmel has used him, Malcolm locks eyes with her, then dramatically informs Tony that the Bible is "full of miracles like the one you've just experienced." As Malcolm walks out of the house, his companion begins to teach a receptive Tony while Carmel looks on in dismay.

The transformations that occur in this film are complex and unexpected. Malcolm has, it appears, abruptly lost his faith but cultivates Tony's to take vengeance on Carmel, who, in the final scene, moves swiftly from fear of exposure to relief to the realization that she has lost control of the situation in an entirely different way than she feared. The film plays overtly with ironies connected with missionaries proclaiming the truth. At the beginning of his confrontation with Tony, Malcolm says, "You cannot live your life in darkness, my friend, or the darkness will grow. I live by the truth, and I'm here to help you see the light." In addition to being encoded with double meaning—the statement could refer to either to Malcolm's proselytizing or his intention to reveal his adultery with Carmel—the statement is also ironic because Malcolm has been lying to his companion and other missionaries to conceal his affair. The statement acquires deeper irony when Malcolm, having seen the light about Carmel's deception, opts to endorse a faith in which he apparently no longer believes to keep Tony in the dark—but now in a way that turns Carmel's deception against her. One would be hard pressed to extract a message from this film, but as a character study, it hinges on, and plays subversively with, the idea that missionaries bring people into light and knowledge and thus alter their lives.

The missionary characters in these films promote epiphanies or transformations far removed from gaining a testimony of the Book of Mormon or being baptized into the LDS Church. Instead, these missionaries inspire a range of activities lurching from the earnest to the parodic: taking meals to people with AIDS, fighting crime with a high-tech sex toy, embracing one's homosexuality, giving up drugs, learning to share with others instead of extorting from them, learning not to fear being single. In one case—*The Saviour*—the transformations wrought by a missionary are morally ambiguous. On the other hand, there is the following to consider: LDS viewers would doubtless find these representations of missionaries inaccurate; many would find them offensive as well. Nevertheless, these images suggest that Mormons have succeeded in forging an association in observers' minds: an encounter with nineteen-year-old boys in white shirts and ties can, however improbably, change your life.

## Conclusion

Like other religious images or goods, the standardized image that LDS elders communicate by their dress, grooming, and material culture can be expropriated as it circulates through public spaces around the globe. This essay has examined how filmmakers from different parts of the English-speaking world have recently replicated, or more loosely evoked, the Mormon missionary image for their own purposes. By metonymy or hybridization, filmmakers have used the missionary image to represent conservative, sectarian Christianity generally. Filmmakers have been particularly interested in using the Mormon elder to represent repressed or unrealized sexuality, gay as well as straight.

Filmmakers often deploy the missionary image in ways that invite viewers to adopt either amused or disapproving attitudes toward people who as appear to operate from the margins of modern life. Nevertheless, filmmakers' expropriations of the missionary image have more in common than one might expect with the meanings that the LDS Church attaches to the image. Observations of LDS missionaries, however casual, have evidently convinced these filmmakers to cast elders (1) as representatives of Christian evangelism, an equation that many evangelical Christians probably contest, and (2) as emblems of moral grounding or the possibility of personal transformation. By encouraging the audiences of their films to associate these meanings with the missionary image, the filmmakers carry out cultural work that may serve Mormon interests to a greater degree than either Mormons or the filmmakers realize.

Recent scholarship on the globalization and materiality of religion has informed this study. David Morgan's work on Protestant visual culture and Colleen McDannell's study of Christian material culture have underscored the roles that images and objects play to make religion happen.[36] This literature participates in a trend within religious studies that examines religion as it takes place in sites other than obvious religious spaces such as churches and temples. These alternative sites include public places, the home, and the body, all of which are relevant to the study of Mormon missionary work. I have conceptualized the Mormon missionary image as a material product manufactured by disciplining elders' bodies through dress and grooming regulations. Although church leaders intend the missionary image to communicate specific religious messages—about the dignity of missionaries' work and their office as ambassadors of the Lord—it becomes expropriatable because it circulates through public spaces. Materially re-created and adapted for film, the missionary image recirculates in ways, and to ends, that Mormons do not intend. However, according to my argument, expropriated versions of the missionary image continue to communicate messages that the LDS Church conveys—for example, that Mormons are Christian.

The use of Mormon missionary images in non-LDS films involves encounter, appropriation, and replacement, dynamics currently of interest to scholars who examine religion and globalization. These dynamics become increasingly relevant to Mormon studies as the LDS Church's international presence expands. The concept of globalization is especially relevant to Mormon expansion because the church's centralized organization remains headquartered in the United States and is still dominated by American leaders, bureaucrats, and culture. Thus, like the dominant cultural goods in today's globalized economy (films, music, popular fashions), Mormon religious goods such as the missionary image customarily originate in the U.S.A. and are then transported to other countries, where they invite acceptance, resistance, indifference, or adaptation. Understanding Mormonism as an international religion entails seeing it as globalized, not simply global. In other words, Mormonism should be understood as a form of globalization. This understanding must include, then, the way Mormons and others receive and use Mormon religious goods around the globe. In addition, the power relations implicated in the production, distribution, and use of Mormon religious goods need to be elucidated. These are areas that invite further scholarship.

Although I have not entirely ignored the question of how Mormons ought to feel about the ways filmmakers have used the missionary image, I have attempted to complicate the dichotomy of fair and sympathetic versus stereotypical and prejudiced that has framed previous studies of Mormons in the media. Key to this attempt has been my reconceptualizing of the missionary image as a manufactured, adaptable, and circulating material good, rather than an abstract reflection—accurate, distorted, or otherwise. None of the films examined here single out Mormonism for commentary: in every case, Mormon missionaries, or hybridized characters with characteristics of Mormon missionaries, function emblematically to make broader comments about conservative, sectarian Christianity. Furthermore, these images function in complicated ways, subverting certain messages that the church intends the missionary image to communicate, yet reinforcing others. The classic antagonism-or-acceptance frame for the study of Mormon media images obscures these complexities.

In this study, then, I have avoided interpreting Mormon media images as if Mormons are objects of commentary (and thus subject either to social stigma or approbation). Instead, I have conceptualized Mormons as contributors to a widely shared cultural lexicon—a public pool of commonly recognized symbols like the missionary image that can be reinterpreted, recombined, and redeployed to multiple, competing ends. This perspective illuminates more clearly the plurivocal nature of Mormon media images and pushes against rhetoric about Mormon victimization by highlighting the way Mormons assemble and circulate self-representations that inform outsiders' representations of them. At the same time, this perspective underscores the impossibility of Mormons' controlling public images of themselves. The LDS missionary image would not be available for expropriation as a symbol immediately recognized by viewers around the world if church leaders had not invested so much effort in maintaining "a unified and dignified image" for missionary elders.[37] Ironically, the church tries so hard to control the missionary image worldwide that it enables filmmakers to take over that image for their own ends.

## Notes

1. Although single women and married couples also serve missions, single men constitute by far the majority of full-time missionaries. The number of LDS missionaries called rose dramatically, and more or less steadily, after 1960, jumping as much as forty-six hundred from one year to the next. The number of missionaries serving reached a high point of more than sixty-one thousand in 2002, then declined to fifty-six thousand in 2004. *2005 Church Almanac*, 630, 635. Recently the *Church Almanac* discontinued publishing statistics for missionaries serving but continues to track the number of new missionaries called. The recent decline in the number of missionaries is probably due to the "raising of the bar" on standards for missionary service that church leadership announced in 2002. Apropos arguments later in this essay about sectarianism and sexuality in representations of Mormon missionaries, the stricter standards included cracking down on sexual transgression, violations of the church's proscriptions on tobacco and alcohol, vulgar language, and, in general, a "semicommitted" attitude toward the church. Ballard, "The Greatest Generation of Missionaries." 46–48.

2. Vásquez and Friedmann Marquardt, *Globalizing the Sacred*; Morgan, *The Sacred Gaze*. Morgan defines expropriation as "the application of images to religious or political ends other than those sought by the missionary." He distinguishes expropriation from appropriation: appropriation occurs when converts "adapt nonnative motifs to the visual rhetoric and vocabulary of their own rather than the missionary's culture" (151), whereas expropriation results when outsiders adapt a tradition's religious images. The examples of expropriation in the text come from Vásquez and Marquardt, 214–15 (the Guatemalan hotline); and Morgan, 164–65 (the Sallman painting).

3. Lambert, "The Image of Mormons in Films," 12–15; Nelson, "From Antagonism to Acceptance," 58–69; D'Arc, "Mormons, Image of: Film," 2:947–48; and Astle and Burton, "A History of Mormon Cinema," 12–163. See also Nibley, "How Mormons See Themselves in Film," 14–17, which urges Mormons to be less defensive about the way they are represented in films. The phrase "treat the Church fairly and positively" comes from Astle and Burton, 121. The expression "Mormon-exploitation films" comes from Astle and Burton, 124; and "screen persecution" comes from Nelson, 65.

4.  For discussions of recent missionary-themed films by LDS filmmakers, see Astle and Burton, "A History of Mormon Cinema," 135–47; and Givens, *People of Paradox*, 274–79.
5.  Morgan and Promey, *The Visual Culture of American Religions*, 15–17.
6.  *Missionary's Hand Book* (1937), 55; *Missionary Handbook* (1973), 13; *Missionary Handbook* (1986), 9–10.
7.  The March 3, 1975, circular, signed by Ezra Taft Benson, president of the Quorum of the Twelve Apostles, is reproduced in *Missionary Training Program Binder* (1983), A8. For similar photos of acceptable haircuts in information packets for newly called elders, see *Missionary Appearance and Grooming* (1988); and *General Instructions for Full-Time Missionaries* (1991).
8.  The 1998 revision to *Dress and Grooming Guidelines for Elders* dropped the requirement about boots needing to look like business shoes.
9.  *Dress and Grooming Guidelines for Elders* (1995); *Dress and Grooming Guidelines for Elders* (1998).
10. Sonntag, "The Faith of Our People"; and Buys, "Making Friends" both mention that missionary elders can wear *ta'ovalas*..
11. *Culture for Missionaries*, 124.
12. *Mission President's Handbook* (1985), 14; *Manual del presidente de misión* (1990), 15; *Manual del presidente de misión* (1997), 48. I had to consult some editions of the mission president's handbook in Spanish due to the seemingly inconsistent restrictions on church leadership manuals at the LDS Church History Library and Archives (e.g., the library gave me access to a 1997 Spanish edition of the handbook but not to the 1996 English edition). A church librarian who examined the restricted materials for me reported that the 1996 and 2001 English editions of the handbook contain "no specifications for missionary name-tag use." Letter from Brittany Chapman, LDS Church History Library and Archives, Salt Lake City, June 12, 2008.
13. For accounts of missionaries in Romania and Russia not being allowed to wear badges for a time, see the Stout Papers and the Varney Papers. (The papers are restricted, but relevant information about badges appears in the publicly available summaries in the library's electronic catalogue.) Also church service missionaries are not required to wear badges; see instructions in *Name Tag Order Information* (1999).
14. For photos of the changing badge styles, see Heslop, "Language Training," 8–10; "Lady Missionaries Use Hymns to Teach Gospel Discussions," 15; "News of the Church," 141; *Ensign*, March 1979 cover image; and *Ensign*, May 1981, 12, 26, 30, 32–33, 35. For instructions to mission presidents about not using alternative or altered badges, see *Mission President's Handbook* (1985), 14; and *Manual del presidente de misión* (1990), 15.
15. *Name Tag Order Information* (1999).
16. Reproduced in *Missionary Training Program Binder* (1983), A8.
17. *Dress and Grooming Guidelines for Elders* (1998).
18. *Mission President's Handbook of Instructions* (c1961), M-4. For other uses of the term *conservative* in connection with missionary dress, see *Missionary's Hand Book* (1937), 55; *Missionary Handbook* (1973), 13; *Mission President's Handbook* (1981), 22; *Missionary Handbook* (1986), 9; *General Instructions for Full-Time Missionaries* (1991); and *Dress and Grooming Guidelines for Elders* (1995).

19. *Dress and Grooming Guidelines for Elders* (1998).
20. *Dress and Grooming Guidelines for Elders* (1995); *Missionary's Hand Book* (1937), 55; *Name Tag Order Information* (1999).
21. Distribution data was obtained from Box Office Mojo, available at http://www.boxofficemojo.com, accessed March 25, 2008. "Widest release" refers to the number of theaters where a film plays at one time, not the total number of theaters that screen the film over its entire release period (which will be higher).
22. Information about festival screenings and awards came from the Internet Movie Database, available at http://imdb.com, and GayVN Awards, available at http://www.gayvnawards.com.
23. In the audio commentary accompanying the DVD, director C. Jay Cox states that all the actors portraying missionaries in the film wore temple garments as part of their costuming. ("That's just one more reason that I'm going to hell for this movie," Cox remarks.) He does not explain how he obtained the garments. *Latter Days*, directed by C. Jay Cox, DVD. Aaron's dramatically stripping off the garment before having sex for the first time—an act meant to symbolize stripping off his inhibitions, according to Cox's audio commentary—is similar to a scene in Tony Kushner's play *Angels in America, Part II: Perestroika,* when Mormon Joe Pitt pulls off his garment at a beach to show that he's willing to give up everything to be with his male lover. In the film version of *Angels in America,* directed by Mike Nichols, Joe and his wife, Harper, wear garments in an earlier scene while they talk in their bedroom. As in *Latter Days,* the makers of *Angels in America* obtained actual temple garments: the marks on them are visible in some shots.
24. While it is conceivable that the display of garments in *Latter Days* or *Angels in America* may have helped prompt the new policy, church leaders were more likely responding to the much-publicized desecration of a temple garment by a protestor at the October 2003 General Conference. See "At Conference Time, Temple Square Becomes Battle Ground," 74; "Religious Leaders Denounce Garment Desecration," 77; and "Church Issues New Policy for Selling Garments," 55.
25. All about the Mormons?" 2003.
26. This interview appeared at http://www.oscar.com on a page featuring *The Saviour* as an Academy Award nominee for best live-action short film in 2007. The page was last accessed in early January 2008; it went off-line after the nominees for the 2008 Academy Awards were announced.
27. Zack Stratis recounts this encounter in the audio commentary accompanying the DVD of *Could Be Worse.*.
28. Shipps, *Sojourner in the Promised Land,* 341, 346–47, 350–51.
29. Audio commentary, *Latter Days,* directed by C. Jay Cox, DVD.
30. Another instance of Mormon missionaries as emblems of opposition to same-sex marriage is a controversial television ad produced during the Proposition 8 debates by the Courage Campaign, an organization lobbying against the proposed ban on same-sex marriage. Titled "Home Invasion: Vote NO on Prop 8," the ad depicts two young men in white shirts and ties knocking on the door of a suburban lesbian couple. The young men identify themselves as representatives of the LDS Church, using the church's

full name. The missionaries then muscle their way into the couple's home, confiscate their wedding rings, and rip up their marriage license.

31.  Nelson, "From Antagonism to Acceptance"; Astle and Burton, "A History of Mormon Cinema," 30–35. Compare Terryl Givens's discussion of Mormon images in nineteenth- and twentieth-century popular literature, where sexual deviance is one persistent theme. Givens, *The Viper on the Hearth*, chaps. 7–8.

32.  On a similar note, Terryl Givens has remarked that in the late-twentieth century, "it is now because Mormons occupy what used to be the center that they fall into contempt. The embrace of ultraconservative values, not their flagrant rejection, is now construed as the source of Mormon perfidy" *Viper on the Hearth*, 164. Givens's tone is aggrieved in a way I tried to avoid in this study, but I agree that the reasons Mormons are perceived as deviant have shifted as a result of changing cultural values after their postpolygamy transformation.

33.  See note 26.

34.  From an interview with Jerry Douglas in *eXposed: The Making of a Legend*, directed by Pam Dore, DVD. *eXposed* is a playful, but not satirical, documentary about the making of *Buckleroos*.

35.  "All about the Mormons?" 2003. Astle and Burton offer a similar reading of *Orgazmo* and the *South Park* episode: "While *Orgazmo* has its share of inaccuracies and cheap barbs, in the end Mormon values are rewarded and the faith defended, something that has also proven true—with the expected jokes and irony—in Parker's subsequent project, the animated series *South Park*" "A History of Mormon Cinema," 125.

36.  Morgan, *The Sacred Gaze*; Morgan and Promey, *The Visual Culture of American Religions*; McDannell, *Material Christianity*.

37.  *Name Tag Order Information* (1999), front side, no pagination

## Bibliography

"All About the Mormons?" Episode 712 in *South Park*. Comedy Central, November 19, 2003.

Astle, Randy, and Gideon O. Burton. "A History of Mormon Cinema." *BYU Studies* 46, no. 2 (2007): 12–163.

"At Conference Time, Temple Square Becomes Battle Ground." *Sunstone*, October 2003, 74.

Ballard, M. Russell. "The Greatest Generation of Missionaries." *Ensign*, November 2002, 46–48.

*Buckleroos*, directed by Jerry Douglas and John Rutherford TLA Releasing, 2004.

Buys, Callie. "Making Friends: Benjamin and Molitika Tuione of South Jordan, Utah." *Friends*, March 2005, 17–19.

*California Sunshine*, directed by David Mackenzie. Sigma Films, 1997.

Church of Jesus Christ of Latter-day Saints. *Dress and Grooming Guidelines for Elders*. Salt Lake City: Church of Jesus Christ of Latter-day Saints, 1995.

———. *Dress and Grooming Guidelines for Elders*. Salt Lake City: Church of Jesus Christ of Latter-day Saints, 1998.

————. *General Instructions for Full-Time Missionaries*. Salt Lake City: Church of Jesus Christ of Latter-day Saints, 1991.

————. *Manual del presidente de misión*. Salt Lake City: Church of Jesus Christ of Latter-day Saints, 1990.

————. *Manual del presidente de misión*. Salt Lake City: Church of Jesus Christ of Latter-day Saints, 1997.

————. *Missionary Appearance and Grooming*. Salt Lake City: Church of Jesus Christ of Latter-day Saints, 1988.

————. *Missionary Handbook*. Salt Lake City: Church of Jesus Christ of Latter-day Saints, 1973.

————. *Missionary Handbook*. Salt Lake City: Church of Jesus Christ of Latter-day Saints, 1986.

————. *The Missionary's Hand Book*. Salt Lake City: Church of Jesus Christ of Latter-day Saints, 1937.

————. *Missionary Training Program Binder*. Salt Lake City: Church of Jesus Christ of Latter-day Saints, 1983.

————. *Mission President's Handbook*. Salt Lake City: Church of Jesus Christ of Latter-day Saints, 1985.

*Could Be Worse*, directed by Zack Stratis. Aquarian Productions, 2004. DVD.

*Culture for Missionaries: Guatemala Indian*. Provo, UT: Missionary Training Center, 1980.

D'Arc, James V. "Mormons, Image of: Film." *Encyclopedia of Mormonism*, edited by Daniel H. Ludlow, 2:947–48. New York: Macmillan, 1992.

Douglas, Jerry. Interview in *eXposed: The Making of a Legend*, directed by Pam Dore. 2006. DVD.

Givens, Terryl. *People of Paradox: A History of Mormon Culture*. New York: Oxford University Press, 2007.

————. *The Viper on the Hearth: Mormons, Myths, and the Construction of Heresy*. New York: Oxford University Press, 1997.

Heslop, J. M. "Language Training." *LDS Church News*, February 15, 1969, 8–10.

"Lady Missionaries Use Hymns to Teach Gospel Discussions." *LDS Church News*, August 19, 1973.

Lambert, Linda. "The Image of Mormons in Films." *New Era*, May 1972, 12–15.

*Latter Days*, directed by C. Jay Cox. 2004. DVD.

McDannell, Colleen. *Material Christianity: Religion and Popular Culture in America*. New Haven, CT: Yale University Press, 1995.

*Me Myself I*, directed by Pip Karmel. Gaumont, 1999. DVD.

Morgan, David. *The Sacred Gaze: Religious Visual Culture in Theory and Practice*. Berkeley and Los Angeles: University of California Press, 2005.

Morgan, David, and Sally M. Promey, eds. *The Visual Culture of American Religions*. Berkeley and Los Angeles: University of California Press, 2001.

Nelson, Richard Alan. "From Antagonism to Acceptance: Mormons and the Silver Screen." *Dialogue: A Journal of Mormon Thought* 10, no. 3 (Spring 1977): 58–69.

"News of the Church." *Ensign*, January 1974, 141.

Nibley, Paul. "How Mormons See Themselves in Film." *Sunstone*, July 1993, 14–17.

*Orgasmo*, directed by Trey Parker. Kuziu Enterprises, 1998. DVD.

"Religious Leaders Denounce Garment Desecration." *Sunstone*, December 2003, 77.

*The Saviour,* directed by Peter Templeman. Australian Film, Television, and Radio School, 2005. DVD.

Shipps, Jan. *Sojourner in the Promised Land: Forty Years among the Mormons.* Urbana: University of Illinois Press, 2000.

Sonntag, Phillip T. "The Faith of Our People." *Ensign,* November 1984. http://www.lds.org.

Stout, Diane Elizabeth Weaver. Stout Papers, 1999–2003, MS 18406. LDS Church Archives.

*2005 Church* Almanac. Salt Lake City: Deseret News, 2004.

Varney, Aaron Cassidy. Varney Papers, 1999–2001, MS 17143. LDS Church Archives.

Vásquez Manuel A., and Marie Friedmann Marquardt. *Globalizing the Sacred: Religion across the Americas.* New Brunswick, NJ: Rutgers University Press, 2003.

# 6

# "I Constructed in My Mind a Vast, Panoramic Picture"

The Miracle Life of Edgar Mint *and Postmodern, Postdenominational Mormonism*

MARK T. DECKER

Most contemporary portrayals of Mormonism are heavily influenced by the nineteenth century. It has been more than a hundred years since mainstream Mormonism officially encouraged the scandalous behaviors—polygamy and blood atonement, for example—that generated the river of lurid tales that flowed from nineteenth-century presses. Yet despite the passing of time and the gradual taming of Mormonism, contemporary authors and auteurs tend to portray the religion in ways that invite comparison with their pulpy forebears. Television and film provide the most recent examples, with HBO's *Big Love* and 2007's limited-release film *September Dawn* playing, or at least attempting to play, to popular culture's appetite for portraying Mormonism's putative penchant for sexual aberration and violence.

Meanwhile, in Mormon literary and intellectual circles, some still yearn for the realization of nineteenth-century Mormon apostle and University of Utah Chancellor Orson F. Whitney's prediction that someday Mormon Miltons and Shakespeares will arise. Although a healthy regional market for LDS fiction and films has evolved in the Intermountain West, Whitney dreamed of the day when nationally and internationally visible Mormon literati would take the message of Joseph Smith "to the high and mighty, even to kings and nobles,"[1] spreading the Mormon gospel through compelling poetry and prose.

The stark polarity between the generally unappealing portrayal of Mormonism in contemporary popular culture and the artful proselytizing some Mormons would like to see gracing the *New York Times*'s best-seller list or breaking box-office records hides a fundamental similarity beyond their debt to the nineteenth century: both modes of representation make assumptions about Mormonism as a whole. For non-Mormons writing to a national audience, Latter-Day Saints are deviant and/or delusional and, as such, worthy of caricature. For the faithful who write for a Mormon audience, the Saints are followers of a divinely inspired gospel and, as such, worthy of hagiography. While these two formulations have been successful in generating sales in the national and Mormon markets respectively, they are both artistically and ideologically limiting. Setting aside the question of whether Joseph Smith was a fraud—the issue fueling the dichotomy—it is easy to realize that a religion with millions of adherents contains not just a Mormon experience but many Mormon experiences; that the devout head of a large household in rural Utah who can trace his ancestry back to Brigham Young probably describes Mormonism in a very different way from a woman in, say, Atlanta who dimly remembers allowing herself to be baptized years before by a persistent missionary. Clearly, Mormonism is experienced locally.

Indeed, instead of relying on existing condemnatory or hagiographic metanarratives, it would be better to assume that adherents experience *any* religion in ways mediated by social forces and individual proclivities. Consequently, a religiously marked literary character's experience would not speak to the theological claims made by that character's religion in a totalizing way. Such a portrayal of localized Mormonism exists in *The Miracle Life of Edgar Mint*. In this novel, Brady Udall creates a postmodern, postdenominational version of Mormonism that is compelling precisely because it caricatures the religion while still granting it a level of spiritual validity.

*Edgar Mint*, a picaresque tale of a biracial Apache boy's quest to find the man who ran over his head with a mail jeep, is not primarily about Mormonism. Both Edgar's conversion to that faith and his stay with a Mormon family, the Madsens, however, are key to the book's structure and Edgar's development. Edgar lives in Richland, a fictional small Utah town, with the Madsens because for a brief time he is part of the LDS Church's Indian Student Placement Program, a now-defunct effort to give Native American children on reservations access to a better education by having them spend the school year living with middle- and upper-class Mormon families. During the program's existence, most Mormons also believed that Native Americans were the descendants of the Lamanites, a group of people who play a prominent role in the Book of Mormon.[2] Consequently, most Mormons assumed that this program was also designed to convert the descendants of Book of Mormon characters Laman and Lemuel to Mormonism. Because most of America did not believe that sending Native American children to live with middle-class white people during the school year represented the fulfillment of predictions by ancient prophets, however, non-Mormons saw the program as problematic.

The relatively few academic investigations of the program have provided a more nuanced picture, however. A study conducted in the early 1970s with the assistance of LDS Social Services and headed by an investigator who was a professor at Brigham Young University revealed a disheartening "failure of such a dramatic change in environment to produce some changes in these children that would lead to increases in educational competency."[3] Writing a few years later, University of California San Diego anthropologist Martin Topper did concede in a largely critical article that the program "spared the children the depersonalizing experiences that many of the parents had suffered when they attended B.I.A. boarding schools" and that it was "less traumatic for the child than placement in a distant missionary boarding school."[4] More recently Tona Hangen conducted an oral-history project that focused on placement alumni whom the LDS Church could view as "success stories." Yet Hangen was surprised by the "depth of ambiguity" her interviewees expressed. Most of these placement alumni described "painful memories of belonging to two worlds and yet to neither."[5]

Udall could have employed a variation of either one of the extant master narratives describing Mormonism to frame Edgar's experience with the Madsens, presenting it as one more instance of the implicit white supremacy of America's homegrown religious fanatics or an illustration of the beneficial wisdom of the institutional Mormon Church. Instead, his subtler approach resonates with the academic investigations, making Edgar's experiences encompass elements that discredit as well as praise the Church of Jesus Christ of Latter-day Saints and therefore ultimately only explain Edgar Mint. Before his baptism, Edgar imagines "a vast panoramic picture" of what life in the placement program will be like. He pictures "a little town with painted houses and" green lawns that are "weedless and perfectly square." He also sees "children riding on bicycles down smooth blacktop streets, trailing a truck that played music and made ice cream available to anyone who wanted it."[6] Clearly Edgar hopes that his new religion will bring him a life as neatly plotted and safe as those portrayed on a sitcom.

Yet Edgar's actual experience humorously contrasts with this initial vision in part because his lived Mormonism is an idiosyncratic perspective, not the artificially panoramic picture of missionary tracts or anti-Mormon screeds. An important part of the contrast between Edgar's panorama and the Mormonism he actually encounters lies in Udall's portrayal of the host family. Instead of Mormon versions of Ward and June Cleaver or Jim and Margaret Anderson, Udall depicts a couple engaged in a rarely articulated, yet complex, negotiation with a religion that purports to offer answers to every question. Because in important ways they are on their way to becoming postmodern spiritual seekers like him, Edgar bonds with his host family in spite of very real cultural differences and the ultimate failure of Mormonism to give him a lasting spiritual home. At the end of the novel, Edgar is no longer Mormon, but it is also clear that his experience as a Mormon living in a Mormon family has not been without spiritual and emotional benefit. It is easy to understand why he abandons the religion, but it is also easy to see why he holds no bitterness and carries pieces of the religion with him. To understand fully *Edgar Mint*'s panorama of personal spiritual experience, however, we must also explore the impact of postmodernism on spirituality in the United States, examining the postdenominationalism that is gradually transforming organized religion. We will also investigate Udall's relationship to Mormonism and historicize his use of the Indian Placement Program.

*Postmodern* is a contested term, but this essay simply stipulates that there are many ways of describing the postmodern—and rightfully so—while employing Jean-Francoise Lyotard's contention, forcefully articulated in *The Postmodern Condition*, that "incredulity toward metanarratives" is the hallmark of postmodernity.[7] According to this definition, *The Miracle Life of Edgar Mint* is a postmodern text. Edgar is the child of an Apache woman and a white man from Connecticut and is reared not only by his mother but also by hospital staff and patients, a Mormon foster family, and a Filipina who lives in rural Pennsylvania and is a devout member of the Joy of All Who Sorrow Ukrainian Orthodox Church. This hybrid biology and polyglot upbringing make it impossible to explain him solely by referring to Apache culture.[8] Edgar's accident bequeaths him a memory rivaling that of Borges's "Funes the Memorious." According to Edgar, "there is no such thing as forgetting, nothing is hazy or vague. I can remember it all: every name, every glance, every word, every throwaway scrap of a moment." This debilitating level of recall leaves him "obsessed with memory, with facts, with history on the smallest scale."[9]

In addition to his memories, Edgar possesses a "secret collection of odds and ends" that he believes are "pieces of some vast, complicated puzzle," yet he cannot see a coherent pattern in the data he collects. This distresses Edgar, who enjoys reading western because they are the "most straightforward" and "the easiest to understand." Despite his fondness for the clarity of Louis L'Amour, however, Edgar comes to the conclusion that his life "could be contained in a word": accidents.[10] In other words, like Oedipa Maas trying to figure out who or what the Trystero is, Edgar seeks a unifying narrative that will explain his life, even though he doubts that such a narrative can exist.

If Lyotard's way of describing postmodernity is particularly useful when dealing with the overall tone of *The Miracle Life of Edgar Mint*, his contentions also help illuminate the novel's commentary on religion. In spite of the evidence he gathers for the chaotic nature of the universe, Edgar holds out hope that his memories and collections can prove that there is some divine force guiding his existence. As Edgar explains, his life has left him unable to tell the difference "between an accident and a miracle."[11] Edgar is thus a postmodern seeker chasing an ever-receding traditional religious metanarrative, and his ultimate disappointment speaks volumes about the inability of conventional religions to hold onto their postmodern flocks. Because they posit an all-powerful and all-knowing God and an easily understood teleology, most religious traditions have found themselves gradually losing influence in post-modern society. Powerful at the beginning of the nineteenth century, the Christian metanarrative found itself becoming unfashionable as the rational skepticism underpinning the scientific and industrial advances of the past two centuries created the intellectual conditions necessary for postmodernity to emerge. As Lyotard argues, "Science, 'smiling into its beard' at every other belief," taught the inhabitants of the nineteenth, twentieth, and twenty-first centuries "the harsh austerity of realism."[12] While atheism is not new, the collision between scientific rationalism and religious faith left many believing something on one level that they knew was implausible on another. As more and more people developed the ability to keep two contradictory narratives at bay within the same psyche, the intellectual and emotional ground-work was laid for the multiplicity of micronarratives that defines the postmodern condition, which is deftly depicted in Edgar's inability to tell accidents from miracles.

Edgar would not even be able to think about miracles, however, if religious metanarrative had been completely discredited. Instead, the proliferation of micronarratives—as Frederic Jameson offers in his foreword to the English edition of *The Postmodern Condition*—has given established metanarratives "continuing but now *unconscious* affectivity as a way of 'thinking about' and acting" in a given situation.[13] In this formulation, religious metanarrative—which obviously hasn't disappeared from popular discourse and is therefore not necessarily unconscious in the way Jameson suggests—becomes a cognitive strategy available to those who are comfortable thinking in that idiom. Instead of explaining everything, religion explains some things some of the time—some things may be miracles after all—and a character like Edgar Mint can pick up a vigorously totalizing religion like Mormonism, use it until it no longer helps him understand the world, and then put it down again. This strategic rejection is apparent in Edgar's reaction to the violent death of Cecil, his best friend from Willie Sherman, a reservation boarding school:

> I tried very hard to convince myself that God and Jesus and the
> resurrection were just a bunch of lies told by some well-meaning
> anglos, but it was no use. God was out there. He had touched me
> and I had felt his presence, which was more than I can say about
> my own father . . . but because I believed He existed did not mean
> that I had to trust Him, or even like Him. . . . I could come to only
> one of two conclusions: either God was a crazed lunatic or He was
> just plain mean.[14]

Though Edgar feels betrayed by his new religious beliefs, the core of the metanarrative cannot be dismissed. As Jameson suggests, Edgar significantly rewrites that metanarrative to account for his current situation. God is still real and knowable through religious doctrine and participation. He has, however, been changed from a loving father into a cruel sociopath.

Edgar's pattern of seeking spiritual solace through an established religious tradition, followed by the rejection and reconfiguration of that tradition, is not confined to his interaction with Mormonism. After Edgar leaves the Madsens, he moves to rural Pennsylvania to find and forgive the man who ran over his head. Though the mailman has passed away, his wife, Rosa, welcomes Edgar into her home. Edgar eventually begins attending the Joy of All Who Sorrow Ukrainian Orthodox Church with her. Even though his commitment to this congregation lasts for more than a decade, he finds no fulfillment

> when it comes to matters of the spirit. Though I have gone to
> church every week with Rosa, prayed with her over meals and
> before bedtime, stood with her through countless vespers and lit-
> urgies, and faithfully fasted with her the forty days of Lent, God
> and I have come to no real understanding. Unlike Rosa, I can see
> no divine purpose behind the tangle of this existence, no ordering

hand. It is all a mystery, or more accurately, a mess. There are no
heroes or villains, no saviors or demons or angels . . . None of this
will keep me from believing in God. I believe in him. I just don't
know that I will ever have faith in Him.[15]

Clearly Edgar is juxtaposing his postmodern religious sensibility against
Rosa's determined invocation of Christianity's teleological metanarrative: his own view that his life has been a series of accidents against
Rosa's contention that life is governed by an indiscernible plan that
eventually led Edgar to her.

It is difficult to doubt the sincerity of Edgar's quest for spiritual
understanding. His method of pursuing enlightenment—with its seemingly facile shifts from religious tradition to tradition—can be described
as consumerist, however. After periods of enthusiasm and moments of
spiritual clarity, Mormonism and then the Ukrainian Orthodox Church are
discarded because they do not work anymore. Edgar's behavior matches
the increasing tendency of postmodern spiritual seekers to act like shoppers. Both literary theorists and theologians from mainstream Protestant
churches, in their own fashion, have noted that God can now be purchased
on easy terms. Jameson has observed that postmodernity has brought "the
penetration of commodity fetishism into those realms of the imagination
and psyche which had, since classical German philosophy, always been
taken as some last, impregnable stronghold against the instrumental logic
of capital."[16] This commodification of the spiritual has had a profound
impact on traditional religious denominations. No longer do all of their
congregants see a particular institutional church structure as the only
means of spiritual guidance and fulfillment. Instead, many congregants
pick and choose sources of spiritual sustenance the way they would pick
and choose groceries or clothing from a number of different retail chains.

The consumerist religious culture at the beginning of the twenty-
first century is rooted in historical changes to the concept of denomi-
nationalism. Sociologist of religion Robert Wuthnow reminds us that,
in the United States, denominational affiliation was high in the years
immediately after World War II. Furthermore, denominational differentiation was also high, and the tensions these religious distinctions created sometimes led to political conflicts such as the controversy in the
1940s surrounding some public school districts' decision to use their
busses to transport children to Catholic schools.[17] As the decades passed,
however, social forces associated with postmodernity gradually wore
down the geographic and interpersonal boundaries that contributed to
denominational differentiation.

During the twentieth century, the American economy relied to a increasingly greater extent on highly educated professionals. Three developments associated with this trend eventually caused a significant number of people to reevaluate their commitment to their religious denomination. First, corporate capitalism required more people to get college degrees. Although some attended denominational colleges, many more went to secular schools where they interacted with students of other faiths and other denominations, causing many to reevaluate their view that, say, Methodists were radically different from Presbyterians. Second, it became more common for careers to require people to relocate frequently. This further broke down barriers because denominations were often concentrated in specific regions. So a devout Catholic from Philadelphia, seeking corporate employment, might move to Atlanta, where she or he lived and worked with Southern Baptists and probably began to feel quite comfortable around them. Unsurprisingly a great increase in the amount of interaction among people of different denominations and faiths led to the third development: a marked increase in intermarriage. In turn the increasing number of denominationally hybrid households created fertile ground for postdenominational religiosity.

Yet while cogently describing the historical forces behind a profound weakening of denominational differentiation, Wuthnow posits that the "vast majority of Americans who claim some religious identity still use denominational labels to characterize themselves." It should be apparent, however, that these labels do not signify what they once did. Moving farther away from essentializing descriptions of ingrained cultural traits, denominational nomenclature becomes increasingly a malleable demographic indicator. Wuthnow does not make a comparison to a consumer's fondness for a particular brand of automobile or detergent, but the atmosphere of "denominational switching" he so clearly describes invokes consumerism, if it is not already implied.[18]

While Wuthnow's copious empirical data is now decades out of date, more recent scholarship and commentary suggest that the trends he detected have proceeded apace. According to Presbyterian Church (U.S.A.) official Joseph Small, this "decline in denominational loyalty and . . . demise of denominational hegemony" has "been apparent for years." Blaming this decline on "the triumph of market consumerism throughout the culture," Small contends that it has also led to "the multiplication of special-interest groups" within denominations like the Presbyterians.[19]

Given that this disintegration of denominational power is both concurrent with and attributed to cultural trends associated with postmodernism, it is not surprising that the rubric *postdenominational* has appeared in religious studies. As Congregational theologian Steven A. Peay explains, the "postmodern emphasis upon the 'web of relationships,'" best exemplified by Internet religious communities, represents a new kind of loyalty, not to "a name or juridical structure, but to an ideal and, even more importantly, to a community of persons. Coupled with ever increasing mobility and the pervasive consumer mindset this pluralistic approach leads to the era of the 'Church shopper' and the 'Church hopper' who looks and moves according to how 'felt needs' are met in any given situation."[20] In other words, church hopping becomes the realization of Jameson's allusion to the instrumental logic of capital breeching the supposedly inviolate psyche, as the desiring self of late capitalism completely overthrows the more medieval devoted self that was the ideal subject of religious metanarrative.

Of course, church hopping is nothing new in Protestant America, with its long history of revivals and rebellious congregations. But at this historical and cultural juncture, the practice of denominational shopping has taken on a new significance. According to Peter Jankowski, an evangelical psychology professor, postmodernity's relentless "elevation of the subjective experience" has led to the interpretation of "religious traditions and sacred writings with the assumption that they must be understood through the lens of subjective experience."[21] The faithful, in other words, no longer seek to conform their personal experiences to the metanarratives of their religion but instead interpret the sacred practices of a religion in terms of their personal experiences. And since a given theology rarely meets all the needs of an individual, many move from church to church, engaging in acts of spiritual bricolage that cannibalize the metanarratives of the denominations they encounter.

Because of this change in the felt experience of religiosity, some suburban megachurches—massive congregations that sometimes meet in converted sports arenas—have attempted to retool their spiritual product for today's savvy spiritual consumers. *Christian Century* columnist Martin E. Marty has noted that some megachurches are downplaying their denominational ties and even dropping denominational nomenclature because "entrepreneurial or do-it-yourself identifiers appeal most directly" to potential congregants,[22] who see themselves engaged in an act of self-creation by means of religious observance. Within the megachurch movement is a youth-oriented cohort that has been dubbed the Emerging Church. According to a feature article in *Christianity Today*, the pastors involved in this movement are quite frank about embracing the consumer impulses of their congregants. They are reaching out to devout young adults, who are nevertheless looking for "a faith that is colorful enough for their culturally savvy friends."[23] In other words, they are trying to reach potential congregants in search of a faith that has the cachet of, say, a boutique hotel.

While the institutional LDS Church has strongly resisted these postmodern and postdenominational pressures, individual Mormons are becoming more and more like the spiritual shoppers targeted by the Emerging Church because they often inhabit the same sociocultural milieu as the hipper participants in mainstream Protestantism and, as a group, are subject to the same social forces weakening denominational differences. This immersion in postmodern culture has only exacerbated tensions that already existed within Mormon culture and have already found expression in literature written by Mormons. As LDS critic Terryl Givens's recent book-length treatment of Mormon high culture indicates, there has always been conflict over "how to salvage individualism and authenticity in a culture supersaturated with norms, programs, commandments, and expectations" within literature produced by LDS authors.[24] *Edgar Mint* offers a postmodern presentation of the dilemma posed by Givens in a work targeting a national audience largely because its author appears to have a postdenominational relationship with Mormonism.

With missionary service in Brazil, an undergraduate degree from Brigham Young University, and a last name recognizable as potentially Mormon in the Intermountain West, Udall is at least historically LDS. He also has an MFA from the University of Iowa, has taught at non-Mormon universities, and clearly writes for a national audience. Statements Udall made to reviewers while he was promoting *Edgar Mint* unsurprisingly reveal a complex relationship with the faith he was reared in. For example, during a June 2001 interview with the *Salt Lake Tribune*, Udall refers to himself as a "practicing member of the LDS Church" yet worries about the way the novel will be received in his culture.[25] A 2003 interview with the Portland *Oregonian* includes suggestions that Udall's missionary experience was positive because Mormon theology changed the lives of the people he taught.[26]

In a 2002 interview with London's *Daily Telegraph*, however, Udall complains that his family is embarrassed by him because they are "extremely devout Mormons" who "have a hard time understanding why I choose to write about people who drink, curse and masturbate." He also gives a decidedly negative impression of his missionary service, describing it as "the worst kind of sexual suffering," One could accuse Udall of being a canny interviewee, appearing at least relatively faithful in American newspapers likely to have religious readers and cynical about faith in a European newspaper. Yet he goes on to say that he believes "the search for God is the defining purpose of human existence. The only problem for me is that He seems pretty hard to find sometimes."[27] It is therefore easier to see Udall examining his religion like the spiritual consumers already discussed. The author rejects the more rigid features of Mormonism—the narrow-mindedness of typical adherents and the restrictions on sexual expression—while accepting the spiritual experiences he believes are genuine. Edgar's own spiritual search is structured in a similar way, and that is what removes his encounter with Mormonism from the paralyzing polarity discussed at the beginning of this essay and places it within the uncertain spiritual landscape of postmodern, postdenominational America.

Udall's presentation of Mormonism is not without caricature, however. In keeping with his critique of the LDS Church's policing of sexuality best exemplified by the requirement that nineteen-to-twenty-one-year-old males enter a period of closely monitored celibacy, most of the satire centers on teenaged Edgar's inability to match ideal Mormon behavior with his rapidly developing sex drive. For example, while attending church in Richland with the Madsens, Edgar quietly hums the hymn "How Great Thou Art" to take his mind off Brenda Hollander's exposed bra strap. He also masturbates in the Madsen's fields late at night, hoping that God will give him "a little credit for leaving the Madsen house out of it." Yet Edgar never directly criticizes the LDS Church. Indeed, the only important character who is openly abusive toward Mormonism is Barry Pinkley, the doctor who operated on Edgar after the incident with the mail truck. After saving Edgar's life, however, Pinkley becomes obsessed with his young patient, loses his job, and turns to drug dealing so he can afford to stalk Edgar. When this obviously troubled person warns Edgar that the Mormons will "do anything to keep you in their clutches," but "the minute you start to go your own way, they'll throw you right out on your ear," careful readers realize that these words are best understood as a con man's come-on and treat them accordingly.[28]

Evidence that Udall portrays Mormonism as having a core spiritual validity rests on his explanation of the way Edgar comes to join the church. Finding Edgar after his unsuccessful suicide attempt, two missionaries begin teaching him about Mormonism. Edgar is anything but credulous and highlights the implausibility of what the elders are telling him. For example, after hearing that Joseph Smith translated the Book of Mormon, Edgar laconically asks if he typed it. He is not converted by the seemingly far-fetched story the elders tell but by their apparent spiritual power. When the missionaries place their hands on Edgar's head and pray for him to recover, for example, Udall's protagonist immediately feels "a warmth at the crown of" his head, "a light, liquid tingling that slowly moved down into my neck and chest" that makes his eyes spill "tears." After this experience, Edgar concludes that he "had been touched by God." After confessing his sins during a mandatory interview before his baptism, Edgar feels "as if all the buckles and clasps inside of me had been unlatched, leaving me loose and free and able to breathe." And during the baptism itself, Edgar reports that he "lay back, suspended in that perfect moment before I was lifted up with one great rushing pull . . . blinking and sputtering and weightless, made of nothing but air." The lightness and pleasure of Edgar's experience with Mormon religious ritual is obvious and uncontradicted in the text. Clearly Edgar is not converted by the theology—the metanarrative—the missionaries present. Instead, like any postmodern spiritual seeker, his decision to participate in Mormonism is based on the way the religion makes him feel.[29]

If Edgar's conversion suggests that there is some spiritual heft to Mormonism in spite of its problematic metanarrative, his actual experience with Mormonism indicates that the religion is experienced locally by people who cannot be fully explained by either the diktats of their theology or widely held assumptions about their religious culture. The best way to understand how Udall expands his portrayal of postmodern, postdenominational Mormonism beyond Edgar is to examine how he deploys the Indian Placement Program in his novel. He clearly has more than a passing acquaintance with both the history and critical assessments of the program. Edgar's experience takes place in the fictional Richland, Utah, while the Indian Placement Program began in Richfield, Utah, in 1947, when Helen John, a seventeen-year-old Navajo migrant worker asked an LDS family if she could stay with them and attend the local high school. Udall is also aware that the program is largely remembered either as a murky affair that, despite its announced good intentions, was little more than an attempt to bribe Native American children into Mormonism through exposure to the middle-class lifestyles of their host families or as a spiritual high point in LDS relations with Native Americans. This knowledge translates into careful juxtaposition of these two narrative strands in his novel.

Edgar is very aware of the mixed motives driving many of the participants in the program, hearing from other students at Willie Sherman before his baptism that if he joins the LDS Church, he will be sent "to live with a rich anglo family somewhere. Utah, mostly."[30] Udall does not pretend that Edgar does not have an easily understandable financial motivation to join the Mormon Church. After all, the poverty clearly described in the novel roughly approximates the situations of most program participants, and these children were often permitted to participate to alleviate family financial issues.

And the clear disjunction between the material conditions of their foster families and their own homes did not go unnoticed. Topper's study clearly illustrates the psychological impact of placement with a Mormon family with an income "far above the national average" when he asserts that to "a child who has grown up in a hogan, a two-room cinder block house, or a small trailer, it is an almost overwhelming experience suddenly to have its own bedroom, to have many bathrooms instead of an outhouse, to be able to go to the refrigerator and eat at will, to receive new clothes frequently, and to be generally free of the pain of never having enough of the necessities of life."[31] This passage provides a good summary of Edgar's reaction to the Madsens' home. He, too, remarks on the bathroom and the material abundance, noting that it was "hard for me not to steal anything" because "the house was so full of *stuff.*"[32] Edgar's conversion has brought him to a kind of paradise, but it is an earthy paradise easily explained by the economic disparities between white and Native American families.

The missionaries who convert Edgar, however, present the Indian Placement Program as a form of salvation. They seem sincerely motivated to remove Edgar from the depressing reservation school he attends to "someplace where evil isn't staring you in the face everywhere you turn."[33] Udall's fictional elders would definitely agree with the sentiments of Golden Buchanan, a deputy director of a Mormon ecclesiastical unit similar to a Catholic diocese in the late 1940s, who was instrumental in turning Helen John's experience into a churchwide program. Buchanan enthusiastically proclaimed that participants in the program would "see the Church at work and learn the blessings of service to God and fellow men." He not only envisioned them demonstrating their conversion to Mormonism by "going on missions," but he also saw them attaining more secular success by "attending and graduating from college" and returning to the reservation to help their people, teaching "by precept and example all they had learned from the Latter-day Saints."[34]

*Edgar Mint* clearly portrays both assessments of the Indian Placement Program. But Udall does not use his novel to resolve the contradiction he skillfully presents. Instead, he creates a historically grounded reimagination of a small corner of the program that multiplies its ambiguity and argues that human experience isn't easily categorized. Key to this narrative strategy is Udall's characterization of the Madsens, Edgar's host family. Unsurprisingly the relationship between the Native American children and their white hosts was emotionally charged and could transcend the limitations of the institutional structure of placement. For example, while "none of the placement students" in Topper's sample "are now regularly attending members of the Mormon church," he found that some of them "hold sympathetic feelings for their Mormon foster parents."[35] Once again Topper's article provides a prescient gloss for *Edgar Mint's* plot. Edgar becomes emotionally involved with the Madsens—so involved that he gives Barry a lethal overdose when it becomes apparent that the former doctor is trying to break up his host parents' marriage.[36] Such loyalty would be misplaced if it were inspired by cookie-cutter white oppressors or spiritual uplifters. Instead, Edgar, the postmodern spiritual seeker, comes to love the Madsens because he recognizes them as fellow postdenominationalists.

In addition to having their middle-class stability certified, host families in the Indian Placement Program were carefully vetted to ensure devotion to the Mormon Church. Yet even a casual reader of Udall's novel should quickly realize that the Madsens do not conform to positive or negative stereotypes of small-town Mormons. Lana, Edgar's foster mother, works at the State Wildlife Office and has "a doctorate in zoology." She is a progressive "political activist of sorts," affiliated with the Audubon Society and the Sierra Club. She campaigns for the Democratic candidate for Congress, even though he "didn't have a shadow of a chance in Richland or anywhere else in Utah." Although apparently more politically conservative than his wife, Clay, Edgar's foster father, has a beard that makes the stricter members of their congregation complain that he looks "like one of them bumble-minded hippies." And although portrayed as an honest man, Clay is not so rigidly devoted to following the rules that he cannot bribe a hospital orderly so that Edgar can see the body of his friend Cecil.[37] In addition to Lana and Clay's individual nonconformity, the family they have created is far from orthodox. Although a two-child family composed of a wisecracking and flirtatious teenage girl and a bright, yet socially maladroit, preadolescent boy might seem unremarkable in a sitcom, it is far from the small-town-Utah Mormon norm, especially in the mid-1970s.[38]

The Madsens do not lack a large family because of a cavalier attitude toward their community's social norms, however. Instead, they are still mourning the death of their youngest son, Dean, who suffocated after becoming caught in the vertical slats of a crib that had "been built by Clay's great-grandfather only a few months after his family had crossed the plains."[39] Although the symbolism is a bit heavy handed, it clearly points to a failure—at least for the Madsens—of a key component of the Mormon metanarrative: the belief that large, intergenerationally linked families are necessary for salvation. Having one's ancestors—even if only metaphorically—break the link in this chain is very traumatizing. When Edgar comes into their family, the Madsens are at a spiritual impasse. Though their participation in the Indian Placement Program suggests that Mormonism is working for them, their marriage has become difficult because Lana wants to move to another state to escape—figuratively, if not literally—the ghost of her dead son and perhaps the religion that brought Clay's crib-making ancestors across the plains.

Although Lana's nascent affair with Barry is the plot device Udall employs to move Edgar from Utah to Pennsylvania—and remove Barry from the narrative—most of the Madsens' personal spiritual questing takes place outside of the narrative. Nevertheless, Udall provides a tantalizing coda to the questions about the Madsens that Edgar's flight leaves unanswered. After Edgar moves to Pennsylvania, he keeps in touch with the Madsens through their daughter, Sunny, who is "married and divorced" and living "in Denver," making "good money writing marketing copy for the Coors Brewing Company." Given Mormonism's emphasis on marriage and teetotaling, this strongly suggests that she has, like Edgar, amiably wandered away from the faith. In the final pages of the novel, Udall has Edgar quote extensively from a letter Sunny writes to describe Lana and Clay's thirtieth wedding anniversary: "They celebrated it back in Richland, in the old community center packed with neighbors and family and friends and nine different kinds of Jell-O salad. *You should have seen it,* Sunny wrote. *Food and streamers everywhere and my folks dancing out there in the middle of all these old people, my dad swinging his hips and yelling to the music, 'That's the way, uh-huh, uh-huh, I like it, uh-huh, uh-huh . . .'* I could have sworn they were all drunk."[40] After reading this letter, Edgar tells his readers that he "nearly bawled with joy." Yet it is not entirely clear why Edgar would be so moved. Because he has been in touch with Sunny, he must be aware that Clay and Lana survived the affair, moved to Olympia, Washington, and managed to negotiate a more stable marriage. By itself, then, Sunny's mention of the longevity of her parent's marriage would not be a surprise to Edgar and would therefore lack enough emotional punch to trigger Edgar's uncharacteristic reaction.

It is much more likely that Edgar's intense joy is triggered by his realization that the Madsens have, in their own way, begun a spiritual journey much like his own, that they have freed themselves from the tyranny of the metanarrative that brought so much tension into their lives. Edgar sees that the Madsens have become post-Mormon—both part of and outside the faith of their forebears. Udall's mention of nine different kinds of Jell-O salad—though done for comic effect—and the Madsens' deliberate return to Richland to celebrate an important anniversary indicate that they still feel tied to Mormon culture. Jell-O is still comfort food, and rural Utah is home. Yet the Madsens have left that home for a life outside the band of Mormon political and cultural influence centered in Utah. While they still may have a taste for Jell-O, they are depicted joyfully dancing in the middle of a group of supposedly staid, elderly Mormons, who, along with the Madsens, appear drunk. Although the details of the Madsens' involvement with the Mormon Church are not stated, they have clearly reconfigured their relationship in a more livable way. Udall's novel strongly implies that the Mormonism that they have assembled is much more responsive to their needs and therefore superior to the institutional version they have abandoned.

At the end of *The Miracle Life of Edgar Mint,* the central characters with significant attachments to the Mormon Church have radically altered their relationship with this regimented faith, becoming more like the postmodern spiritual seekers creating postdenominational America's spiritual landscape. Of course, the degree of distance from the church's institutional metanarrative varies. For Edgar, converted before he was an adult to a religion he had not known before, it was possible to walk away effortlessly when his personal experiences with Mormonism began to be painful, rather than light and effortless. For the Madsens, with the weight of their ancestors—as Marx might suggest—pressing down on their minds like nightmares, outright rejection was not possible, but remapping their relationship with the faith of their mothers and fathers, thanks to the geographic and cultural mobility of postmodernity, was relatively simple. Although the section of the novel dealing with Edgar's stay in Richland is populated with minor characters that conform to well-established literary stereotypes about Mormons, Edgar and the Madsens experience that religion locally and idiosyncratically, comprehending both its spiritual and ridiculous components.

If new cultural and political conditions call for new means of crafting narratives, and postmodern narrative has already established itself as a tool available to mainstream writers, it is encouraging that Brady Udall has successfully applied this narrative strategy to Mormonism. It is time that commercially and critically successful portrayals of Mormons intended for national audiences left the nineteenth-century ghetto that has imprisoned them for so long. This is not to say that

Mormonism's unsavory past is not fair game for fictional portrayal, or that the institutional metanarrative of the Mormon Church should not be questioned in fiction. Nor does it mean that devout Mormons should not continue to publish—and profit from—hagiographic fiction. Instead, it is a request that the literary panorama of Mormon portrayals become truly vast by including a locally experienced, subjective Mormonism that resonates with our postmodern, postdenominational society.

## Notes

1. Whitney, "Home Literature," paragraph 10.
2. Recent attempts to establish an ancestral link between Native Americans and the Semitic people purportedly inhabiting the Book of Mormon by DNA analysis have failed, and LDS culture is now quietly backing away from the strong claims made during most of the twentieth century.
3. Cundick, Gottfredson, and Willson, "Changes in Scholastic Achievement and Intelligence of Indian Children," 819.
4. Topper, "Mormon Placement," 145.
5. Hangen, "A Place to Call Home," 60.
6. Udall, *The Miracle Life of Edgar Mint: A Novel*, 235.
7. Lyotard, *The Postmodern Condition*, xxiv.
8. Edgar's hybrid background has often escaped the notice of critics. For example, P. Jane Hafen's review of the novel, "Speaking for Edgar Mint," asserts that "Edgar's Indian identity influences every major plot development" and then proceeds to catalogue Udall's problematic treatment of Native American characters. While Hafen makes a cogent case for Udall's insensitivity to Native Americans, however, she is wrong to assert that he is "assuming the first-person voice of Apache boy Edgar Mint," 180. From the beginning of the novel, Edgar is explicitly presented as something other than simply Apache, and his ability to assume and discard different identities suggests that the problematic depictions that Hafen mentions may be a clumsy part of Udall's commentary on a postidentity society.
9. Udall, *Miracle Life of Edgar Mint*, 38, 14.
10. Ibid., 47, 53, 29.
11. Ibid., 41.
12. Lyotard, *The Postmodern Condition*, 41.
13. Jameson, foreword to *The Postmodern Condition*, xii (italics in the original).
14. Udall, *Miracle Life of Edgar Mint*, 311.
15. Ibid., 418.
16. Jameson, foreword to *The Postmodern Condition*, xv.
17. Wuthnow, *Restructuring of American Religion*, 72ff.
18. Ibid., 97, 88.
19. Small, "Signs of the Postdenominational Future," 509.
20. Peay, "Heart to Heart," 21.
21. Jankowski, "Postmodern Spirituality," 70–71.
22. Marty, "Faith in Fashion," 47.

23. Crouch, "Emergent Mistique," 38.
24. Givens, *People of Paradox*, 308.
25. Griggs, "Udall Mints a Dickens of a Tale in 'Miracle Life.'"
26. McMullen, "The Oregonian Book Club," D1.
27. Cox, "Class of 2002 Novelist Brady Udall," 10.
28. Udall, *Miracle Life of Edgar Mint*, 273, 279, 294.
29. Ibid., 224, 225, 233, 236.
30. Ibid., 188.
31. Topper, "Mormon Placement," 148.
32. Udall, *Miracle Life of Edgar Mint*, 257 (italics in the original).
33. Ibid., 229.
34. Buchanan, quoted in Birch, "Helen John," 125.
35. Topper, "Mormon Placement," 158.
36. Udall, *Miracle Life of Edgar Mint*, 373.
37. Ibid., 252, 258, 302, 306.
38. Although readers are given to understand that the text of his novel comes from Edgar's voluminous diary, Udall does not make explicit dates part of his narrative. He does, however, make references to popular culture that make approximation possible. When Edgar arrives in Stony Run, Pennsylvania, from Richland, he watches *Police Woman* and *The Rockford Files* on television in the evening. *Miracle Life of Edgar Mint*, 411. Both were in first run during the mid-1970s. During the 1970s, according to Michael B. Toney and his collaborators in "Residence Exposure and Fertility Expectations of Young Mormon and Non-Mormon Women in Utah," Utah's birthrate increased at the same rate it did during the 1950s, while the overall birthrate for the United States saw historically unprecedented declines, 459.
39. Udall, *Miracle Life of Edgar Mint*, 288.
40. Ibid., 420 (italics in the original).

## Bibliography

Birch, J. Neal. "Helen John: The Beginnings of Indian Placement." *Dialogue: A Journal of Mormon Thought* 18, no. 4 (1985): 119–29.
Cox, Tom. "Class of 2002 Novelist Brady Udall." *Daily Telegraph* (London), January 5, 2002, 10.
Crouch, Andy. "Emergent Mistique." *Christianity Today*, November 2004, 36–41.
Cundick, Bert P, Douglas K. Gottfredson, and Linda Willson. "Changes in Scholastic Achievement and Intelligence of Indian Children Enrolled in a Foster Placement Program." *Developmental Psychology* 10, no. 6 (1974): 815–20.
Givens, Terryl L. *People of Paradox: A History of Mormon Culture*. New York: Oxford University Press, 2007.
Griggs, Brandon. "Udall Mints a Dickens of a Tale in 'Miracle Life.'" *Salt Lake Tribune*, June 17, 2001. http://www.sltrib.com/2001/Jun/06172001/Arts/106266.htm.
Hafen, P. Jane. "Speaking for Edgar Mint." *Dialogue: A Journal of Mormon Thought* 35, no. 1 (2002): 179–81.
Hangen, Tona J. "A Place to Call Home: Studying the Indian Placement Program." *Dialogue: A Journal of Mormon Thought* 30, no. 1 (1997): 53–69.

Jameson, Frederic. Foreword to *The Postmodern Condition,* by Jean-Françoise Lyotard, vii–xxii. Minneapolis: University of Minnesota Press, 1984.

Jankowski, Peter J. "Postmodern Spirituality: Implications for Promoting Change." *Counseling and Values* 47 (2002): 69–79.

Lyotard, Jean-Françoise. *The Postmodern Condition: A Report on Knowledge.* Translated by Geoff Bennington and Brian Massumi. Theory and History of Literature 10. Minneapolis: University of Minnesota Press, 1984.

Marty, Martin E. "Faith in Fashion." *The Christian Century,* November 2, 2004, 47.

McMullen, Peggy. "The Oregonian Book Club: 'If I Could Tell You Only One Thing about My Life,'" *Portland Oregonian,* February 1, 2003, Sunday sunrise edition, D1.

Peay, Steven A. "Heart to Heart: Congregationalism as a Post-Denominational Ecclesial Spirituality Expressed through Relationship, Worship, and Fellowship." *International Congregational Journal* 4, no. 2 (2005): 17–40.

Small, Joseph D. "Signs of the Postdenominational Future." *The Christian Century,* May 5, 1999, 506–9.

Toney, Michael B., Banu Golesorkhi, and William F. Stinner. "Residence Exposure and Fertility Expectations of Young Mormon and Non-Mormon Women in Utah." *Journal of Marriage and the Family* 47, no. 2 (1985): 459–65.

Topper, Martin D. "Mormon Placement: The Effects of Missionary Foster Families on Navajo Adolescents." *Ethos* 7, no. 2 (1979): 142–60.

Udall, Brady. *The Miracle Life of Edgar Mint: A Novel.* New York: Vintage Books, 2002.

Whitney, Orson F. "Home Literature." *Contributor* 9 (July 1888) http://mldb.byu.edu/homelit.htm (accessed August 10, 2007).

Wuthnow, Robert. *The Restructuring of American Religion: Society and Faith since World War II.* Princeton, NJ: Princeton University Press, 1988.

# 7

# Jane Austen in Mollywood

*Mainstreaming Mormonism in Andrew Black's* Pride & Prejudice

JULIETTE WELLS

In interviews in June 2003, during filming of their feature-length version of Jane Austen's novel *Pride and Prejudice,* director Andrew Black and producer/coscreenwriter Jason Faller made clear their hope of reaching viewers both inside and outside the Church of Jesus Christ of Latter-day Saints, of which they are members.[1] "We're [trying] to make a film that appeal[s] to both insiders and outsiders," the Scottish-born Black explained to a reporter at Brigham Young University (BYU), from which both he and Faller had recently graduated. "It's almost like 'My Big Fat Greek Wedding' where the culture is just a backdrop."[2] Central to this effort was their choice to update Austen's novel, which Black and Faller considered to have broad appeal, especially to women viewers. *Pride and Prejudice* "has a huge following," Faller told the *Deseret News,* a Salt Lake City daily newspaper. "It's kind of like 'Star Wars' for women."[3]

Unlike the 2005 period version of *Pride & Prejudice* directed by Joe Wright, Black and Faller's *Pride & Prejudice,* which is set in present-day Provo, can hardly be said to have reached a huge audience. It was screened in a very limited geographical area—Utah, Arizona, and Idaho—before being released on DVD,[4] and outside that region, it was reviewed only in *Variety* (in an article that noted that "careful grassroots marketing will be required" for the film to succeed financially).[5] Created on a $350,000 budget, *Pride & Prejudice* grossed $373,942 at the box office.[6] In its DVD incarnation, however, the film has indeed benefited from its connection to Austen. Enthusiasts can find *Pride & Prejudice* listed among other adaptations of her novel on the Web site of the Jane Austen Society of North America (JASNA) and the Austen fans' site, the

Republic of Pemberley, whose discussion boards also feature comments about this film;[7] it is also featured in two recently published articles in JASNA's online journal.[8]

What representations of Mormons do viewers outside the LDS Church—say, Austen fans—find when they encounter this version of *Pride & Prejudice?* Black's comment about Mormon "culture [being] just the backdrop" for his film points to a crucial feature of this adaptation: it avoids explicitly mentioning the words "Mormon" and "Latter-Day Saints," even in scenes where characters attend church, and it remains coy about the name of the university (presumably BYU) that its main characters attend. This decision was strategic: Faller has said that he and Black wanted to avoid the tendency toward Mormon in-jokes among recent films aimed at LDS audiences.[9] For the DVD release, the filmmakers opted as well to drop the giveaway subtitle *(A Latter-day Comedy)* that had appeared on posters for the theatrical release. The result is a film that—rather oddly, in the opinions of some viewers and critics—depicts a wide range of young, contemporary Mormons—from the self-aware, ambitious Elizabeth Bennet, to the dating-crazy Lydia, to the pious Collins and Mary—without ever identifying them as such.

To assess the effects of this decision, and the resulting representations, it is necessary to consider more fully what was at stake for Black and Faller in choosing to aim for a crossover audience and specifically to use Austen-inspired content.[10] The next section of this essay examines these issues in the contexts of contemporary Mormon cinema history and Austen adaptations, with special attention to explicitly Christian reworkings of her novels. The later portions of this essay look more closely at *Pride & Prejudice's* handling of those characters who most fully incarnate Mormon stereotypes (Mary and Collins) and critique them (Elizabeth) and particularly the way those interactions with stereotype convey impressions about Mormonism to a non-LDS audience. Faller has said that he sees this version of *Pride and Prejudice* as an example of a *Mollywood* film or, in other words, a "Mormon chick flick";[11] thus, this analysis is informed by recent scholarship on chick flicks. *Pride & Prejudice,* it is argued, aims to replace popular perceptions of "peculiar" Mormons with characters who, like the filmmakers themselves, have chosen to embrace LDS life in ways that suit their own personalities and aspirations. The result is a film that presents contemporary Mormonism as appealing and rewarding, rather than—as those outside the LDS Church have often depicted it—restrictive or strange. The conclusion of the essay compares this reading of the film to ones from critics and reviewers, the majority of whom see *Pride & Prejudice* as flawed.

# Crossing Over:
# Aiming for a Wider Audience through Austen

Film scholars Randy Astle and Gideon O. Burton assert that a majority of films made during what they call the "fifth wave" of Mormon cinema, beginning in 2000, shared a "crossover desire."[12] Yet directors and critics disagree strongly about the way to achieve this goal. "What's It Gonna Take to Crossover into Mainstream?" asks LDS film critic Thomas Baggaley in the title of his 2004 article for *Meridian Magazine,* an online forum that bills itself as "The Place Where Latter-day Saints Gather." Baggaley reminds LDS filmmakers that many American viewers outside the church seek, as do those inside, "Hollywood quality storytelling and filmmaking—without all the garbage. . . . They want good, entertaining stories they can trust to not offend their sensibilities." Part of "Hollywood quality," in Baggaley's view, is casting actors with name recognition since "stars are the brand names audiences associate most with to decide whether they want to watch a film." Finally, he advises filmmakers seeking broader audiences to think about their projects' Mormon content: "If the characters absolutely have to be LDS for the particular story you tell, so be it. If they don't, then don't make them LDS. Just make them good people who may very well be LDS."[13]

Richard Dutcher, the filmmaker who is widely credited with having inaugurated the contemporary renaissance of Mormon cinema through his 2000 film *God's Army,* and who has since publicly separated himself from the church, holds an opposing view.[14] In a 2006 interview with *Christianity Today,* Dutcher pointedly criticized those LDS filmmakers who optimistically imagine that their products will appeal to wider audiences: "Lifetime Mormons who've never been outside of Utah have no idea what would make a film cross over to another community. They have such a limited view of the religious world, they just don't have a clue how to make a film that might appeal to other people." Furthermore, Dutcher feels that avoiding Mormon content in a bid for more viewers prevents serious Mormon cinema from developing: "I think most Mormon films are expressions of 'the Mormon aesthetic,' and have very little to do with anything at the heart of Mormonism. I mean they're really not about doctrine or history; there's really no thought put into it. It's just simply a trifle, a piece of entertainment, something that won't offend."[15]

Many Mormon film scholars agree with Dutcher that the motive of avoiding offense—the heart, according to Baggaley, of what would appeal to outsiders about an LDS film—ultimately impedes the development of Mormon cinema. Audiences as well as directors are to blame for this evasion of controversy, argue these scholars. In the introduction to the recent special issue of *BYU Studies* devoted to Mormons and film, Gideon O. Burton contends that "Mormon cinema will not have a chance to arrive as long as Mormons are prepared only to ascertain what is morally wrong in films they see, and remain uninterested in seeking out, discriminating, or creating what is right (morally or aesthetically) in film."[16]

Scholars of mass media have investigated the extent to which such standards for media consumption are influenced by LDS leaders' teachings, which themselves have changed over time. Daniel A. Stout observes that church leaders' recommendations regarding media choices— which, in the early- to midtwentieth century, invoked "artistically and intellectually grounded criteria—shifted by the end of the century to "a rules-based approach focusing almost exclusively on the avoidance of media depictions considered inconsistent with church teachings (e.g., violence, sexual intimacy, etc.)."[17] Stout and David W. Scott identify "three distinct approaches to media literacy" among groups of LDS Church members surveyed: "*belief-based media literacy,* where audience members emphasize religious teachings and predetermined sets of guidelines in their media selections; *personal media literacy,* which is the evaluation of media according to the fulfillment of individual needs and objectives; and *interactional media literacy,* where media use revolves around relationships and church members often defer to other family members in making media selections."[18] Those who take the second approach are most likely, according to Stout and Scott, to choose media on the basis of aesthetic criteria, rather than, or in balance with, moral imperatives.

While many church members approach commercial films (as well as other media) with care—if not suspicion—the church itself has long used film as a tool, as Mormon film historians have pointed out. Burton asserts that "film has been central to how The Church of Jesus Christ of Latter-Day Saints instructs its members and presents itself to the world," and he cites as worthy of further study "unique LDS cultural practices such as the ward movie night or the use of filmstrips in proselytizing."[19] Randy Astle's "History of Mormon Cinema," written with Burton, cites "Institutional (Church) Films" as one of its four central types.[20] Furthermore, Astle identifies what he calls a "unifying potential" in LDS-made films posted online, which, in his view, can "creat[e] a global cinematic *web* of Saints" and thereby act "as a crucial component of our discipleship."[21]

One might expect to find film credited as well with the potential to influence those who are not yet members of the LDS Church: in other words, to support proselytizing. Acknowledgment of this potential function of LDS-made film is, however, almost completely absent from the critical and scholarly discussions on crossover impulses among LDS filmmakers. This gap is especially surprising in the light of the widespread popular association of the LDS Church with missionaries and conversion.[22] A rare exception is John-Charles Duffy's brief remarks during a panel discussion at a 2006 symposium, where he explores the differences between LDS and other forms of Christian and "minority" film in this regard. Unlike LDS filmmakers, he argues, Catholics and evangelical Protestants "are overt about their interest in using film for evangelization: for bearing witness of Christian truth and promoting Christian values"; Duffy offers a few theories regarding this difference but does not fully explore it.[23]

Two of Duffy's observations are especially pertinent to my discussion of *Pride & Prejudice*'s effort at mainstreaming Mormonism. Comparing the aspirations of LDS filmmakers to those articulated by the organizers of the San Francisco Jewish Film Festival, Duffy recognizes shared ground only in the sense that LDS filmmakers do "present images of Mormons that serve as a counterpoint to Hollywood images and media stereotypes." He notes, too, that "one important function of [films made by] evangelicals is to legitimize their subculture, literally by giving evangelicalism screentime in mainstream venues."[24]

Austen's *Pride and Prejudice* afforded Black and Faller the opportunity to "legitimize their subculture"[25] —to borrow Duffy's words—by linking it to a novel that is both canonical and enduringly popular among general readers. Their choice is exceptional among recent LDS filmmakers, who have not opted for literary adaptation.[26] "I looked high and low for a good story from local writers and found [them] wanting," Faller explained to one interviewer, "so I decided that I'd go to a story that was tried and tested. . . . 'Pride and Prejudice' is a great story."[27] Those associated with this *Pride & Prejudice* stress the ability of Austen's world to map convincingly onto that of the young dating Mormons in their film: "You have to be quite careful where you set" *Pride and Prejudice*, commented Orlando Seale, who played Darcy, "because most societies no longer share the same social morals as the societies did about which (the novel) was written. I think what's clever about this adaptation is that they found a context which works very well with the original story."[28] Similarly Black has claimed that "it would be hard for the story to work in a secular culture, but in an environment like LDS culture, it is a great fit."[29]

Seale's and Black's assertions that Mormon culture is somehow uniquely comparable to Austen's beg analysis, not least because the filmmakers were clearly quite aware of—and strongly influenced by— Amy Heckerling's 1995 *Clueless*, which transposes the plot and characters of Austen's *Emma* to a Beverly Hills high school. Faller brought up *Clueless* in one interview where he defended his and Black's decision to make *Pride & Prejudice* "even more light-hearted and fun."[30] A much-praised adaptation, *Clueless* certainly succeeded in finding a wholly secular context that worked with Austen's original. Updated fictional versions of *Pride and Prejudice*—of which Helen Fielding's *Bridget Jones's Diary* (1996) is the best known—also demonstrate the capacity of this particular novel to be transposed effectively into mainstream contemporary culture,[31] while Gurinder Chadha's 2004 film *Bride & Prejudice* locates a compelling parallel to Austen's social world in present-day Amritsar, India. Austen fans coming to Black's *Pride & Prejudice* are likely to be familiar with some, if not all, of these versions of Austen's novel and would thus see the Mormon setting of this film as one of many possibilities.[32]

Especially relevant counterparts to this *Pride & Prejudice* are the evangelical Christian approaches to Austen's novels recently published by Sarah Arthur and Debra White Smith, which I have analyzed at length elsewhere.[33] Arthur's dating guide based on *Pride and Prejudice*, titled *Dating Mr. Darcy: The Smart Girl's Guide to Sensible Romance* (2005), takes as its premise that both the courtship culture and moral assumptions of Austen's era are fully recognizable to modern young evangelicals. Furthermore, Arthur suggests that by studying and reflecting on *Pride and Prejudice*, readers can deepen their relationship with God at the same time that they increase their chances of success on the dating market. Likewise, albeit less didactically, Smith's novel *First Impressions* (2004)—a version of *Pride and Prejudice* that is part of a six-novel series of Christianized Austen updates by this author—integrates its characters' spiritual journeys with their search for mates. Smith's advice guide *What Jane Austen Taught Me about Love and Romance* (2007) further emphasizes the ability of Austen's characters to function as moral guides.

As I argued in my earlier article, both Smith and Arthur acknowledge the challenge of adapting Austen's novels for their own audience of believers. Arthur in particular anticipates and addresses the concern that the world of Austen's novels—and indeed Austen herself—is not *Christian* in the sense that Arthur and her readers understand the term. A comparable anxiety about the appropriateness of Austen's novels arises in Kenneth R. Morefield's article in *Persuasions*, the journal of JASNA, when he discusses his past experience teaching in what he calls "a fundamentalist environment."[34] "Are there really readers," asks Morefield, "who can and do have moral objections to reading or assigning Jane Austen? The answer to that question, as difficult as it is for those who teach in secular (or more enlightened Christian) institutions, is yes."[35]

No such worry crops up in Black's *Pride & Prejudice* or his and Faller's interviews about the film. Understandably Black and Faller were less concerned about possible objections to Austen from LDS viewers—who, if opposed to this author, would simply not see the film—than with the potential of the Austen association to draw viewers from outside the church. In other words, as ambitious but still little-known filmmakers, they hoped to trade on Austen's name recognition. This effort recalls film critic Thomas Baggaley's recommendation that LDS filmmakers in search of a crossover audience appeal to those viewers by casting well-known actors: Austen *is* the star, as it were, of *Pride & Prejudice*. In this respect, Black's film shares common ground with other recent screen adaptations of Austen's novels. As Harriet Margolis asserts, the "identification of a project in marketing terms through Austen's name is meant to guarantee an audience. . . . Through clever marketing, Austen's cultural status, her cultural capital, translates into commercial success and economic capital for producers such as BBC, or Columbia, or Miramax, or A&E."[36]

## Collins and Mary: A Match Made in Stereotype

*Pride & Prejudice*'s depiction of Mormonism is strongly affected by one of its most notable departures from the plot of Austen's novel: the establishment of a romance between Mr. Collins and Mary Bennet. In Austen's original, Mr. Collins—a pedantic clergyman and distant cousin of the Bennet sisters who stands, thanks to a legal entail, to inherit the Longbourn estate where the Bennets live—marries Elizabeth's close friend, Charlotte Lucas, after Elizabeth turns him down. Mary, Elizabeth's younger sister, would have been next in line had Mr. Collins continued down the list of Bennet daughters, and Austen indicates that the equally pedantic Mary considers him a good match.[37] That, in Black's version, Mary and Collins's similarities indeed bring them together is implied by the film's original casting call, which describes William Collins as "self-absorbed, self-righteous, anxiously seeking wife" and Mary Haywood as "self-absorbed, self-righteous, anxiously seeking Collins."[38]

The casting call further characterizes Collins as "geeky/nerdy" and Mary as a "plain, religiously devoted girl, who desperately seeks attention." The latter description is significant as the only hint in the casting notice of the film's cultural context. At this stage of production, the film's subtitle was *A Utah Comedy*—a less-explicit reference to Mormonism than the later choice, *A Latter-day Comedy*. Actors consulting this casting notice would learn only that the planned film was "a modern, comedic adaptation of Jane Austen's novel. . . . a comedy about love, reality and feminine persuasion."[39] Of course, actors who noticed in Andrew Black's biography that he was set to graduate from BYU in June 2003 could draw their own conclusions.

Black's decision not to emphasize the LDS aspect of the production in his notice resulted in a cast where only approximately one-fifth of the actors were church members. Publicity pieces for the film often suggested that such a diverse cast bode well for the film's appeal to a crossover audience.[40] In interviews Black and his cast members stressed as well the educational experience, for nonchurch members, of working on the film. Black noted in one interview that Kam Heskin, who played Elizabeth, "was very familiar with LDS culture because she grew up in Colorado where about half the people were members. The other actors to varying degrees did their own research. They had some questions for me, but while they were in Utah they immersed themselves in the culture for the duration of shooting, and a few even went to church a couple times."[41] One of those less-well-informed cast members was Orlando Seale, who played Darcy. "Making a film with LDS undertones [was] an eye-opening experience" for Seale, another article reported, quoting him as saying that "it would be a great thing if this film helped people see this is just a normal community, that there's nothing mysterious about it. . . . Because there is that (mysterious) perception."[42]

As the film's most devout characters—and also some of its most relentlessly satirized— Collins and Mary are crucial to the question of whether *Pride & Prejudice* depicts the Mormon world as "normal" or "mysterious" (read "peculiar"). Before looking closely at a few key scenes that develop these characters, it is worth noting that Mr. Collins in particular has proved troubling for other adapters working within Christian frameworks. Austen's character is a clergyman whose pomposity and willingness to grovel to his patroness, Lady Catherine de Bourgh, render him ridiculous in the eyes of Elizabeth and her father— and presumably to most readers. While Austen—herself the daughter and sister of Anglican clergymen—evidently had no qualms about creating a character who united silliness and ordination, both Sarah Arthur and Debra White Smith find ways to explain away this combination, apparently to avoid offending their evangelical readers. Arthur blames the early-nineteenth-century Church of England's lax standards of selecting clergymen, while Smith reinvents Collins altogether as the vice president of an oil company.[43]

Black's *Pride & Prejudice* dodges this challenge, in part, by not identifying Collins as any kind of leader within the LDS Church. Collins does, in one scene, address the congregation of his church in an extended monologue, but context and the personal content of his remarks suggest to the non-LDS viewer that this is a form of witnessing, rather than a sermon. Moreover, the film's screenwriters—Anne K. Black, Katherine Swigert, and Faller—make it clear that Collins's ideas, far from being representative of present-day LDS beliefs, are distinctly old-fashioned. They signal this by having him brandish and quote to Elizabeth from a church magazine that he says is dated 1978. He wants to share with her, he says, "a great article on the glories of womanhood," and as he reads through the titles of the other pieces, he remarks on one (titled "Provoke Not Your Children") that it is "as true today as when it was written." Elizabeth's scornful sneer conveys to the viewers that she considers all these ideas to be passé in the extreme. That Collins has brought this antiquated magazine to a party—at which he, alone, is formally attired in a suit and tie—further accentuates his unappealing conservatism.

While Collins's traditional views alienate Elizabeth, they obviously attract Mary. Later in the same party scene, Collins tries to renew conversation with Elizabeth by remarking that he "was reading in the church news last week and . . . read an article on the pioneer trek." Not Elizabeth, bored as ever by Collins, but the eager Mary takes up the thread, exclaiming, "Oh, the reenactment! My great-great-great aunt Chestyna crossed with that company. One night it was so cold, she had to sleep inside a buffalo!" Mary has commemorated this event in her cross-stitched family tree, which she hastens to show to both Collins and Elizabeth. This exchange is an excellent example of this film's ability to be interpreted on different levels by viewers with varying acquaintance with Mormon history and culture. Someone with no knowledge will grasp that Collins is broadcasting his "geeky/nerdy" qualities by referring to a church publication at a party and asking Elizabeth to a reenactment as a kind of date. Mary's enthusiasm for and family connection to the trek likewise identify her as Collins's counterpart even to a viewer unaware of the nuances of the trek or the significance of Mormon lineage. That Mary has brought her elaborate cross-stitch project to the party further underscores her similarity to Collins.

Collins, however, is not yet ready to acknowledge that Mary is better suited to him than Elizabeth. Why he finds Elizabeth so attractive is not fully answered in this film; he only mentions, when proposing to her, that he "always thought that [he] would marry an old-fashioned girl" but finds Elizabeth's "forward feminist ways very exciting." Austen's Mr. Collins, of course, was motivated in his courtship of Elizabeth by his family relationship and his desire to benefit one of the Bennet daughters, whose house he would inherit. Black and his screenwriters have preserved only the essential absurdity of Collins imagining a match between himself and Elizabeth, as well as her main reason for refusing him: "I'm really flattered, but you wouldn't make me happy, and I know I wouldn't make you happy," this Elizabeth says to Collins in a reasonably close echo of Austen's heroine's declaration that "you could not make *me* happy, and I am convinced that I am the last woman in the world who would make *you* so."[44]

By transforming Austen's Bennet sisters into roommates, this version of *Pride & Prejudice* removes the parental characters who, in Austen's novel, play such crucial roles in Mr. Collins's courtship of Elizabeth (as, of course, in the narrative as a whole). Memorably Mr. Bennet backs up Elizabeth's decision to place her happiness ahead of certain financial security, while Mrs. Bennet, desperate to marry off advantageously as many daughters as possible, condemns Elizabeth's refusal of what she sees as a very eligible proposal.

Black's *Pride & Prejudice* does, however, provide Collins with an occasion to criticize Elizabeth's decision in a manner somewhat comparable to Mrs. Bennet's outburst in Austen's novel. This is the scene, already mentioned, when Collins addresses fellow church members at great length (underscored by shots of a wall clock advancing) on his disappointment. The views Collins expresses in this monologue are consistent with his earlier comments: "If a young, worthy man proposes, it seems that it's the woman's duty to accept. . . . And why wouldn't she accept, if she's smart? I mean, she gets someone to protect her and provide for her for the rest of her life. So that she can drop out of school and stay at home like she is supposed to." As he did earlier, Black cues the audience to mock Collins's ideas as old-fashioned, this time by showing those assembled responding to the monologue. Not only does Elizabeth look furious and Mary enraptured (hardly surprising in either case), but several middle-aged male congregants demonstrate their disapproval of Collins's sentiments by rolling their eyes and exhibiting skeptical expressions; one of them subsequently escorts Collins firmly away from the podium and expresses frustration with the length of his address. Once again the film stresses that Collins's notions, though shared by Mary, are not representative of their church generally.

In mating Collins with Mary, this version of *Pride & Prejudice* not only unites two characters that Austen suggests are well suited but also avoids the disturbing issues raised by the marriage Austen has Mr. Collins make. In the novel, Charlotte Lucas's pragmatic acceptance of Mr. Collins, which follows her concerted—though quick—campaign to gain his notice and favor, alarms Elizabeth, who cannot imagine sacrificing her happiness (as she sees it) for a home of her own.[45] No such sacrifice occurs within this film. Rather, we see Elizabeth helping Mary get ready for a date with Collins, preparation that involves removing Mary's glasses, applying new makeup, and creating a new hairstyle, as movie makeovers of plain girls always do. Rainy Kerwin, playing Mary, replaces her earlier sour and overeager expressions with a shy smile that matches the one that Collins now wears.

Though the film does not depict subsequent stages in the Mary/Collins romance, Elizabeth announces in voice-over in the final sequence that "Collins proposed to Mary after a long courtship. They honeymooned on a pioneer trek reenactment. They did not have to sleep inside a buffalo." Strikingly, Elizabeth does not mention anything further about this marriage, although elsewhere in her voice-over she specifies that the Kitty Bennet character has married and has five daughters, while the Caroline Bingley character has three children. One expects no fewer from the traditionally minded Mary and Collins, especially since in his proposal to Elizabeth, he reminded her that "we've been commanded to multiply and replenish the earth." At the very end, if not before, Black relaxes his insistence on heaping Mormon stereotypes on these two characters: they do not engender an astonishingly large family. Instead, he allows Collins and Mary to appear as two awkward, but rather endearing, young people, who, both feeling isolated within their peer group, find happiness in choosing and sharing their own version of LDS culture. The film's snapshot-style wrap-up, where Elizabeth comments on the future fates of all of the central characters, reinforces the conclusion that the earnest Mary and Collins represent one possible path for young Mormons, rather than Mormonism in general.

## "Frustrated . . . but not rebellious": Elizabeth Finds a Place within the Church

From a different perspective, Elizabeth, too, feels disenchanted with the flirtation-heavy, marriage-minded culture that surrounds her in this film. She makes her position plain in the film's opening line, which she speaks in voice-over: "It is a truth universally acknowledged that a girl of a certain age and of a certain situation in life must be in want of a husband." The twist on the first line of Austen's *Pride and Prejudice* is obvious: what is at issue here is not, as in Austen, the "possession of a good fortune"[46] by an unmarried man but simply the pressure—amply evident in Austen's novel as well—imposed by a woman's advancing age in a culture that considers her to be settled only when married. The phrase Elizabeth uses in Black's film about "a certain situation in life" obliquely refers, of course, to her position as a member of the LDS Church, which strongly emphasizes marriage and family life. As Elizabeth reveals later in this opening voice-over, she is focused more on her vocation—to "be a great writer," in her words—than on securing a husband. Her priorities place her at odds with her friends and fellow undergraduate students, especially her man-chasing housemate, Lydia.

Rather than spend all her time primping, working out, and flirting, Elizabeth is absorbed in her classes (including one scene where her professor discusses Austen), her part-time work at a bookstore (where, to her distaste, she has to shelve copies of the so-called Pink Bible, a guide to catching men), and her efforts at novel writing, which culminate in her submission of a manuscript to a literary agency that turns out to be co-owned by Darcy. Marriage, Elizabeth makes clear, is on the back burner until she finishes her studies. (Why she is still an undergraduate at twenty-six is never explained in the film; viewers familiar with Mormon culture may infer that she served a mission.) Her insistence on discriminating among suitors is evident in her rejection of not only Collins but George Wickham, who in this version torpedoes his chances with Elizabeth by coming on too strong physically. (In Austen's novel, Elizabeth's attraction to Wickham dies not because of any pivotal encounter but after she hears that he has become engaged to an heiress; she subsequently learns from Darcy about Wickham's past seduction of Darcy's sister.)

Indeed, Elizabeth's resistance to Wickham's advances in this film, together with her disdain for flirting and excessively feminine self-display, complicate our understanding of what Collins describes as her "forward feminist ways." What distinguishes Elizabeth is her insistence on thinking of herself as complete without a man, not any supposedly liberated notions about sexuality or even authority. Her response to Collins's marriage proposal, while firm, is entirely polite: "Please, no. . . . I'm not sure what I did to lead you on, but please stop." Only in a fantasy sequence does Elizabeth challenge Collins's public rebuke of her at church: she imagines throwing a book at his head and watching the congregation erupt in cheers. In actuality, as already mentioned, an older male congregant simply escorts Collins away from the lectern. Elizabeth may gripe in monologues, or to her favorite housemate, Jane, but she doesn't vent in any public venues. As the film's casting notice describes her, she is "frustrated by the society she lives in, but not rebellious"[47]—an apt description as well of Austen's Elizabeth Bennet, who finds much to object to in the mores of her culture but stops well short of transgressing them.

The distinction this film draws between frustration and rebellion is clearest in a brief scene where Elizabeth is evidently addressing an audience of fellow church members. This scene is one of several presented in an extended sequence over upbeat music, showing Elizabeth taking charge of her life after a period of despondency. She stands in front of a blackboard, dressed up and gesturing toward her listeners, all of whom seem to be women (only the backs of a few heads are visible). She holds a thick book open in her hand—presumably a book of scripture, given the list of references visible in the middle of the blackboard. On the left is written "Pascal's Christ"; on the right is a chart (empty so far), headed "Lust" and "Love." Elizabeth's face shows her enthusiasm for her subject matter, in marked contrast with her demeanor in the earlier church scene as she listened to Collins denounce her. While the film does not linger on this episode of Elizabeth lecturing, the image of her as a spiritual instructor is powerful and memorable. This scene indicates both that Elizabeth finds satisfaction in exploring her ideas within the framework of devotion and that her fellow believers welcome her efforts. That thoughtful, ambitious Elizabeth feels at home in her church and is listened to by fellow members constitutes this film's strongest positive portrayal of Mormonism.

In focusing on Elizabeth's endeavor to pursue her goals and maintain her convictions, this version of *Pride & Prejudice* performs the work that Suzanne Ferriss and Mallory Young describe as characteristic of recent women's films in the *chick flick* genre. Chick flicks, write Ferriss and Young, "raise questions about women's place—their prescribed social and sexual roles, the role of female friendship and camaraderie— and play out the difficulties of negotiating expectations and achieving independence."[48] Nor is *Pride & Prejudice* alone among chick flicks in exploring this territory without depicting overt sexuality: Ferriss and Young point out a subgenre of films that "have returned to the subtle promotion of chastity . . . offering the chaste kiss at the end as the only expression of sexuality."[49] *Pride & Prejudice* fits as well into the subgroup of chick flicks derived from Austen novels: Ferriss and Young cite *Clueless, Bridget Jones's Diary, Bride & Prejudice*, and Joe Wright's 2005 *Pride & Prejudice*. Austen-inspired films are representative, in turn, of a broader trend identified by Karen Hollinger of "a return to classic woman's literature as a source of female-centered plots and characters," which she identifies as a change brought about by "women's greater involvement in filmmaking" beginning in the mid-1990s.[50] Such literary adaptations, argues Hollinger, "represent not only a conservative return to what is presented as a simpler, better past, but also the attempt of female screenwriters, directors, stars and production executives to recapture for a contemporary female audience the distinctive voices of prominent women of the past."[51]

Creating a Mormon version of Austen's most popular novel, in contrast, is not an effort at "return" or "recapture" but instead asserts the existence of common ground among groups that may seem distant: Austen's characters and contemporary Mormons, LDS filmgoers and mainstream cinema audiences. Black has said that he views his own religious history as key to this attempt: "I hope and believe that the film can play to an LDS and non-LDS audience. I am a convert and relatively new to the LDS culture. I don't think I am capable of making a movie for an exclusive LDS audience."[52] By reinventing Elizabeth Bennet as an aspiring writer, Black encourages the viewer to see her as a version of himself as creator (as well as, possibly, an updated incarnation of Austen). Like Elizabeth, Black recognizes and satirizes the foibles of members of his church, but his criticism does not reach the church itself—and need not since Mormonism, as Black presents it, offers space for such very different characters as Collins, Mary, and Elizabeth to become the best and happiest versions of themselves.

## Conclusion

Within the community of LDS film critics and scholars, Black's portrayal of Mormonism in *Pride & Prejudice* has not, on the whole, been praised. Most appreciatively, Eric Samuelson has described it as a "flawed but perfectly watchable comed[y]" that demonstrates its director's "provocative visual sense for style and shot composition."[53] More typical is Randy Astle's faulting of this film's "attempts at crossing over by watering down the Mormonism."[54] According to Astle, "the more authentic the depiction of Mormonism, the more engaging [a] movie will be."[55]

As an adaptation of a classic literary text to the context of a particular, often-misunderstood religious culture for a diverse audience, *Pride*

*& Prejudice*'s authenticity or fidelity has been debated from many angles. Are its depictions of flirtatious young Mormons true to life or over the top? The anonymous author of a capsule review at the Web site lds-video.com[56] vigorously defends these portrayals:

> the most frequent complaint about [this film] I have heard is that people say that many of the characters, all of whom are LDS, are not all very good examples: Many seem shallow, selfish, obsessed with dating, clothes, and other worldly things. It just makes me wonder, have the people who are complaining about thes[e] characters actually spent any time in a BYU singles ward? . . . . I definitely recognize and remember the types of situations and people in Jane Austen's novel, and now in Andrew Black's movie. . . . Yes, these are flawed characters, and some of them are pre-occupied with marriage. But they also are serious about important values and morality, without it seeming odd or unfashionable to be that way. [57]

Another question of fidelity for this film, as for any adaptation, concern sits relation to its source text. LDS film critic Thomas Baggaley, a strong detractor of this *Pride & Prejudice*, asserts a particular relationship between these two forms of authenticity: "I just didn't really get the sense that the characters were actually LDS in any way other than name. . . . Instead, the film stays slavishly true to the original book. . . ." In Baggaley's opinion, this film's fidelity to Austen's novel ensures that "fans of Jane Austen's *Pride and Prejudice* (the book) will probably enjoy" it, even if he did not.[58]

Baggaley's view is borne out by the generally positive comments from Austen fans posted on the Republic of Pemberley's discussion boards. "Surprisingly well done" is a typical assessment,[59] with several viewers expressing particular enthusiasm about Orlando Seale's performance as Darcy. Response to Black's film from Austen scholars has been more mixed. Jennifer Mary Woolston commends this version for its fidelity: "Rather than moving away from Austen's original tale, Black's re-imagining reinforces the basic need for women to tell, show, and share their experiences, providing a light-hearted commentary hauntingly congruous with what Austen originally impressed upon the reading audiences of her day."[60] Linda Troost and Sayre Greenfield, in contrast, call attention to the extent to which Black's film shares the limitations of other recent "global" adaptations of Austen. These films, argue Troost and Greenfield, "wish to use Austen for a celebration of women's triumphs, but their heroines must have professional abilities in addition to moral worth. The films appropriate Austen as a vehicle to celebrate community, family, and friendship but are not willing to adopt her critical eye toward these social entities."[61]

To an audience with no connection to the LDS church, *Pride & Prejudice*'s depictions of Mormons do certainly convey—in the words of the anonymous critic already quoted—a seriousness "about important values and morality, without it seeming odd or unfashionable to be that way." To communicate such seriousness while remaining entertaining is a feat comparable to Austen's: arguably it is on this level, rather than any parallels in courtship cultures, that this *Pride & Prejudice* comes closest to its source. Given the positive—though oblique—presentation of Mormonism in this film, a non-LDS viewer may well be motivated to find out more about the church, just as a viewer new to Austen may be inspired to seek out the original novel. Crossing over works both ways.

## Notes

1.   Following the convention established by critics of Mormon film, I use the abbreviation LDS to denote members of the Church of Jesus Christ of Latter-day Saints and the broader term of Mormon when referring to the culture generally; see Astle and Burton, "A History of Mormon Cinema," 15. Another note on terminology: Black's film is titled *Pride & Prejudice* (with an ampersand) in its opening credits and on the DVD box, and I always refer to it that way, although some quotations from other sources render it as *Pride and Prejudice*. In my usage, *Pride and Prejudice* refers to the title of Austen's novel.
2.   Bennett, "A Novel Approach to LDS Comedy."
3.   Hyde, "Let's Hear It for Mollywood."
4.   Culver, *"Pride and Prejudice."*
5.   Foundas, review of *Pride & Prejudice.*
6.   The budget figure was reported on the Internet Movie Database (www. IMDb.com) when the film was in production; the information from that posting is archived at http://www.ldsfilm.com/Pride/PrideAndPrejudice2. html. The box-office gross is available at IMDb (http://us.imdb.com/title/ tt0366920/business) and is also reported by Eric Samuelson in his article "Finding an Audience, Paying the Bills," 225. Samuelson's chart on the same page allows an easy comparison of profits and losses among LDS-associated films released since 2000.
7.   See "The Jane Austen Society of North America: *Pride and Prejudice* Film Adaptations"; and Parrill, "Jane Austen Adaptations Filmography."
8.   Woolston, "It's Not a Put-Down, Miss Bennet; It's a Category"; and Troost and Greenfield, "Appropriating Austen."
9.   Van Valkenburg, "On TV: Big Screen a Reality for Utah Stars."
10.  Two recent novels based on Austen's writings, created by LDS members and aimed at a wide audience, bear comparison to Black's *Pride & Prejudice*. Stephenie Meyer's wildly popular teen vampire novel *Twilight* (2005) is a

loosely updated version of *Pride and Prejudice*, while in Shannon Hale's *Austenland* (2007), a young woman finds her own version of Mr. Darcy while participating in a kind of fantasy camp for Austen fans. Unlike Black's film, however, both *Twilight* and *Austenland* lack even indirect references to Mormonism.

11. Hyde, "Let's Hear It for Mollywood."
12. Astle and Burton, "History of Mormon Cinema," 138.
13. Baggaley, "Reviews of Recent LDS Films and a Question."
14. Samuelson, "Finding an Audience, Paying the Bills," 222.
15. Moring, interview with Richard Dutcher, November 14, 2006.
16. Burton, "Establishing Shot," 8. See also Travis T. Anderson's critique of the concept of "wholesomeness" as applied to both entertainment and art in "Seeking after the Good in Art, Drama, Film, and Literature," 231–46.
17. Stout, "Protecting the Family," 88.
18. Stout and Scott, "Mormons and Media Literacy," 149 (italics in the original).
19. Burton, "Establishing Shot," 6, 10.
20. Astle and Burton, "History of Mormon Cinema," 17.
21. Astle, review of *Angie*, 329–30 (italics in the original).
22. Viewed from the inside, of course, the missionary experience has been central to many recent LDS films, as John-Charles Duffy mentions in his essay in this volume.
23. Duffy, "Remarks for Panel Discussion."
24. Ibid.
25. Ibid.
26. For an overview of independent LDS films released from 2002 to 2004, see Astle and Burton 138–47. Astle and Burton do note the 2007 release of what they describe as "Brian Brough's modernization and Mormonization of *Beauty and the Beast*," 146—a folk tale, of course, rather than a classic novel.
27. Bennett, "Novel Approach to LDS Comedy."
28. Taylor, "*Pride* Odd for Actors."
29. Culver, "Pride and Prejudice."
30. Van Valkenburg, "On TV: Big Screen a Reality for Utah Stars."
31. Other noteworthy updated fictional versions of *Pride and Prejudice* include Melissa Nathan's *Pride, Prejudice and Jasmin Field* (2000), Kate Fenton's *Lions and Liquorice* (1995; published in the U.S. as *Vanity and Vexation: A Novel of Pride and Prejudice*), and Paula Marantz Cohen's *Jane Austen in Boca* (2002).
32. Troost and Greenfield discuss Black's adaptation of *Pride and Prejudice* together with the film version of *Bridget Jones's Diary*, *Bride & Prejudice*, and the Tamil-language Bollywood musical *Kandukondain Kandukondain* (2000), a version of *Sense and Sensibility*. I have previously compared Black's version of *Pride and Prejudice* with those of Joe Wright (2005), Gurinder Chadha (2004), and Simon Langton (1995): see "Filming the 'Really Accomplished' Woman: Performance and Gender in Recent Adaptations of *Pride and Prejudice*," in "The Public's Open to Us All": Essays on Women and Performance in Eighteenth-Century England.
33. See Wells, "True Love Waits."
34. Morefield, "Emma Could Not Resist," 198.
35. Ibid., 199.
36. Margolis, "Janeite Culture," 27, 29.

37. "Mary might have been prevailed on to accept him. She rated his abilities much higher than any of the others; there was a solidity in his reflections which often struck her, and though by no means as clever as herself, she thought that if encouraged to read and improve himself by such an example as hers, he might become a very agreeable companion." Jane Austen, *Pride and Prejudice*, 139–40.

38. "Casting Notice." Mary's last name appears as Lambton (an allusion to a place name in Austen's novel) in the credits for the finished film.

39. Ibid.

40. See, for example, Bennett, "Novel Approach to LDS Comedy."

41. Culver, "Pride and Prejudice."

42. Hyde, "Let's Hear It for Mollywood."

43. See Wells, "True Love Waits."

44. Austen, *Pride and Prejudice*, 120 (italics in the original).

45. Austen's presentation of Charlotte's decision, and the tendency of film adaptations to cast aspersions on it, are discussed fully by Ruth Perry in "Sleeping with Mr. Collins," in *Jane Austen and Co.: Remaking the Past in Contemporary Culture*, 213–28.

46. Austen, *Pride and Prejudice*, 3.

47. "Casting Notice."

48. Ferriss and Young, "Introduction: Chick Flicks and Chick Culture," 4.

49. Ibid., 6.

50. Hollinger, "Afterword: Once I Got Beyond the Name *Chick Flick*," 223. Additional Austen-inspired films mentioned by Hollinger in this context are *Sense and Sensibility* (1995) and *Mansfield Park* (1999).

51. Ibid., 224. Of course, Black's *Pride & Prejudice*—with a male director, producer, and coscreenwriter—has a more gender-mixed group of creators than Hollinger envisions. Many recent screen adaptations of Austen's novels have featured male directors and/or screenwriters as well: major examples include Joe Wright's direction of *Pride & Prejudice* (2005), Ang Lee's direction of *Sense and Sensibility* (1995), and Andrew Davies's scripts for television versions of *Pride and Prejudice* (1995), *Emma* (1995), and *Northanger Abbey* (2007). Other noteworthy examples of male creators reworking Austen material range across the spectrum of popular to high culture: consider Seth Grahame-Smith's *Pride and Prejudice and Zombies* (2009); John Kessel's 2008 Nebula Award–winning story "Pride and Prometheus," included in *The Baum Plan for Independence and Other Stories*, 2008; and Ian McEwan's critically praised novel *Atonement* (2001). My article "Shades of Austen in Ian McEwan's *Atonement*," 101–12, discusses McEwan's debt to Austen.

52. Culver, "Pride and Prejudice."

53. Samuelson, "Finding an Audience, Paying the Bills," 224, 228.

54. Astle and Gordon, "History of Mormon Cinema," 140.

55. Ibid., 135.

56. See http://www.ldsvideo.com/index.asp?PageAction=Custom&ID=7. ("Our goal is to be the most incredible source possible for LDS-made videos and DVDs.")

57. Anonymous review of *Pride & Prejudice* posted at http://www.ldsvideo.com/index.asp?PageAction=VIEWPROD&ProdID=320.

58. Baggaley, "Reviews of Recent LDS Films and a Question."

59. Comment posted by Faith R. on June 28, 2007, on http://www.pemberley. com.
60. Woolston, "It's Not a Put-Down, Miss Bennet; It's a Category."
61. Troost and Greenfield, "Appropriating Austen."

## Bibliography

Anderson, Travis T. "Seeking after the Good in Art, Drama, Film, and Literature." *BYU Studies* 46, no. 2 (2007): 231–46.

Anonymous. Review of *Pride and Prejudice*, directed by Andrew Black. http://www.ldsvideo.com/index.asp?PageAction=VIEWPROD&ProdID=320.

Astle, Randy. Review of *Angie*, produced by the Tom Russell family. *BYU Studies* 46, no. 2 (2007): 324–30.

Astle, Randy, and Gideon O. Burton. "A History of Mormon Cinema." *BYU Studies* 46, no. 2 (2007): 12–163.

Austen, Jane. *Pride and Prejudice*. Edited by Pat Rogers. Cambridge: Cambridge University Press, 2006.

Baggaley, Thomas. "Reviews of Recent LDS Films and a Question: What's It Gonna Take to Crossover into Mainstream?" *Meridian Magazine*, 2004. http://www.meridianmagazine.com/arts/041008crossover.html.

Bennett, Elizabeth. "A Novel Approach to LDS Comedy." *BYU NewsNet*, June 26, 2003. http://newsnet.byu.edu/story.cfm/44740.

Burton, Gideon O. "Establishing Shot: The Scope of Mormon Cinema." *BYU Studies* 46, no. 2 (2007): 5–11.

"Casting Notice." http://www.ldsfilm.com/Pride/PrideAndPrejudice2.html.

Culver, Sarah "*Pride and Prejudice*: Behind the Scenes." *Meridian Magazine*, February 21, 2004. http://www.meridianmagazine.com/arts/040212industryprint.html.

Duffy, John-Charles. "Remarks for Panel Discussion: 'Mormon Cinema at Five.'" April 22, 2006. http://www.unc.edu/~jcduffy/mormoncinema. pdf.

Ferriss, Suzanne, and Mallory Young. "Introduction: Chick Flicks and Chick Culture." In *Chick Flicks: Contemporary Women at the Movies*, edited by Ferriss and Young, 1–25. New York: Routledge, 2008.

Foundas, Scott. Review of *Pride and Prejudice*, directed by Andrew Black. *Variety*, November 25, 2003. http://www.variety.com/index.asp?layout=print_review&reviewid=VE1117922526&categoryid=31.

Hollinger, Karen. "Afterword: Once I Got Beyond the Name *Chick Flick*." In *Chick Flicks: Contemporary Women at the Movies*, 221–32.

Hyde, Jesse. "Let's Hear It for Mollywood: Filmmaker Says LDS Version of 'Pride and Prejudice' Has a Market." *Deseret News*, June 21, 2003. http://www.ldsfilm.com/Pride/PrideAndPrejudice2.html.

"The Jane Austen Society of North America: *Pride and Prejudice* Film Adaptations." http://www.jasna.org/film/pp.html.

Margolis, Harriet. "Janeite Culture: What Does the Name Jane Austen Authorize?" In *Jane Austen on Screen*, edited by Gina Macdonald and Andrew F. Macdonald, 22–43. Cambridge: Cambridge University Press, 2003.

Morefield, Kenneth R. "'Emma Could Not Resist': Complicity and the Christian Reader." *Persuasions: The Jane Austen Journal* 25 (2003): 197–204.

Moring, Mark. Interview with Richard Dutcher, November 14, 2006. http://www.christianitytoday.com/movies/interviews/richarddutcher.html.

Parrill, Sue. "Jane Austen Adaptations Filmography." http://www.pemberley.com/filmography/filmography.html.

Perry, Ruth. "Sleeping with Mr. Collins." In *Jane Austen and Co.: Remaking the Past in Contemporary Culture*, edited by Suzanne R. Pucci and James Thompson, 213–28. Albany: State University of New York Press, 2003.

*Pride & Prejudice*, directed by Andrew Black. Excel Entertainment Group, 2003.

Samuelson, Eric. "Finding an Audience, Paying the Bills: Competing Business Models in Mormon Cinema." *BYU Studies* 46, no. 2 (2007): 209–30.

Stout, Daniel A. "Protecting the Family: Mormon Teachings about Mass Media." In *Religion and Mass Media: Audiences and Adaptations*, edited by Daniel A. Stout and Judith M. Buddenbaum, 85–99. Thousand Oaks, CA: SAGE, 1996.

Stout, Daniel A., and David W. Scott. "Mormons and Media Literacy: Exploring the Dynamics of Religious Media Education." In *Mediating Religion: Conversations in Media, Religion, and Culture*, edited by Jolyon Mitchell and Sophia Marriage, 143–58. London: T & T Clark/Continuum, 2003.

Taylor, Lindsie. "*Pride* Odd for Actors." *Deseret News*, July 29, 2004. http://deseretnews.com/dn/view/0,1249,595080624,00.html.

Troost, Linda, and Sayre Greenfield. "Appropriating Austen: Localism on the Global Scene." *Persuasions: The Jane Austen Journal On-Line* 28, no. 2 (2008). http://www.jasna.org/persuasions/on-line/vol28no2/troost-greenfield.htm.

Van Valkenburg, Nancy. "On TV: Big Screen a Reality for Utah Stars." *Standard-Examiner* (Ogden, UT), June 29, 2003. http://www.ldsfilm.com/Pride/PrideAndPrejudice2.html.

Wells, Juliette. "Filming the 'Really Accomplished' Woman: Performance and Gender in Recent Adaptations of *Pride and Prejudice*." In "The Public's Open to Us All": Essays on *Women and Performance in Eighteenth-Century England*, edited by Laura Engel, 300–322. Newcastle upon Tyne: Cambridge Scholars Publishing, 2009.

———. "Shades of Austen in Ian McEwan's *Atonement*." *Persuasions: The Jane Austen Journal* 30 (2008): 101–12.

———. "True Love Waits: Austen and the Christian Romance in the Contemporary U.S." *Persuasions: The Jane Austen Journal On-Line* 28, no. 2 (2008). http://www.jasna.org/persuasions/on-line/vol28no2/wells.htm.

Woolston, Jennifer Mary. "It's Not a Put-Down, Miss Bennet; It's a Category": Andrew Black's Chick Lit *Pride and Prejudice*." *Persuasions: The Jane Austen Journal On-Line* 28, no. 1 (2007). http://www.jasna.org/persuasions/on-line/vol28no1/woolston.htm.

# 8

# Reality Corrupts; Reality Television Corrupts Absolutely

KAREN D. AUSTIN

Though reality, television, and Mormons have never been complete strangers, they have become unusually cozy in recent years. Since 2000, Mormon contestants have appeared on shows such as *The Real World, American Idol, So You Think You Can Dance,* and *America's Next Top Model* in proportions far beyond what seems reasonable from their numbers in the general populace. Not only have Mormons appeared on these programs, but they have done well, often winning the shows formatted as season-long contests. Mormons have won *The Biggest Loser* (Ryan Benson and Ali Vincent), *Survivor* (Todd Herzog), *Dancing with the Stars* (Donny Osmond), and *Rebel Billionaire* (Shawn Nelson). While competing on these shows, Mormon contestants have garnered large followings among national and international audiences. "Not since the Mormon Tabernacle Choir was formed in 1847," wrote the *Sunday Times* in 2008, "has America been listening to so many singing Mormons."[1] That same year—when Mormons David Archuleta and Brooke White became two of the final five contestants on Fox's top-rated reality show *American Idol—Newsweek* magazine captured the irony succinctly: "Considering that earlier in this country's history Mormons were threatened with extermination and driven from the United States, it's remarkable that America may now be poised to crown a Mormon as its new 'Idol.'"[2]

Throughout its remarkable reign as America's most popular reality show, *American Idol* has hosted far more than its fair share of Mormon contestants, including Carmen Rasmussen (season two), Jon Peter Lewis (season three)—and Brooke White and David Archuleta (season four). Apparently Mormons not only can sing; they can dance. Returned missionary Benji Schwimmer won the second season of *So You Think You Can*

*Dance*, where he also competed with his Mormon cousin, Heidi Groskreutz. On camera he talked about his mission experience and his standards of modesty, which he found challenged during choreography for his first hip-hop dance with partner Donyelle Jones. In addition to the amateur Mormon dancers on *So You Think You Can Dance, Dancing with the Stars* has featured Mormon professional dancers, including Ashly DelGrosso, two-time champion Julianne Hough, and Julie's brother, Derek, who won the seventh season. Two Mormon dancers—Lacey Schwimmer and Chelsie Hightower—moved from performing as amateurs on the former dance show to appearing as professionals on the latter.[3]

Explanations for the unlikely prominence of Mormons on reality TV are not hard to find, and everyone who has noticed it has an opinion. One critic proposes that the wholesome lifestyle and innocent demeanor of many young Mormons are "ideally suited to mainstream American television, which still eschews nudity and swear words" or that "Mormon family traditions of singing and dancing—stretching back to campfire nights on the great 19th-century Mormon trek to Salt Lake City—give amateur contestants a head start when performing in public."[4] Others argue that "coming from a large family . . . probably helps in [shows like] *Survivor*, with its complicated group dynamics that can mirror sibling rivalry."[5] A casting director from *Survivor* opines that Mormons "have these incredible experiences through their missions and can relate to being dropped off in the middle of somewhere they've never been and having to make it."[6] And as other essays in this collection show, Mormons of all sorts have become increasingly interesting characters in American popular culture during the 1990s and 2000s—exactly the time period represented by the resurgence of reality television.

The more interesting part of the story, however, is the extent to which these Mormons appear *as Mormons*. Their religious identity is part of either the explicit narrative of the production or, even more often, the informal narrative of the fan base that participates in reality-television programs on e-mail discussion lists and Web sites and in chat rooms. Undoubtedly lots of United Methodists and Roman Catholics have appeared on these shows, but these more mainstream denominations have not played nearly as big a part in the narrative building that defines reality television. Mormonism itself functions in these narratives in much the same way that race and sexual orientation do: an off-the-shelf cultural category that functions to build scenarios, create conflicts, and produce resolutions. Reality television has made characters out of average Americans, and as any honest critic will tell you, characterization requires stereotypes. From the comfort of an easy chair, viewers observe recognizable reality show characters from the cast of thousands: nurses, cowboys, aspiring models, people of color, soccer moms, homosexuals, college students, firemen—and even Mormons.

## Reality as Genre

Establishing the presence of reality television is an easier task than defining it as a genre. But we need to attempt a definition to understand the narrative-building strategies that Mormon characters so frequently take part in. The most stripped-down definition characterizes *reality television* as broadcast programming depicting unknown actors in a natural setting reacting in an unscripted manner for purposes unrelated to the presence of a camera. However, the explosion of reality-television programming has breached almost every essential characteristic of this definition. Nevertheless, these core traits are almost entirely exemplified by two pioneers of reality television—*Candid Camera* and *An American Family.*

Coinciding with the inception of regularly scheduled television programs in the late 1940s was the appearance of *Candid Camera,* which featured people filmed outside of a television studio without their knowledge. Creator Allen Funt initially developed the concept as a radio show—*Candid Microphone*—which then crossed into television in 1948 and aired either as an independent show or an element of another program for decades. *Candid Camera* reached its zenith as "one of the top ten US network shows during the 1960s."[7] Yes, Allen Funt and other crew members did manipulate situations to provoke the unaware participants, but other than the setup, the show featured both nonactors' responses to the unexpected and their reactions when the setup was revealed. Whether confronted with a talking mailbox, a car that split in half while moving, or a conveyer belt that delivered cakes at an impossibly fast rate, the average citizen reacted, unaware of the camera or the people who had designed the stunt.

In the early 1970s, television crews exited the Hollywood sound stages and entered the Santa Barbara home of Bill and Pat Loud and their five children. The crews emerged with around three hundred hours of footage, which was cut down to twelve episodes that aired on PBS beginning in early 1973. Unlike the people filmed by Funt, the seven family members knew about the presence of the camera. Supposedly the family would acclimate to the constant presence of the camera and exhibit normal behavior in their private setting, revealing the intimacies of family life for a viewing audience of millions. During the course of the filming, the parents' marriage crumbled and one of the sons shared elements of his life as a gay man with viewers unfamiliar with seeing such topics during the era of *The Brady Bunch* and *The Waltons*.

It is hard to gauge the extent to which the camera itself introduced a Hawthorne-effect alteration of participants' behavior.[8] Even during its first airing, the press erupted with debates about the influence of the camera in this supposed documentary and the collapse of the distinction between private and public spheres. These debates presage many of the current discussions about the significance of today's reality-entertainment programming. Jeffrey Ruoff summarizes the critical reception of *An American Family*, noting that this public television program was "swamped in controversies concerning the American family and sexuality, the state of the nation, the role of television, and the representation of reality."[9] Even anthropologist Margaret Mead weighed in with an article in *TV Guide*, where she described the program as giving birth to a new genre: "I do not think *An American Family* should be called a documentary. I think we need a new name for it, a name that would contrast it not only with fiction, but with what we have been exposed to up until now on TV."[10] Positioned somewhere between the natural and the artificial, the viewer and the viewed, reality television began to expand and take up significant space on the small screen, and, ever since the television writers' strike of 1988, producers have offered more and more programs that forego scriptwriters and professional actors.

Accountants and network executives, however, have also discovered that these stopgap shows were not only a convenient alternative during the strike; they were also cheaper and, in some cases, more popular than scripted shows. Since the year 2000 and the ratings success of early reality shows such as *Survivor* and *Big Brother*, television schedules have been full of programming that allows viewers to more vividly imagine their neighbor or themselves participating in the spectacle on the screen in their living rooms. The presence of such programming is so prevalent that on May 24, 2005, Fox Entertainment Group launched Fox Reality channel, dedicated to the genre. Even traditional networks are filling significant space with reality shows: "By January 2003, one-seventh of all programming on ABC was reality based."[11]

The key phrase here, perhaps, is "reality based." Though reality-TV participants use their real names and present more-or-less factual biographies to viewers, the situations that they encounter are carefully contrived, and the footage that the audience eventually sees has usually been heavily edited to create a narrative effect similar to a scripted drama. Today we also see people participating in reality television who demonstrate an awareness of the camera during the filming itself. Shows that rely on viewers' votes to determine the outcome are particularly prone to having participants play to the camera. *Big Brother* asks contestants to balance the fine line between cooperating with each other enough to avoid nomination for eviction and pandering to the cameras to convince the viewing audience to evict a peer. According to academic media critic Richard Kilborn, there "is a recognition on the part of the contestants [on *Big Brother*] that they are all *dramatis personae* on a television stage specially rigged and designed to encourage the lively interpersonal exchanges on which this type of show feeds."[12] Characters talk to the viewers during confessionals, and they talk to each other about their reception by the viewing public. As more and more fans of these shows move from observers to participants, they bring with them strategies and attitudes that erode reality television's initial qualities of unaware, unscripted, and unrehearsed.

Reality television is still fundamentally a narrative genre, and, as such, requires the same elements as any other story: plots that can be followed; characters that can be loved, hated, and identified with; and, perhaps most importantly, conflicts that can be resolved. These are the elements that make any story interesting; without them Americans could just watch the security-camera footage at their local convenience stores and call that the ultimate reality television. In fact, surveys conducted by media critic Annette Hill point toward this paradox: "The more entertaining a factual [program] is, the less real it appears to viewers."[13] Producers and directors have to manufacture "the real" with a variety of features, from the show's setting to its goals, tasks, and characters. These elements for depicting human behavior in a dramatic setting have existed for centuries and been defined, analyzed and applied not only to human behavior but to works of fiction such as poetry, novels, and dramas and their electronic offspring—film, television and hypertext media.

The exaggerated role of Mormons in reality television stems from this need for drama and the dramatic potential inherent in Mormonism's current position in the larger American culture. Contemporary Mormons are generally perceived as straitlaced, friendly, repressed, and naïve. But they are also impacted by nineteenth-century stereotypes that have not gone away: the Mormon man as a sinister, theocratic, polygamist Svengali; and the Mormon woman as a put-upon, none-too-bright victim of the ultimate patriarchy.[14] These stereotypes provide reality-TV producers with the raw cultural material that they need to shape compelling narratives around any participants in their programs who happen to be Mormon.

## The Mormon Connection:
## Variations on Two Themes

The current relationship between Mormons and reality television began in 2000 with Mormon Julie Stoffer's appearance on MTV's signature reality show *The Real World*. In this program, young, single, attractive people are housed together in an urban setting (in this case, New Orleans) while their interactions are filmed around the clock. Each week audiences watch highlights from this filming that have been carefully selected and woven into a narrative. A key factor of the show's premise is the casting. The producers select people from a variety of backgrounds with the expectation that members will clash in their behaviors and ideologies, creating drama for the viewers at home. What could be more opposite from the stereotypical urban sophisticate than a wide-eyed Mormon from Wisconsin? Under the gaze of the camera, Stoffer faced questions from her more worldly wise housemates about some of their preconceptions about Mormons. Were they allowed to dance? What about their health code? Did they marry young? Did they practice polygamy? What was their feeling about people of color? Or homosexuals? By watching Julie's housemates ask her a series of questions about her religious tradition, general viewers could satisfy their curiosity about a Mormon character without being the people asking the probing questions. Mormon viewers also felt a degree of validation by having one of their own depicted on a popular television show.

In the decade following Stoffer's appearance on *The Real World*, other Mormons on reality-television shows offered a steady stream of variations on the "sweet young thing" image that she had inaugurated. Two examples were Neleh Dennis from season two of *Survivor*, who brought her scriptures with her as a luxury item, and Aimee Wright from cycle ten of *America's Next Top Model*, who expressed anxiety about the possibility of having to do nude modeling on the show. Benji Schimmer from *So You Think You Can Dance* was portrayed as the naïve young man, paired with the more worldly wise dance partner Donyelle Jones. During rehearsals for their first routine, Schwimmer blushed and talked about the way he was "not supposed to" get close to a girl like that "until after marriage."[15] *American Idol* contestant David Archuleta showed his wonder during his homecoming visit with mild expletives such as "gosh" and "gee." Host Ryan Seacrest teased Archuleta during the season about his sex appeal, only to have David blush and the audience laugh at his naïveté.

These plot elements, of course, are made possible by the general cultural perception of Mormons as upright, innocent, and unsophisticated.

Mormons generally accept these characterizations and even embrace them as positive traits. However, within the larger American culture, innocence is often the flip side of intolerance. This dynamic comes through clearly in the portrayal of Julie Stoffer on *The Real World*, where her rural Mormon values were contrasted constantly to those of her more worldly housemates: one of the things that she did not understand was sex; another was diversity; and much of the footage that the audience was shown highlighted this inexperience in ways that caused some of her housemates, and many critics, to label her racist and homophobic.

We need not think that the producers of *The Real World* were simply working with Stoffer's Mormonism as an interesting part of a more coherent whole. She was specifically recruited by casting directors "on a mission to find a faithful Mormon" for the ninth season of their show.[16] By this time, the producers had perfected their shtick into a simple formula: bring naïve, rural teenagers into an urban setting, add racial tension, and stir. In his insightful article "Country Hicks and Urban Cliques," Jon Kraszewski argues that the staging and editing of *The Real World* are designed to provide a simplistic narrative about race and racism:

> The show constructs a reality that frees the audience of any implications in racism by blaming rural conservatives for the problem. And yet, these rural figures contain a certain hip quality, both in their appearance and manners, that in some ways suggests they are urban and liberal. The rural characters discursively experience a dual existence on the program, living partly as members of a liberal urban clique and partly as conservative racist outsiders. The show then constructs serial narratives to expel racism from these characters in order to make them full-fledged, city-dwelling liberals.[17]

Julie Stoffer, who grew up in rural Wisconsin, fits easily into the rural/urban narrative that Kraszewski describes, and her Mormonism extends it even further. Of the thousands of hours that *The Real World* producers filmed, the twenty-two minutes that aired each week were carefully crafted to build, and resolve, this narrative. Stoffer betrayed her lack of experience with diversity when she commented that being in New Orleans was her first real encounter with "colored people" in her life. If she had changed her phrasing to "people of color" and punctuated her observation with "what a great opportunity," then her statement would have been more in line with contemporary liberal ideology. Instead, she was given a quick lesson on the problem with her outdated choice of "colored," which was in broader use before the civil-rights movement of the 1960s. The greater conflict, though, is the distance between the sweet Mormon character and the broader culture's more "way of the world" sensibility. To resolve this conflict, Stoffer had to symbolically give up her Mormonism in much the same way that other characters had to relinquish their rural sensibilities. The administration of Mormon-owned Brigham Young University collaborated with the producers brilliantly, if unintentionally, when they suspended Stoffer for living with housemates of the opposite sex.

As the decade unrolled, other Mormon contestants began to challenge and complicate the Mormon stereotype, such as the frat boy Chet Cannon from season twenty-one of *The Real World*, set in Brooklyn. Chet was intent on showing his ability to be cool and religious at the same time. The more radical challenge to the Mormon stereotype, though, took the form of three gay Mormon participants: Rafe Judkins, who placed third in the eleventh season of *Survivor*; Todd Herzog, who placed first in the fifteenth season of *Survivor*; and Keith Bryce, who participated in the fifth season of *Project Runway*. Three contestants across the entire reality genre are hardly enough to count as a trend, but the phenomenon deserves some comment. *Survivor*, for example, has had five openly gay contestants over eighteen seasons, and two of them (40 percent) have been Mormons—despite the fact that the words "gay Mormon" —for the vast majority of Mormons and non-Mormons alike—embody a fundamental contradiction.

The contradiction, of course, is part of the entertainment value. Gay Mormons on shows such as *Survivor* and *Project Runway* are, for most viewers, something like jackalopes or Hollywood Republicans: people want to see if they are really possible, and the contradictions become part of the narrative. The conflict is not an external one between innocent Mormons and the sophisticated world; rather, it is an internal contradiction within the individuals struggling to reconcile their lifestyles with their cultural upbringing. The struggle—which is played out primarily in the magazines, on the Web sites, and in other forms of fan literature that support the onscreen narratives—is generally successful as contestants discover, or prove to others, that they can reconcile the seemingly irreconcilable parts of their identity into a coherent whole. Rafe Judkins, for example, told reporters after the show that he wanted to participate as a gay Mormon to show the world that "people don't have to fit in one box or another." He wanted to prove to America that "you can be yourself and that people will like you."[18] Todd Herzog, a gay Mormon who actually won the *Survivor* challenge, put it somewhat differently: "If I can survive being a gay Mormon in Utah," he told reporters, "I can survive anything."[19]

## Conclusion

There is no reason to suspect that the producers of *American Idol, Survivor,* and all of the other new reality shows are driven by any ideological agenda larger or more comprehensive than making money. But we can still learn much from the ways that they propose to attract—and succeed in getting—viewers and build narratives around the lives of the participants that they include (after rigorous screening) in their carefully stage-managed slices of real life. Based on the number of Mormon participants in these programs, and the prevalence of Mormonism in the narratives constructed to support them, we can safely conclude that Mormons have begun to play a part in American popular culture comparable to (but certainly not identical with) the role they played in the late-nineteenth and early-twentieth century, when they appeared in such works as Mark Twain's *Roughing It,* Jerome Kern's *The Girl from Utah,* and Zane Grey's *The Riders of the Purple Sage.* After more than a hundred years of relative cultural obscurity, Mormons—as Mormons—appear to be back on the stage.

But what, if anything, can we conclude from the ways that Mormons have been portrayed on reality-television programs during the first decade of the twenty-first century? It is not enough to argue simply that these shows exploit stereotypes of Mormons (and of just about everybody else) and leave it at that. Stories of all kinds require ready-made stereotypes that can be pulled off the shelf and inserted into the narrative to develop characters, plots, and conflicts quickly without sacrificing coherence to endless explication. But stereotypes work because they resonate with a culture's predominant perceptions, and the dramatic surge in Mormon characters in the contemporary reality genre tells us a great deal about the space that Mormonism occupies in the larger American culture. I propose the following three conclusions as minimal "morals of the story" this essay has been telling:

*1. Mormons are still objects of curiosity in American Culture—so much so that just seeing a Mormon up close seems to be inherently interesting to a large number of people.*

A Pew Research Center survey conducted in the fall of 2007 revealed an almost perfect split in people's self-reported knowledge about Mormons: 48 percent of respondents reported that they personally knew a Mormon, and 49 percent said that they knew either "a great deal" or "some" about Mormonism. These findings suggest that Mormonism may be positioned in just the place between familiarity and unfamiliarity that makes some-thing interesting.[20] Members of a common religion (white Protestants, for example) would probably be too familiar to most viewers to sustain inter-esting story lines, while members of an extremely unfamiliar one (say, Hutterites) would be unlikely even to attract much interest.

The general unfamiliarity with Mormonism across a broad spectrum of the population also gives producers a free hand to invoke stereotypes and use them as the basis for creating narratives out of raw footage. The producers of *The Real World* went searching for a Mormon for their ninth season because they knew that the very word "Mormon" would conjure up a set of very distinct characteristics—straitlaced, naïve, conserva-tive, racially insensitive—that fit perfectly into the show's established formula. When characters play into the stereotypes, viewers have their suspicions about Mormonism confirmed. And characters that break free from these stereotypes—such as the gay Mormon contestants on *Survivor*— are all the more interesting for their ability to do so.

### 2. Mormons get a kick out of seeing themselves on TV.

Like members of many small, close-knit subcultures, most Mormons can easily rattle off lists of famous people who share their religious beliefs. In the past, such celebrities might have included the golfer Johnny Miller, the actor Gordon Jump, the baseball great Dale Murphy, and perhaps an Osmond or two. Today the lists are more likely to feature *Twilight* author Stephenie Meyer, former Massachusetts governor and Republican presi-dential candidate Mitt Romney, and *American Idol's* seventh-season run-ner-up, David Archuleta. It is not difficult to understand why Mormons respond this way to the idols of their tribe. Everybody wants respect, and, in a celebrity culture, nothing brings respect to a group faster than a bona fide A-list celebrity. But while the Mormons of the 1970s and 1980s probably did not have an appreciable effect on the standings of the Atlanta Braves or the ratings of *WKRP in Cincinnati*, the call-in vote for-mat of many contemporary reality-TV shows (which does not limit the number of votes a single person can cast) can be influenced dramatically by a core of committed block voters—such as Mormons voting for other Mormons. "In reality-TV terms," writes Sally Atkinson in *Newsweek*, "the Church of Jesus Christ of Latter-day Saints is in a sweet demographic spot: small enough for members to get excited over seeing one of their own in the spotlight, but large enough that they can affect results."[21]

This demographic dynamic gives producers an extra incentive to cast Mormons in reality shows where the voting often becomes part of the extended narrative. When Archuleta became a finalist on *American Idol*, he was joined by fellow Mormon Brooke White. The novelty of two Mormon finalists became part of the season-seven story line, driving ratings sky high in Utah and the Intermountain West, and causing considerable excitement elsewhere as people wondered whether the Mormon bloc would split its vote or unite behind one or the other of their newest celebrities. And the sheer strangeness of two Mormons in the finals of a secular music contest attracted the kind of attention that fuels shows like *American Idol*. "They represent less than 2% of the population, and yet they are 40% of the Idol top five" quipped TV critic Mo Rocca. "Are they simply better at singing than other Christian denominations?"[22]

*3. Mormon characters provide a new opportunity for producers to explore old questions about innocence, corruption, civilization, and assimilation.*

Julie Stoffer and her fellow "naïve-Mormon" reality-show participants end up enacting one of the oldest conflicts in literature: the corruption of the rustic provincial by the savvy city inhabitant. We see this trope in the oldest of literary texts, *The Epic of Gilgamesh*, when Gilgamesh sends a court prostitute to corrupt the wild man, Enkidu, whose closeness to nature is a great threat to the king. When Enkidu, on his deathbed, attempts to curse the prostitute for seducing him into the human fold, no less than the god Shamash appears to rebuke him: "Enkidu," asks the god, "why are you cursing the woman, the mistress who taught you to eat bread fit for gods and drink wine of kings? She who put upon you a magnificent garment, did she not give you glorious Gilgamesh for your companion, and has not Gilgamesh, your own brother, made you rest on a royal bed and recline on a couch at his left hand?"[23] Enkidu sees the error of his ways and realizes that his seduction was, in fact, a good thing. This same dynamic continues throughout the canons of world literature as one naïve character after another must shed his or her innocence to overcome its limitations. Such are Voltaire's Candide and Goethe's Faust, Marjorie of *The Country Wife* and Hester of *The Scarlet Letter*, Pippin and Peer Gynt—and all the way to Olivia Newton-John's black tights and filtered cigarettes at the end of *Grease*.

The popular image of Mormonism in twenty-first-century American culture—formed, as it has been, by a strange combination of transgressive nineteenth-century polygamists and conservative twentieth-century puritans—is especially well suited to this kind of narrative. Americans perceive Mormons as, on the one hand, religious, upright, and virtuous, and, on the other hand, insensitive, intolerant, and intractable.

When Mormon *American Idol* contestant Brooke White said in her audition that she had never seen an R-rated movie—and host Simon Cowell responded, "We can bring you over to the dark side a little bit"—he was not simply joking; he was giving away the secret of the game. While the Mormons' premium on sexual virtue may be quaint and even vaguely admirable on its own, it is bound inextricably with three socially disruptive ideologies: racism, sexism, and homophobia. Since all of these attributes are packaged together, corruption and enlightenment go hand in hand.

In an interview with the LDS-owned newspaper the *Deseret News*, given soon after her experience in New Orleans and before her suspension from BYU, Julie Stoffer demonstrates very clearly that she gets the point: "This whole experience has made me re-evaluate my beliefs and just the way I think about things," she explains, "but it's been in a very positive way, because I walk away from it no longer just believing everything written on paper or everything told to me. . . . I wish more people at BYU—and more people in general—would just open their eyes and get away from what they've always known, and figure out who they are and what they believe."[24]

However, a caveat is in order. The narrative built around gay, or otherwise atypical, Mormon characters often inverts the one constructed around the Julie Stoffer, sweet-young-thing Mormons. Whereas the latter must resolve the narrative conflict by giving up part of their Mormon identity in deference to the more enlightened standards of *The Real World*, the former are often presented as holding onto some part of that same identity despite pressure, and good reason, to shed it entirely. It is this sentiment that Rafe Judkins expresses in an interview, when, despite being invited to renounce his Mormon identity, he instead states that "Mormons are so focused on family and caring for other people, and there are so many things about the Mormon religion that I want to bring to my life. . . . When I have a husband and kids, I want us to have Family Home Evening on Monday nights, and I'll get together and play board games or do whatever. I think the Mormon Church has so much good that you can take from it."[25] This sentiment directly inverts Stoffer's, and the two statements work in tandem to define the end points of a "successful" (according to the ideology of the constructed narratives) integration of Mormonism with the more sophisticated American urban culture. Mormons (this narrative suggests) can be successful when they give up those parts of their identity that are judgmental, self-righteous, and sexually repressive—but hold onto the parts that are strong willed, close knit, and mutually supportive. And this, of course, is simply one more version of the melting-pot myth that has always governed the delicate dance with assimilation required of any subculture seeking admission into the great American popular ball.

## Notes

1. Allen-Mills, "'Mormon Mafia' Storms Reality TV."
2. Atkinson. "America's Next Top Mormon," 52.
3. Lacey Schwimmer was a contestant on season three of *So You Think You Can Dance* and then was cast as a professional in seasons seven and eight of *Dancing with the Stars*. Chelsie Hightower appeared as a contestant on season four of *So You Think You Can Dance* and then performed as a professional in season eight of *Dancing with the Stars*.
4. Allen-Mills, "'Mormon Mafia' Storms Reality TV."
5. Atkinson, "America's Next Top Mormon," 52.
6. Ibid.
7. Hill, *Reality TV*, 21.
8. The Hawthorne effect indentifies a change in a person's behavior merely because of the increased attention received as a subject in a study. The term was coined after a study conducted at the Hawthorne Works (a factory that manufactured electronic equipment). Production levels rose when investigators made changes to the work environment and fell when the study concluded.
9. Ruoff, "Can a Documentary Be Made of Real Life?," 270–96.
10. Mead, "As Significant as the Invention of Drama or the Novel," A61–63.
11. Murray and Ouellette, *Reality TV*, 4.
12. Kilborn, *Staging the Real*, 80 (italics in the original).
13. Hill, *Reality TV*, 57.
14. For a discussion of the way these nineteenth-century stereotypes have entered contemporary popular culture, see Austin's "Troped by the Mormons," 51–71.
15. "Top 20 Performance," *So You Think You Can Dance*, July 14, 2006, Fox network.
16. Atkinson, "America's Next Top Mormon," 52.
17. Kraszewski, "Country Hicks and Urban Cliques," 182.
18. Interview on http://www.post-gazette.com/pg/05347/621267.stm #ixzz0NS0AJELJ.
19. Ward, "Born Survivor," 72.
20. The results of the survey can be found at http://pewforum.org/surveys/religionviews07/#section2.
21. Atkinson, "America's Next Top Mormon," 52.
22. Rocca, quoted in Allen-Mills, "'Mormon Mafia' Storms Reality TV."
23. Sandars, *The Epic of Gilgamesh*, 91.
24. Pierce, "Unlikely Path."
25. Horiuchi, "Gay Mormon Gets Real on 'Survivor.'"

# Bibliography

Allen-Mills, Tony. "'Mormon Mafia' Storms Reality TV." *Sunday Times* (London), May 18, 2008.

Atkinson, Sally. "America's Next Top Mormon: Reality-TV Shows Are Plucking Contestants from an Unlikely Pew." *Newsweek*, May 19, 2008, 52.

Austin, Michael. "Troped by the Mormons: The Persistence of 19th-Century Mormon Stereotypes in Contemporary Detective Fiction." *Sunstone* 21, no. 3 (August 1998): 51–71.

Hill, Annette. *Reality TV: Audiences and Popular Factual Television.* London: Routledge, 2005

Horiuchi, Vince. "Gay Mormon Gets Real on 'Survivor.'" Talk of the Morning: Utah's Prime-Time Connection. *Salt Lake Tribune*, December 1, 2005.

Kilborn, Richard. *Staging the Real: Factual TV Programming in the Age of Big Brother.* Manchester, UK: Manchester University Press, 2003.

Kraszewski, Jon. "Country Hicks and Urban Cliques: Mediating Race, Reality, and Liberalism on MTV's *The Real World.*" In *Reality TV: Remaking Television Culture,* 179–95.

Mead, Margaret. "As Significant as the Invention of Drama or the Novel." *TV Guide,* January 6, 1973, A61–63.

Murray, Susan, and Laurie Ouellette, eds. *Reality TV: Remaking Television Culture.* New York: New York University Press, 2004.

Pierce, Scott D. "Unlikely Path: BYU to MTV." *Deseret News*, June 2, 2000.

Ruoff, Jeffrey. "Can a Documentary Be Made of Real Life?: The Reception of *An American Family.*" In *The Construction of the Viewer: Media Ethnography and the Anthropology of Audiences,* edited by Peter Ian Crawford and Sigurjón Baldur Hafsteinsson, 270–96. Højbjerg, Denmark: Intervention Press in association with the Nordic Anthropological Film Association, 1996.

Sandars, N. K., trans. *The Epic of Gilgamesh.* London: Penguin, 1972.

Ward, Lindsay. "Born Survivor: If I Can Survive Being a Gay Mormon in Utah, I Can Survive Anything." *Toronto Sun,* September 20, 2007, 72.

# About the Contributors

*Karen D. Austin* has spent thirty years studying rhetoric, twenty years teaching composition and literature, eleven years raising kids with her husband, Michael, and almost ten years watching entirely too much reality television. Currently she lives in Wichita, Kansas, where she provides academic support services for students attending Newman University.

*Michael Austin* is provost and vice president for academic affairs at Newman University in Wichita, Kansas. He has published books and articles on a variety of topics in twentieth-century American and eighteenth-century British literature. He is the editor of *A Voice in the Wilderness: Conversations with Terry Tempest Williams,* also published by Utah State University Press, and, most recently, the author of *Useful Fictions: Evolution Anxiety, and the Origins of Literature,* which will be published by the University of Nebraska Press in 2010. He lives in Wichita with his wife and two children.

*Mark T. Decker* is assistant professor of English at Bloomsburg University. He has published essays on William Faulkner, Thomas Pynchon, Richard Wright, and Charles Brockden Brown. He is also interested in the connection between social thought and speculative fiction. His most recent essay on this topic appears in *New Boundaries in Political Science Fiction* (University of South Carolina Press, 2008).

*John-Charles Duffy* is a William N. Reynolds fellow at the University of North Carolina at Chapel Hill, where he is completing a doctoral degree in religious studies. In addition, he holds degrees in English from Brigham Young University and the University of Utah. A former officer in the Association for Mormon Letters, he has published essays on Mormon cultural production, intellectual history, and the politics of diversity in *Irreantum, Sunstone, Dialogue: A Journal of Mormon Thought,* the *Journal of Mormon History,* the *Journal of Ritual Studies, Homosexuality and Religion,* and *Hispanic American Religious Cultures.*

*Cristine Hutchison-Jones* is a PhD candidate in Boston University's Division of Religious and Theological Studies. Her area of interest is the religious history of the United States, with particular focus on the history of Christianity and religious intolerance. She is currently working on a dissertation on non-Mormon representations of the Latter-day Saints in America since 1890.

*Kevin Kolkmeyer* has an MA in English from California State University, Long Beach. He has taught English at community colleges in California and New York for thirteen years. Currently he is a lecturer at the City University of New York (CUNY), teaching developmental and freshman writing and literature courses at the Kingsborough Community College campus in Brooklyn.

*J. Aaron Sanders* is assistant professor of English at Columbus State University. His stories and essays have appeared in *Gulf Coast, Quarterly West,* the *Beloit Fiction Journal, Karamu,* and the *Hawaii Review.*

*Juliette Wells,* associate professor of English at Manhattanville College, is working on a book titled *Everybody's Jane: Austen in the Popular Imagination* (Continuum, forthcoming). Several of her articles on Jane Austen's novels and their cultural legacy have appeared in *Persuasions: The Jane Austen Journal* as well as in *Chick Lit: The New Woman's Fiction* (Routledge 2006) and "The Public's Open to Us All": Essays on Women and Performance in Eighteenth-Century England (Cambridge Scholars Press, 2009). She is a coeditor of *The Brontës in the World of the Arts* (Ashgate, 2008).

# Index

### A

Abraham, 104
*Advise and Consent* (Drury), 19
AIDS, 5, 6, 7, 10, 13, 15, 131, 135
Allen, Mike, 105
Allred, Owen, 49
Al Qaeda, 71
*American Family, An*, 185–86
*American Idol* , 183, 188, 191, 193, 194
*American Massacre* (Denton), 107n25
*America's Next Top Model*, 183, 188
Amish, 113
*Angels in America* (Kushner), 2, 3, 5–26,
  83n15; film, 23–25
Apostolic United Brethren (Allred
  Group), 49
Archuleta, David, 183, 188, 192–93
Arrington, Leonard, 29n38
Arthur, Sarah, 168, 170
Astle, Randy, 165, 166, 176
Augustine, 46
*Austenland* (Hale), 178n10
Avard, Sampson, 90

### B

Baggaley, Thomas, 165–66, 169, 177
Bagley, Will, 92
Barash, David, 47
Barzee, Wanda, 41
Bateman, DeLoy, 69, 73, 79
Beck, Glenn, 1
Benson, Ryan, 183
*Best Two Years, The* (2003 film), 115
Biden, Joe, 39
*Big Brother*, 186, 187
*Biggest Loser, The*, 183
*Big Love*, 2, 3, 19, 37–61, 78, 81, 144
Black, Andrew, 163, 167–68. *See also Pride
  and Prejudice* (2003 film)

Black, Anne K., 171
blood atonement. *See* Mormonism and
  blood atonement
Bloom, Harold, 40, 68, 105
Book of Abraham, 74
Book of Mormon, 12–13, 88, 90, 100, 119,
  121, 122, 123, 124, 125, 135, 145–46, 154
*Brady Bunch, The*, 186
*Bride and Prejudice* (2004 film), 168
*Bridget Jones Diary* (Fielding), 168
Brigham Young University, 146, 153,
  163–64, 170, 177, 190, 194
Brodie, Fawn McKay, 13, 15–16, 74
Buchanan, Golden, 156
*Buckleroos* (2004 film), 115, 120, 122, 126,
  127, 128–29, 131
Burton, Gideon O., 165, 166
Bushman, Claudia L., 67
BYU. *See* Brigham Young University

### C

*California Sunshine* (1997 film), 115, 120–
  21, 123, 126, 127–28, 132, 133
Campbell, Joseph, 89–90, 93
*Candid Camera*, 185
*Candid Microphone*, 185
*Candide* (Voltaire), 193
Catholicism 38–39, 51, 113, 124, 150, 151,
  156, 167, 184
Chadha, Gurinder. *See Bride and
  Prejudice*
Church of England, 171
Civil War, 73
*Clueless* (1995 film), 168
Constitution of the United States, 54–55,
  77
*Could Be Worse* (2000 film), 115, 120, 123,
  129, 130, 133–34
*Country Wife, The* (Wycherley), 193

Cowell, Simon, 194
Cox, C. Jay, 115, 122–23, 128, 140n23
Cradlebaugh, John, 107n26
*Crying of Lot 49, The* (Pynchon), 148
*Culture of Missionaries, A*, 117

## D

*Dancing with the Stars*, 183, 184
Danites, 90–91, 95, 99, 107n14
Deism, 54
DelGrosso, 184
Dennis, Neleh, 188
Denton, Sally, 92
DePillis, Mario, 31n77
Doctorow, E. L., 105
Doctrine and Covenants, 13, 76
Douglas, Jerry, 115, 131
*Dress and Grooming Guidelines for Elders*,
  118
Duffy, John Charles, 167
Dutcher, Richard, 165. *See also God's
  Army* (2000 film)
*Dynamiter, The* (Stevenson), 40

## E

Eckankar, 54
Edmunds-Tucker Act, 44
Emerging Church, the, 152–53
Emerson, Ralph Waldo, 105
*Emma* (Austen), 168
*Epic of Gilgamesh, The*, 193
Evenson, Brian, 4, 89, 93, 104, 105, 106;
  *The Open Curtain*, 96–100, 103
evolutionary psychology, 47–48

## F

Faller, Jason, 163, 167, 171
Faulkner, William, 96
*Faust* (Goethe), 193
Feldman, Noah, 3
Ferris, Suzanne, 175–76
Fielding, Helen. *See Bridget Jones Diary*
*Finding Faith in Christ* (2003 film)
Friedman, Marie, 113
Fundamentalist Church of Jesus Christ
  of Latter-day Saints (FLDS), 1, 2, 49–50,
  58n30, 65, 67, 69–72, 73, 76–77, 81, 82

## G

garments. *See* temple garments
Garner, Stanley B., 15
Girard, René, 91, 100

*Girl from Utah, The* (Kern), 40, 191
Givens, Terryl, 8, 25, 27, 141n31, 141n32
  153
*God Makers, The* (1982 film), 125
*God's Army* (2000 film), 115, 165
Grant, Jedidiah M., 102
*Grease* (1978 film), 193
Great Salt Lake, 65
Green, Tom, 58n19, 77, 83n7
Greenfield, Sayre, 177, 179n32
Groskereutz, Heidi, 184
Gustafson, Sandra, 93

## H

Hafen, P. Jane, 160
Hangen, Tona, 146
Hanks, Maxine, 50–51
Harris, Martin, 123
Haun's Mill Massacre, 71–72
Herzog, Todd, 183, 190
Heskin, Kam, 170
Hightower, Chelsie, 184
Hill, Annette, 187
Hinckley, Gordon B., 81–82, 110n84
Hofmann, Mark, 52
Hollinger, 176
Hough, Derek, 184
Hough, Julianne, 184

## I

immigration, 64, 75
Immigration Reform Act, 75
*In Cold Blood* (Capote), 68
Indian Placement Program, 145–47,
  155–58
*Into the Wild* (Krakauer), 64
Islam, 62, 71–72
*It's a Wonderful Life* (1946 film), 134

## J

Jameson, Frederick, 148–49, 150, 152
Jane Austen Society of North America
  (JASNA), 163–64
Jankowski, Peter, 152
Jeffs, Rulon, 50, 58n30, 73
Jeffs, Warren, 1, 41, 50, 58n30, 77, 81
John, Helen, 155, 156
Joseph, Elizabeth, 57n11, 78
*Journal of Discourses*, 102
Judkins, Rafe, 194
Jump, Gordon, 192
Jung, Carl, 90, 96, 100

## K

Karmel, Pip, 115, 134
Kennedy, John F., 39
Kerwin, Rainy, 173
Kilborn, Richard, 187
Kimball, Spencer W., 73–74
King David, 104
Kingsborough Community College, 62
Kingston, Michael, 78
Krantzen, Allen J., 8
Kraszewski, Jon, 189
Kurtz, Stanley, 44

## L

L'Amour, Louis, 148
Laban, 88–90
LaBute, Neil, 4, 89, 104, 105; *A Gaggle of Saints*, 93–96, 100, 103
Lafferty, Brenda, 67, 87
Lafferty, Dan and Ron, 41, 67–72, 83n7, 87, 89, 97
Lafferty, Erica, 67, 87
*Larry King Live*, 110
*Latter Days* (2003 film), 115, 120, 121–22, 127, 128–33
*Lawrence v. Texas*, 44
LeBaron, Ervil, 50, 97
LeBaron, Joel, 40–41, 50
Lee, John D., 91, 107n25
Lehi, 88
Lewis, John Peter, 183
Lipton, Judith Eve, 47
Loud family. *See American Family, An*

## M

Mackenzie, David, 115
Mailer, Norman, 105; *The Executioner's Song*, 68
Mamet, David, 105
Margolis, Harriet, 169
Marty, Martin, 152
McCain, John, 1
McDannell, Colleen, 136
*Me Myself I* (1999 film), 115, 120, 121, 123, 126, 127–28, 129, 133–34
Mead, Margaret, 186
Melville, Herman, 96
Meyer, Stephanie. *See Twilight*
Mill, John Stuart, 37, 38
*Millennium Approaches. See Angels in America*
Miller, Arthur, 5

*Miracle Life of Edgar Mint, The* (Udall), 2, 4, 144–62
*Missionary Handbook*, 116, 119
Mitchell, Brian David, 41, 77, 83n7
Mollywood, 164
Monson, Thomas S., 82
Moore, R. Laurence, 92
Moorefield, Kenneth, 168–69
Morgan, David, 113, 116, 136
*Mormon America* (Ostling and Ostling), 9, 84n38, 84n39
*Mormon Corporate Empire, The* (Heinerman and Shupe), 9
Mormon fundamentalism, 48–50. *See also* Fundamentalist Church of Jesus Christ of Latter-day Saints (FLDS)
*Mormon Maid, The* (1917 film), 40, 130
Mormon missionaries, 113–143; as agents of transformation, 131–35, 154–55; as typical Christians, 114, 124–26, 136; dress and grooming, 118, 127; and drugs, 127; hair length, 116–117; name badges, 117–118, 119, 120; and sexuality, 128–31, 136, 153–54
*Mormon Question: Polygamy and Constitutional Conflict in Nineteenth-Century America, The* (Gordon), 54–55
Mormon Reformation, 92
Mormon Tabernacle Choir, 183
Mormonism: and blood atonement, 4, 69, 87–112, 144; Christianity of, 114, 124–26, 136; and conservative politics, 11, 16–18, 20, 22, 26, 80–81, 118–19, 137, 157; and family size, 157–58, 173, 184; as a global religion, 137; and homosexuality, 9, 18–19, 43–45; 50–51,94, 188, 190; and Judaism, 8–9; 10–11; and Native Americans, 13, 145–46, 160n2 (*see also* Indian Placement Program); postdenominational, 145, 147, 153, 159–60; and polygamy, 19, 38–40, 53–57, 69–70, 76–77, 110n84, 144, 187, 188; and racism, 69, 73–74, 76; spiritual validity of, 145 154–55; temple ceremonies, 94–95, 97, 109n62
*Mormons, The* (PBS documentary), 81
Moroni, 12, 16, 26, 106n5
Mountain Meadows Massacre, 72, 106, 197n17
Murphy, Dale, 192

## N

*Namesake, The* (Lahiri), 64
National Organization for Women, 78
Native Americans, 55, 145–46, 155–57
Nelson, Shawn, 183
Nephi, 88–91, 92, 94–95, 96, 98, 100, 103, 104, 110n77
Nigeria, 114

## O

O'Neil, Eugene, 5
Olsen, Mark, 43–45, 55
Orgazmo (1997 film), 2, 3, 115, 120–22, 124–28, 130, 132–33, 141n35
Osmond, Donny, 183
Osmond family, 192
Other Side of Heaven, The (2001 film), 115
Otterson, Mike, 69

## P

Palmer, Debbie, 77–78
papal infallibility, 38–39
Parker, Trey, 115, 122–23, 124, 127, 132–33, 141n35
*Peristroika. See Angels in America*
Peterson, Levi, 89, 93, 105, 106; *The Backslider*, 100–104
*Pippin* (Schwartz), 193
polygamy: and homosexuality, 43–45, 50–51; legality of, 41, 70, 77–78; naturalness of, 46–48. *See also Mormonism and Polygamy*
postdenominationalism, 152–53. *See also* Mormonism, postdenominational
*Postmodern Condition, The* (Lyotard), 147–49, 159–60
postmodernism, 147–49, 151–52
Powers, Perry Kerry, 93
Presbyterian Church (U.S.A.), 151
*Pride and Prejudice* (Austen), 163, 168, 174, 177–78; evangelical approaches to, 168
*Pride and Prejudice* (2003 film), 4, 163–182
*Project Runway*, 190
Proposition 8 (California), 2, 43, 51–53, 82, 129, 140n30

## Q

Quinn, Michael, 48–49, 59n35, 87n38

## R

Reagan, Ronald, 5, 17, 25, 26
reality television, 183–96
*Real World, The*, 183, 188, 189–90, 191, 194
*Rebel Billionaire*, 183
Reid, Harry, 1, 37
Reilly, Adam, 39
Republic of Pemberly (website), 163–64, 177
*Reynolds v. United States*, 55
*Riders of the Purple Sage* (Grey), 19, 40, 42, 191
*Romer v. Evans*, 44
Romney, Mitt, 1, 37–39, 56, 81, 105, 125, 192
Rosaldo, Renato, 66
Rosenberg, Warren, 104
Rouff, Jeffrey, 186
*Roughing It* (Twain), 40, 191
Rutherford, John, 115

## S

Sallman, Warner, 113
Samson, 104
Samuelson, Eric, 176
*Saviour, The* (2005 film), 115, 120, 121, 123, 124, 126, 127, 128, 130, 134–35
Savran, David, 15
Scalia, Antonin, 44, 57n18
*Scarlet Letter, The* (Hawthorne), 193
Schaffer, Will, 43–45
Schlesinger, Arthur Jr., 72–73
Schwimmer, Benji, 183–84, 188
Schwimmer, Lacey, 184
Scientology, 54
Scott, David W., 166
Seacrest, Ryan, 188
Seale, Orlando, 167–68, 170
September 11 attacks, 72, 75
*September Dawn* (2007 film), 105–6, 144
Short Creek raid, 82
Sikhism, 54
slavery, 70, 72, 74
Slotkin, Richard, 90, 91–92
Small, Joseph, 151
Smart, Elizabeth, 37, 41, 78
Smith, Deborah White, 168, 171
Smith, Joseph, Jr., 8, 12, 13, 15–16, 17, 25, 26, 40, 70, 74, 77, 88, 89–91, 105, 122, 144–45, 154
*So You Think You Can Dance*, 183–84, 188